The Real Jimmy Carter

The Real Jimmy Carter

How Our Worst Ex-President Undermines
American Foreign Policy, Coddles Dictators,
and Created the Party of Clinton and Kerry

S T E V E N   F.   H A Y W A R D

Since 1947
REGNERY
PUBLISHING, INC.
An Eagle Publishing Company • Washington, DC

Cataloging-in-Publication Data on file with the Library of Congress

ISBN 0-89526-090-5

Published in the United States by
Regnery Publishing, Inc.
An Eagle Publishing Company
One Massachusetts Avenue, NW
Washington, DC 20001

Visit us at www.regnery.com

Distributed to the trade by
National Book Network
4720-A Boston Way
Lanham, MD 20706

Printed on acid-free paper

Manufactured in the United States of America

10 9 8 7 6 5 4 3 2 1

Books are available in quantity for promotional or premium use. Write to Director of Special Sales, Regnery Publishing, Inc., One Massachusetts Avenue, NW, Washington, DC 20001, for information on discounts and terms, or call (202) 216-0600.

To Allison, for the usual reasons

Contents

CHAPTER ONE

The Conscience of the World

"America's anti-President: a psalm-singing global circuit rider and moral interventionist who behaved, in a surreal and often effective way, as if the election of 1980 had been only some kind of ghastly mistake, a technicality of democratic punctilio."[1]

—LANCE MORROW, *Time* magazine, on Jimmy Carter

On the surface, it is astonishing that someone whose four years in the presidency are widely judged to have been a horrendous failure continues to attract front-page headlines and exert influence on the world stage—even winning the Nobel Peace Prize— more than twenty years later. Among professional historians, former president Jimmy Carter is enjoying the now-predictable "reappraisal" phase, wherein a "fresh look" shows an apparently failed president to have been better than we first thought.

This book argues, on the contrary, that Jimmy Carter's presidency really was as bad as we thought at the time, or worse; that his lasting and dominant impact on the Democratic Party of today—the party of John Kerry and Hillary Clinton—has been calamitous; and that his supposed status as a "model" ex-president is the reverse of the truth, unless one's idea of a model statesman is Jesse Jackson.

Every leader has some bad luck, and every public figure deserves to have myths and inaccuracies debunked, but Jimmy Carter's failures are rooted in the character and ideology of the man himself. This would be less important were it not for the fact that Carter continues to insert himself in the nation's business, both at home and around the world.

The Smiley-Face Candidate

For many, Carter emblemizes the 1970s, a forlorn decade whose iconography, from rounded typefaces to disco music (but thankfully not leisure suits), is back in vogue. Perhaps the most memorable 1970s icon was the smiley face, so it is not surprising that the smiley-face decade would produce a smiley-face candidate: Carter's most prominent attribute as a politician was a grin toothier than a Cheshire cat's. As with the Cheshire cat in Lewis Carroll's story, what lay behind the grin was mysterious and sometimes disconcerting. Hamilton Jordan, one of Carter's chiefs of staff, referred candidly to what he called Carter's "weirdness factor."

In the early stages of Carter's extraordinary campaign for the presidency in 1976, a common response to his candidacy was "Jimmy who?" In some respects, we are still asking that question today, almost thirty years after he emerged suddenly on the national stage. He has a Jekyll and Hyde quality unlike almost any other American politician. He is certainly a better person than Bill Clinton; at least Carter lusted after women only in his heart. Yet there are aspects of Carter's character and political views that are more troubling than Clinton's unprincipled opportunism and lasciviousness.

Carter presents layer upon layer of difficulty to untangle. His one-time speechwriter Patrick Anderson observed that in Carter's hometown of Plains, Georgia, neighbors said of him that after an hour you love him, after a week you hate him, and after ten years you start to understand him. He added that anyone who didn't have a personality conflict with Carter didn't have a personality. Anderson also described Carter as a combination of Machiavelli and Mr. Rogers. The

Washington Post's Sally Quinn similarly observed: "The conventional image of a sexy man is one who is hard on the outside and soft on the inside. Carter is just the opposite."[2] Fellow Southern Baptist Bill Moyers said, "In a ruthless business, Mr. Carter is a ruthless operator, even if he wears his broad smile and displays his southern charm."[3] Part of the mystique of Carter is his careful and successful positioning as someone "above politics." He gives off an air that he is too good for us, or certainly better than the rest of his peers in politics. Carter exemplifies the paradox of taking pride in denouncing the sin of pride. He also displays a talent for combining self-pity and self-righteousness, sometimes in the same sentence.

He is a maddeningly contradictory figure. He first achieved statewide office in Georgia with a cynical race-baiting campaign, and then immediately proclaimed that the time had come for the South to repudiate its racist ways. An avatar of morality and truthfulness, Carter bends the truth and has a singularly nasty side to his character that ultimately contributed to his loss in 1980. Longtime NBC and ABC broadcaster David Brinkley observed of Carter: "Despite his intelligence, he had a vindictive streak, a mean streak, that surfaced frequently and antagonized people."[4] Eleanor Randolph of the *Chicago Tribune* wrote: "Carter likes to carve up an opponent, make his friends laugh at him, and then call it a joke....[He] stretched the truth to the point where it becomes dishonest to call it exaggeration."[5] *New York Times* reporter James Wooten called Carter "a hyperbole addict." And Gary Fink, author of a generally favorable study of Carter's governorship, notes that "Carter usually claimed the moral and ethical high ground" but "practiced a style of politics based on exaggeration, disingenuousness, and at times outright deception."[6]

Carter seldom, if ever, repents of his nastiness or asks forgiveness. Instead, when called out for an egregious personal attack, he displays the advanced skills of evasion that made him such an effective presidential candidate, at least until the public caught on in 1980.

The man with the legendary smile can be unfriendly and cold. "There were no private smiles," said one disgruntled campaign aide in 1976. Carter's personal White House secretary, Susan Clough, recalled that Carter rarely said hello to her as he walked by her desk. Not a "Happy Thanksgiving," or a "Merry Christmas." Nothing, she says. Arthur Schlesinger, Jr. judged Carter to be a "narcissistic loner." "Carter was never a regular guy," Patrick Anderson observed; "the sum of his parts never quite added up to that.... Carter talked his way into the presidency, yet in some profound way he never learned the language of men."[7]

Why Not the Best?

Carter's 1975 campaign autobiography, *Why Not the Best?*, proclaimed that he was "optimistic about America's third century," but he became a tribune of "limits to growth" pessimism, diminished expectations for the future, and a national "malaise." Margaret Thatcher, among others, noted the trouble with this, writing that Carter "had no large vision of America's future so that, in the face of adversity, he was reduced to preaching the austere limits to growth that was unpalatable, even alien, to the American imagination."[8]

Carter campaigned on the slogan of giving us "a government as good as the people," and then, at the climactic moment of his presidency, complained that the people were no good. As a champion of human rights and critic of (at least pro-American) autocratic dictators while president, ex-president Carter compiled a record of meeting with and subsequently praising some of the world's most loathsome dictators, often strengthening their political stature. Yet he was always quick to criticize anyone else who associated with dictators. He is the only person elected to the presidency to have filed a UFO-sighting report with the Air Force. "I don't laugh at people anymore when they say they have seen a UFO because I've seen one myself," Carter said at a 1975 press conference.[9] He is the only president to nearly provoke the resignation of his vice president due to a loss of confidence.

Self-righteousness is another of Carter's obvious hallmarks. Biographer Betty Glad noted that, as governor, Carter "seemed to experience opposition as a personal affront and as a consequence responded to it with attacks on the integrity of those who blocked his projects. He showed a tendency [which will become even clearer as other facets of his career are explored] to equate his political goals with the just and the right and to view his opponents as representative of some selfish or immoral interest."[10]

This aspect of Carter's character cannot be unraveled without looking deeply into the self-proclaimed sources of his political thought, and especially his political religion. In keeping with the biblical injunction to "judge not," one should be cautious about evaluating Carter's faith, but it is clear that the trouble with Carter has to be sought in his peculiar blending of religion and politics.

As we shall see, there is an alarming superficiality to his political religion, which journalists and biographers have noticed but not analyzed with sufficient seriousness. Biographer Kenneth Morris wrote that "when he became governor and then president, Carter continued to show himself bereft of a solid intellectual foundation for his political views."[11] Betty Glad reached a similar conclusion: "He lacks, it seems, a well-thought-out conceptual framework to guide his concrete political choices. . . . Carter's political views rest on a simplistic moralism."[12]

Some of Carter's critics think he is a religious charlatan. Reg Murphy, editor of the *Atlanta Constitution* during Carter's years as governor, called Carter "one of the three or four phoniest men I ever met."[13] Despite instances of hypocrisy that can be pointed out in Carter's political career, it is precisely his sincerity and authenticity that are most disturbing. He is sincere about his beliefs, and is an authentic representative of a segment of Christianity that modern liberalism has corrupted and politicized. Douglas Brinkley regards Carter as "the most principled American president since Harry Truman." The core of the problem with Carter is that his principles are wrong.

Giving Peace a Chance: The Legacy

There is a contemporary urgency to understand Carter and Carterism, because Carter's perspective has become the dominant perspective of contemporary liberalism and his Democratic Party successors. While neither Carter nor the leading Democrats today are explicitly pacifist, they have adopted a de facto pacifist bias that believes any conflict can be resolved through negotiations and good intentions. While this strain of thinking always reserves the use of force as "the last resort," in practice there is no point at which certain kinds of contemporary liberals—the Howard Deans, the John Kerrys . . . and Jimmy Carter— will give up on "dialogue." Carter always believes that the "peace process" has not been "given a chance." If Carter or his successors were in charge, Afghanistan would still be ruled by the Taliban, Saddam Hussein would still be in power, and Libya's Qaddafi would still be building weapons of mass destruction.

In other words, although the voters decisively dispatched Jimmy Carter in 1980, his legacy lives on in potent form today and is likely to survive his death. It is important that it be understood clearly. His story offers a valuable object lesson into the realities of modern politics and international statecraft. In the century of terrorism, it is crucial that our leaders get the lesson right.

It is obvious that on the international stage, many have gotten the lesson wrong. When Jimmy Carter was awarded the Nobel Peace Prize in the fall of 2002, many of his supporters thought it was long overdue, that he should have received it for helping consummate the Camp David peace accord between Israel's Menachem Begin and Egypt's Anwar Sadat, who shared the award instead. According to one Nobel insider, Carter was passed over in 1978 for the simple reason that he was not nominated in time.[14] It was an oversight Carter would not let happen again. His repeated nominations were typically sponsored by the American Friends Service Committee, a Quaker pacifist group with decidedly leftist leanings. The nominations arrived early, and (thanks to intense lobbying behind the scenes) his name would be promoted as a short-list candidate.

Up until 2002, all this work was for naught. On the *Today Show*, Katie Couric once quipped to Carter: "You're kind of the Susan Lucci of the Nobel Peace Prize"—a comparison to the soap opera actress perennially nominated for a TV Emmy that surely made Carter wince.

When he finally won, the prize came surrounded with controversy.

The chairman of the Nobel Prize committee, a leftist Norwegian politician named Gunnar Berge, told the media in announcing Carter's prize that "it should be interpreted as a criticism of the line that the current [George W. Bush] administration has taken" in the war on terrorism, and particularly Iraq. "It's a kick in the leg to all that follow the same line as the United States," Berge added for the benefit of America's British, Polish, Spanish, Czech, and other European allies in the Iraq war. The other four members of the politically appointed Nobel awards committee rushed to say that Berge was expressing only his personal opinion and not that of the committee.[15]

Michael Kinsley has shrewdly defined a "gaffe" as an instance where someone unaccountably tells the unvarnished truth, and the disclaimers of the other committee members fooled no one. Berge's sin was his candor. The Nobel committee's official commendation for Carter used more subtle language to make Berge's point: "In a situation currently marked by threats of the use of power, Carter has stood by the principles that conflicts must as far as possible be resolved through mediation and international cooperation based on international law, respect for human rights, and international development." The deputy chairman of the Nobel committee told *Time* magazine that "one should read our statement very carefully," as it "contains clues to our motivation and philosophy."

No need to parse that statement. The *New York Daily News* editorialized that "The most prestigious award in the world has been tainted. . . . By extension, it is a slap in the face of the American people, since our duly elected representatives have just voted to fully support the administration's Iraq policies."[16] Even the *New York Times* understood the anti-American politicization of the prize. *Times* reporter Michael Wines noted, "Jimmy Carter won [the prize] 'for his decades of untiring effort to find peaceful solutions to international conflicts'—and, by the declaration of the prize panel's chairman, *for his labors as a critic of the Bush administration's pistols-cocked brand of geopolitics."* (Emphasis added.) The *Daily Telegraph* wrote that "By convention, former American presidents do not criticize their successors, so it could be said that Carter should not have accepted the award if it was going to be taken as a public rebuke of Bush." President Bush took no notice of the ruckus; he promptly telephoned Carter to pass along his congratulations.

Carter did not find it awkward or embarrassing to be used in a way that was an explicit criticism of American foreign policy, telling CNN merely, "The Nobel Prize itself encourages people to think about peace and human rights, so I'm very grateful and honored by this." Carter brought actress Jessica Lange, actor Anthony Hopkins, country singer Willie Nelson, and rocker Carlos Santana along with him to the Oslo award ceremony. (Bob Dylan, Carter's favorite philosopher/poet, was apparently unavailable.) Lange was as forthright as the Nobel committee on the meaning and purpose of Carter's prize: "It is time to move beyond this terrible and dangerous agenda set by our current government." Willie Nelson sang "Georgia on My Mind" at a three-hour "peace concert."

Carter's two-step—letting others fire the heavy bombardments while he attempted to stay above the fray—continued in his acceptance address and subsequent remarks to the media. Carter criticized President George W. Bush's Iraq policy without naming Bush. "For powerful countries to adopt a principle of preventive war may well set an example that can have catastrophic consequences," Carter said. "I feel very strongly about" Iraq, Carter told the media after the ceremony. "But I didn't think it was appropriate to mention it. *I haven't spent the last twenty-two years walking around saying what I would or wouldn't do if I were still president."* (Emphasis added.)

But that is exactly what Carter has done in the more than two decades since American voters expelled him from the White House in a landslide. In one sense, the Nobel dust-up is business as usual for Carter; low-grade controversy seems to follow him the way a dust cloud shadows Pigpen in the "Peanuts" comic strip.

The Overlooked Meddler

Carter has assembled a record of egregious behavior that is invariably forgiven and forgotten. The most notable instance came in late 1990 and early 1991, as the George H. W. Bush administration assembled its international coalition to expel Saddam Hussein from Kuwait. Carter opposed the prospective Gulf War, saying it would be "a massive, self-destructive, almost suicidal war." But he didn't stop there.

In November 1990, and without informing the Bush administration, he wrote to several heads of state represented in the United Nations Security Council—including François Mitterrand, Margaret Thatcher, and Mikhail Gorbachev—and to more than a dozen other leaders, appealing for "negotiations," deploring President Bush's "line in the sand" rhetoric, calling for the UN Security Council to stop the United States from launching a military campaign, and declaring that the Arab League, not the United States, should be the agent to work out a diplomatic solution. The Bush administration learned of Carter's letters only when Canadian prime minister Brian Mulroney telephoned Defense Secretary Dick Cheney to ask what Carter was up to. Cheney was shocked, later telling Carter biographer Douglas Brinkley that Carter's actions were "reprehensible, totally inappropriate for a former president."[17]

Carter didn't let up. In the early weeks of 1991, Carter wrote in the *New York Times* that the imminent war to evict Saddam Hussein from Kuwait could be avoided if Israel would end its occupation of the West Bank. In the days leading up to the UN's January 15 ultimatum to Hussein, Carter continued his behind-the-scenes meddling. Carter wrote on January 10 to Saudi Arabia's King Fahd, Egypt's Hosni Mubarak, and Syria's Hafez Assad, urging them to break from Bush's painstakingly assembled coalition. "I urge you," Carter wrote, "to call publicly for a delay in the use of force while Arab leaders seek a peaceful solution to the crisis. *You have to forgo approval from the White House, but you will find the French, Soviets, and others fully supportive.*" (Emphasis added.) While Carter had belatedly informed the Bush administration of his November communiqués, after Mulroney called Cheney, his January missives he kept secret from Bush, who did not find out about them until several years later. Brinkley notes that Carter never apologized to Bush for his interference, though he did admit, after intense media scrutiny in 1993, that they were "not perhaps appropriate."

Carter also opposed President George W. Bush in the run-up to the Iraq war of 2003, at one point questioning not only Bush's policy but his Christian faith. Writing in the *New York Times* a week before Bush gave the final "go" order, Carter argued that the prospective war violated Christian teaching on just war.[18] No former president had ever before criticized an American commander in chief on the brink of war as acting immorally.

But this is par for the course with Carter. As we shall see, he both openly and covertly sought to undermine President Reagan's ultimately successful policy toward the Soviet Union, at times making direct contacts with Soviet officials to subvert American policy.

It is episodes like these that prompted *Time* magazine's Lance Morrow to comment that some of Carter's "Lone Ranger work has taken him dangerously close to the neighborhood of what we used to call treason." Despite these breaches of protocol and good judgment, Carter continues to bask in bipartisan acclaim. As disastrous as his presidency was, many Americans have a warm spot in their heart for Carter, sympathizing with his intentions, admiring his charitable good works, and hopeful about his globetrotting efforts on behalf of peace. *People* magazine—which Carter criticized during his presidency for its focus on self-absorbed celebrity—generously remarked on his winning the Nobel Prize that: "Almost everyone agrees that Jimmy Carter was not our best President, but as former Presidents go, he's tops," while *Time* magazine wrote that Carter is the "consensus best ex-President."

Another former chief of staff, Jack Watson, remarked effusively that Carter is "the only man in American history who used the United States presidency as a stepping stone to greatness." Even his political enemies tend to agree. Richard Nixon, who disliked Carter, expressed to his research assistant Monica Crowley kind thoughts about Carter's good deeds: "Look, although I have problems with Carter personally and politically, he has done some very decent things as a former president. While Ford is playing golf, which he should do if that's his idea of retirement, Carter is out there banging nails into houses for the poor. At least Carter puts his money where his mouth is. He practices what he preaches, and for that I give him credit."[19] Another Republican elder statesman, former senator Howard Baker of Tennessee, said in the 1980s that "history will be kind to Jimmy Carter."[20]

The question is: Should it be?

CHAPTER TWO

The Plain Man from Plains

"We of my generation have lost one line of fortifications after another, the old South, the old ideals, the old strengths."[1]

—WILLIAM ALEXANDER PERCY, *Lanterns on the Levee*

Jimmy Carter can claim a long lineage in America. His first American ancestor, Thomas Carter, arrived in Virginia in the 1630s. The family didn't stay in the Old Dominion, however, gradually drifting to new farming locations farther south until Kindred Carter arrived in Georgia in 1787, the year the U.S. Constitution was written. Kindred started a farm on 307 acres "ceded from the Cherokees" (according to the euphemism of one of Carter's biographers) in northeast Georgia, near Augusta, which he operated with the help of ten slaves.[2] The colorful family (one of Kindred's grandsons was murdered in a bar fight in 1874; another Carter descendant was killed by gunshot in 1903) bounced around to several other farming locations in Georgia during much of the nineteenth century, until at length Alton Carter, Jimmy's grandfather, moved the family in

1904 to the southwest Georgia town of Plains, about 120 miles straight south of Atlanta.

Jimmy's father, James Earl Carter, was a hardworking businessman whose shrewd investments in farm and timberland, a grocery business, and a peanut brokerage made him, by the standards of the time, prosperous as well as locally prominent. The Carter family farm was not a grand, colonnaded plantation in the image of Tara in *Gone with the Wind*; think of Grant Wood's *American Gothic* with magnolia trees and Spanish moss instead of waving fields of corn and wheat. Jimmy's family lived in a small clapboard house without running water. Despite his father's industriousness, farm life was always precarious. Years later, Jimmy wrote, "I remember my father often walking back and forth in the yard looking up at the sky, praying that the weather would be clear enough to plow up the crop before it rained again." He added that "the amount of labor expended compared to any sort of cash return [from the farm] was almost unbelievable."

"Mr. Earl," as Jimmy's father was known throughout Sumter County, married Lillian Gordy, a nursing student from a politically prominent Georgia family, in 1923. Three months later she became pregnant, and on October 1, 1924, James Earl Carter, Jr.—"Jimmy"— was born. Two sisters and a brother—the infamous Billy—would later round out the family.

One of the odder bits of Jimmy Carter trivia is that he was the first American president to be born in a hospital, but this was about the only modern appurtenance of Plains. Southwest Georgia in 1924 was very much in the mainstream of the old South, far removed from the advancing frontier of industrial progress that Southern agrarians deplored. There were few paved roads. Plains, with a population of about six hundred when Jimmy Carter was born, wouldn't get electricity for another ten years, courtesy of the New Deal's Rural Electrification Administration. "It is deplorable," Herman Clarence Nixon wrote in the famous 1930 anthology of agrarian resistance to the twentieth century, *I'll Take My Stand*, "that the South's agricultural philosophy is imperiled by a non-philosophical pattern of society in which the highest aim of life is success in industry."[3]

Earl Carter probably sympathized with Andrew Lytle's sentiment that "A farm is not a place to grow wealthy; it is a place to grow corn." Like many Southern planters, Earl was incensed when FDR's agricultural production controls came into effect, requiring the slaughter of "unneeded" animals and the plowing up of "surplus" crops in an effort to prop up farm prices. "He never again voted for Roosevelt," Jimmy wrote years later. Earl may not have voted for FDR again, but he was not above receiving several New Deal agricultural subsidies as the Depression wore on. (One irony between Carter and Ronald Reagan is already apparent; Reagan's father, rescued from destitution by the New Deal, worshipped FDR.)

Jimmy and the "New South"

Jimmy Carter would grow up as the South self-consciously transformed itself into the "New South," what C. Vann Woodward called "the Bulldozer Revolution." The upheaval of World War II prompted much of the South's modernization; Bertram Wyatt-Brown remarked that the South changed much more starting in 1940 than it had changed between 1865 and 1940.

The distorting lens of the civil rights movement colors our retrospective understanding of the South today. When Jimmy Carter was growing up, lynchings were not unheard of, but race relations were generally cordial in Plains. At the peak of the family farm's prosperity, Earl Carter employed more than 250 black workers, paying the men $1 a day, the women 75 cents, and the children 25 cents.[4] Carter provided free housing for many of his workers, and threw a sumptuous barbeque on July 4 every year to which he invited everyone in the area, including most of the black families. Most of young Jimmy's playmates were black. Although other farm families kept their black field laborers out of their home, Lillian Carter would invite black children into the house to eat lunch with Jimmy in the kitchen. The

Carters did, however, attend a segregated Southern Baptist church on Sunday, where Earl Carter taught Sunday school. "We never went to the same church or school," Carter wrote later of his childhood black playmates. "Our social life and our church life were strictly separate....Despite the black playmates of my youth, I can remember that I was literally a grown man before I was thrown into social situations in which I routinely met and talked with black men and women on an equal basis."[5]

Like his eventual rival Ronald Reagan, Carter's childhood has been described as a Huckleberry Finn existence. Carter himself portrayed it in a spare but affecting style in his autobiography, *Why Not the Best?* He spent the summer months barefoot and shirtless, fishing for eels and catfish in local creeks and streams, learning to shoot rifles, swimming in ponds, riding horses, and climbing trees. He was exuberant enough in his boyish pursuits that he broke his arm twice. (And, on another occasion, a school bus ran over both his feet.) In between his idylls he performed the full spread of farm chores that were typical for farm families in those years.

In elementary school Carter became known as an obedient, well-behaved, and hardworking pupil. In the third grade he won a prize for reading the most books, and he purportedly read Tolstoy's *War and Peace* when he was twelve. He was naturally outgoing, and would introduce himself in the same manner in which he later ran for president, sticking out his hand and saying, "Hi, I'm Jimmy Carter." Even in childhood, Carter displayed some of the grasping traits that would later arrest his critics, and many admirers as well. He stole a penny from a church collection plate one Sunday, for which he received a whipping from his father. "It was the last money I ever stole," Carter laconically recorded. On another occasion, he persuaded his younger sister Gloria to bury a nickel he had paid her for picking peanuts, telling her it would grow into a money tree. Jimmy then dug up the nickel.

In later years it would be said that Carter judged people harshly according to whether they agreed with him, taking disagreement as a personal moral affront rather than allowing for honest difference of

opinion. In *Why Not The Best?*, Carter offers a perhaps unintentionally revealing portrait of his judgmentalism:

> Even at that very early age of not more than six years, I was
> able to distinguish very clearly between the good people
> and the bad people of Plains. The good people, I thought,
> were the ones who bought boiled peanuts from me! [Carter
> had set up a small peanut stand on Main Street to sell
> peanuts from the family farm.] I have spent much time
> since then trying to develop my ability to judge other peo-
> ple, but that was the simplest method I ever knew, despite
> its limitations. I think about this every time I am tempted
> to judge other people hastily.[6]

Carter recalled this episode in a book of poems he published in
1995:

> Long before I was ten years old
> I learned to judge the whole community,
> My standards just as good as those of preachers
> Or scholars, who would teach philosophy
> Or write their books.
> I knew the good folks were
> The ones who bought their boiled peanuts from me.[7]

The Early Years

There is no clear point in the timeline of Carter's young life at which
his interest in politics was first manifest, though he told a reporter in
the early 1970s, when he was governor, that he had been "intensely
interested" in politics starting at the age of eight. But he wrote in
1975, "It is difficult for me to remember when my interest in politics
began." In high school he was on the debating team and built as a
class project a small replica of the White House. At college he ran—
and lost—a campaign to become freshman class president. But aside

from some college classmates who recalled—in the 1970s—that Carter boasted he would one day be governor of Georgia, there are few recollections that he showed any serious interest in politics. One thing was clear about Carter, though: his intense competitiveness. He graduated at the top of his high school class in the fateful year of 1941, narrowly missing out on being the class valedictorian.

Earl Carter had only a tenth-grade education, and constantly impressed upon young Jimmy that he needed to study hard and earn a college degree after high school. Jimmy says that even before he started the first grade he knew he wanted to attend the U.S. Naval Academy at Annapolis. He wrote to Annapolis for admission information while still a grade school student. Despite his father's connections to the local congressman, Representative Stephen Pace, Jimmy did not receive the coveted nomination to Annapolis after he graduated from high school. He enrolled instead at Georgia Southwestern College, a two-year college in nearby Americus.

The following year, 1942, Carter did receive Congressman Pace's nomination, contingent upon his completion of some prerequisite science courses at Georgia Tech in Atlanta. He passed the next year as a science and engineering student, where he finished in the top 10 percent of the class and made the honor roll. "He did not discuss politics much, or show any great interest in it," biographer Betty Glad wrote of Carter's interlude at Georgia Tech.[8]

In the Navy

Carter arrived at the Naval Academy in the fall of 1943. He weighed only 121 pounds, barely above the minimum for entrance into the Academy. Except for brief vacation visits, it would be eleven years before Carter returned to Plains. Although he was formally a member of the class of 1947, the necessity of wartime led the Naval Academy to accelerate its curriculum by a year so that it turned out a class of newly minted officers in three years instead of four. Carter ended up graduating in 1946. He ranked in the middle of his class throughout the first two years, but rose to finish fifty-ninth out of 820 in his final year. Betty Glad noted that "Carter did not win prominence as a class leader," and quoted an anonymous classmate's recollection: "He didn't show any signs of greatness, and I don't recall that he held any strong political or religious views....I think we were all amazed when he became governor of Georgia, and positively astounded when he ran effectively for President. I still can't get over it."[9]

While home from the Academy in the summer of 1945, Jimmy Carter met and began dating Rosalynn Smith, then a sophomore at Georgia Southwestern College. Jimmy kissed her on their first date—unheard of in those days—and announced to his mother when he arrived home that he intended to marry Rosalynn. They corresponded faithfully after Carter returned to complete his final year at Annapolis, and married in the summer of 1946, a few weeks after his graduation.

Carter was at sea in the North Atlantic when President Harry Truman's announcement came that the U.S. had dropped the atomic bomb on Hiroshima, heralding the imminent end of World War II. Carter and his classmates had all assumed that they were destined to be in major action in the Pacific against Japan, and the sudden, unexpected end of the war changed Carter's vistas. He performed his required two years of ship duty on a series of decrepit and undermanned ships as the Navy rapidly downsized. "The postwar Navy was in bad shape," Carter recalled. "It was a time of great discouragement because we were undermanned....I became disillusioned with the Navy, and the military in general." Carter said he probably would have resigned had he not, as an Annapolis graduate, been serving "at the pleasure of the President."

Chafing at what he saw as a narrowing field of opportunity, he decided to apply for a Rhodes scholarship. He didn't get it. At a regional screening interview, Carter lost out to someone whose student expertise was in Elizabethan poetry, even though Carter said he was able to answer all the interviewers' questions across a wide range of topics. "It was the first time in his life that Jimmy was forced to face a significant failure," biographer Peter Bourne wrote, "and he was depressed for several weeks."[10]

Carter did not refer to this episode in *Why Not The Best?* (though he did discuss it with numerous journalists at the time), but did not allow his disappointment to slow him down for long. He shrewdly judged that the way ahead within the Navy would be to join the submarine program; with all the talk of developing nuclear power for a new generation of submarines, that was where the action would be. Carter's engineering background made him ideally suited to move into the program.

He entered the submarine service first as an electronics officer on the USS *Pomfret*, based out of Pearl Harbor. Once, when the *Pomfret* was recharging its batteries on the surface during a strong storm in the western Pacific, a large wave swept Carter overboard. When the wave receded, Carter luckily landed on the aft deck gun, where he clung to the gun barrel until he could make his way back to the bridge. "Had the currents been even slightly broadside instead of from forward to aft," Carter reflected later, "I would never have landed on the ship as the wave receded, and would undoubtedly have been lost at sea."

In 1952, Carter was promoted to full lieutenant and posted to the submarine *K-1*, based out of Groton, Connecticut. In the fullness of time, he could expect to be given command of a submarine. He won a reputation on the *K-1* as a supremely confident, hardworking officer, and as a straight arrow. One fellow crewman told Betty Glad, "It's hard to believe about anybody in the Navy, but there are no sea stories about Jimmy Carter."[11] Carter was now beginning to show some overt signs of interest in politics. On both the *Pomfret* and the *K-1* Carter occasionally discussed politics; in 1948, on the *Pomfret*, he argued in favor of Harry Truman's election. Recollections of Carter from this period tend to be vague and unspecific beyond wide praise for his dutifulness, intelligence ("smart as hell," one fellow officer said), and competence as an officer. Carter, by most accounts, remained aloof from his fellow sailors, even within the close confines of a submarine. One of his commanding officers on the *K-1* told Peter Bourne that "I sure couldn't tell you who his buddies were."[12] Carter himself says, "My contact with political life was transient and super-ficial while I was in the Navy."

His application to join the Navy's nuclear program brought him face-to-face with one of the dominant personalities of mid-century America: Admiral Hyman Rickover. Rickover was to the Navy's sub-marine program what J. Edgar Hoover was to the FBI for more than four decades: imperious, intimidating, arrogant, unorthodox, but with unparalleled mastery of the whole scene. And like Hoover, Rickover made himself indispensable, and could not be gotten rid of. To his critics, he was something of a latter-day Captain Bligh. (One of Rick-over's favorite books was *The Caine Mutiny*.) Years later, when Carter was governor of Georgia, he would say that there was one sentence that would still make him break out into a nervous sweat: "Gover-nor—Admiral Rickover on the line."

Meeting Rickover would be a turning point in Carter's life in more than merely professional terms. Carter would later say that "Admi-ral Rickover had a profound effect on my life—perhaps more than anyone except my own parents." Rickover sought total loyalty in his underlings, and made it his practice to personally interview every applicant to the nuclear program. He liked to make his interviewees sweat. It was his form of a stress test. Carter's interview lasted over two hours. The wide-ranging questions grew progressively more dif-ficult, and Carter wrote, "I was saturated with cold sweat." Carter thought he had regained the initiative by telling Rickover that he had graduated fifty-ninth out of his class of 820 at Annapolis. Rickover bore in on the self-satisfied young lieutenant: "Did you always do your best?" Carter candidly admitted, as most humans would, "No, sir, I did not always do my best." He recorded the aftermath:

> He looked at me for a long time, then turned his chair around to end the interview. He asked one final question, which I have never been able to forget—or to answer. He said, "Why not?" I sat there for a while, shaken, and then slowly left the room.[13]

How Carter's interview compared to those of other applicants to Rickover's program is unknown, but the decisive fact is that Rickover accepted Carter into his ranks. It was from this episode that Carter derived his theme, later used in the title of his autobiography: *Why Not the Best?* The indelible impression made on Carter by the Rickover episode led to a rhetorical habit that became a Jimmy Carter signature—using superlatives. He would always claim that his campaign, his transition to office after winning election, each department and bureau in his administration, even his transition out of office in favor of Ronald Reagan in 1981, was or would be "the best" in history. Even some of Carter's closest confidantes and aides would find this rhetorical tic to be annoying and grandiose.

Carter's overuse of superlatives seems closely related to his penchant for exaggeration, which became another signature of his political style, as we shall see. Exaggeration comes with the political trade; it is an ineluctable and perhaps necessary component of that overweening sense of self that all successful politicians exhibit to some degree. A catalogue of whoppers can be collected on nearly every modern president. One thinks in this regard of Lyndon Johnson falsely claiming that an ancestor fought at the Alamo; Bill Clinton claiming (among other things) to recall black church burnings during his childhood in Arkansas, when historical records show there were none; and Al Gore exaggerating nearly every aspect of his life. In this respect Carter's occasional whoppers and frequent petty exaggerations do not especially stand out. But they are incongruous with his self-declared Christian wariness of the sin of pride and profession of the virtue of humility.

One of the first instances of a small but telling Carter exaggeration has its origin in his period in the Rickover program. When he ran for president in 1976, Carter would claim, among his other credentials, that he was a nuclear *physicist*. Betty Glad explains:

> Though Carter was to later call himself a nuclear scientist,
> it is apparent that his formal training in that field was

limited; he had had no training in nuclear physics at Annapolis and his subsequent graduate work at Union College [in New York] consisted of a noncredit, one-semester course. One professor who taught the course says that "No one who took that program could be classed as a nuclear engineer—it was at quite an elementary level."[14]

While Carter exaggerated his scientific credentials, there is no slighting his subsequent experience with nuclear technology, which included working a hazardous cleanup at a Canadian nuclear reactor that had suffered a partial meltdown in 1952.

At this point, the twenty-nine-year-old Carter could have every expectation of a distinguished naval career ahead of him. Given his ambition and intelligence, he was a possible admiral, maybe even Chief of Naval Operations. "My job was the best and most promising in the Navy," Carter reflected later. But just a year into Rickover's nuclear program, Carter received news that brought his naval career to an abrupt end and resulted in the second major turning point in his life. Back in Plains, his father was dying of cancer.

CHAPTER THREE

Rising Politician

> "Our personal problems are magnified when we assume
> different standards of morality and ethics in our own lives as we
> shift from one responsibility or milieu to another."
>
> —JIMMY CARTER, *Why Not the Best?*

Carter lay on his bed and wept when he heard the news of his father's terminal illness. Jimmy, like many men of his generation, did not have a close relationship with his father. But he sought immediate leave from the Navy, and in the hours and days spent at his father's bedside over the following weeks, son and father grew very close. One pressing worry was the fate of the family business. By the early 1950s, Earl Carter had accumulated more than five thousand acres of farmland, and his seed and fertilizer business was thriving. Jimmy saw his father as more than just the family patriarch; he was in some ways the commercial linchpin of the local economy. But while the business was asset-rich, it was cash-poor and potentially insolvent. Among Earl Carter's more generous but precarious business practices was extending credit into six figures—a massive sum in those days—to his customers. A bad year for his customers could take the Carter family business down.

Jimmy's brother, Billy, then only sixteen, was too young to take his father's place. Jimmy's mother, Lillian, urged Jimmy to do it. Over the strenuous objections of his wife, Rosalynn ("It was the first really serious argument of our marriage," Carter wrote in *Why Not the Best?*; in 1992, he described Rosalynn as "violently opposed"), and after much agonizing, Carter decided to do it.

Years later, Carter told his most sympathetic biographer, Peter Bourne, that "God did not intend for me to spend my life working on instruments of destruction to kill people," but this seems a post hoc justification crafted to suit his contemporary image.[1] In *Why Not the Best?*, Carter wrote that he had been attracted to the Navy's nuclear program out of a desire to develop peaceful uses for atomic energy, while another sympathetic biographer, James Wooten, wrote that "Carter himself had been dejected about missing a chance actually to fire torpedoes in anger."[2] His Navy colleagues recall that at the time, Carter was deeply conflicted about what he should do; concerns of higher morality never entered his conversations. At his own request, Carter was honorably discharged from the Navy in October 1953, three months after his father's death.

The Peanut Farmer

Returning to the remote confines of Plains to take up the life of a farmer is surely the most counterintuitive step ever taken by a future president. His first few years as a farmer could not have been encouraging. Peanut prices were depressed in 1953; Carter says he netted a profit of only $200 his first year. He performed much of the warehouse labor himself (filling seed and fertilizer bags, for example, while Rosalynn did the bookkeeping). Facing $12,000 in debts, Carter applied for a loan from a local bank in 1954. He was turned down. When his mother accepted a job as housemother for a fraternity at Auburn University, Jimmy was fearful people might think it due to declining family fortunes. So he bought her a brand-new white Cadillac to keep up appearances.

Bolstered by better weather and Carter's improved production techniques, the farm's fortunes started to turn around, and Carter's political career began. He joined local civic associations like the Lions Club and the Jaycees; he also served on the boards of the Sumter County Library Association and the local hospital authority, where he led a fund-raising drive to bring a full-time doctor to Plains. Carter's stature in the community led to his first real political job. In 1956, he was appointed to fill an unexpired term on the local school board. He served on the board until 1961.

This was a momentous time to be on a school board in the rural South, coming just two years after the U.S. Supreme Court's *Brown v. Board of Education* decision, which ordered Southern public school districts to desegregate "with all deliberate speed." Carter's record on the central issue of Southern politics during this period is elusive. In *Why Not the Best?*, Carter affected simple ignorance about the dimensions of segregation. "It seems hard to believe now," Carter wrote, "but I was actually a member of the county school board for several months before it dawned on me that white children rode buses to their schools and black children walked to theirs! I don't believe any black parent or teacher ever pointed out this quite obvious difference."[3] This seems a convenient rationale for explaining why, whatever his private sentiments about racial issues, he appears to have been content to ride with the tide of Southern public opinion, which steadfastly resisted desegregation. (Georgia's governor at the time, Herman Talmadge, had publicly proclaimed that Georgia would not abide by the *Brown* decision.)

Most of Carter's actions upheld the dual school system then prevalent in rural Georgia. Biographer Betty Glad scoured the records of the Sumter County school board, discovering that in 1956 Carter offered the motion to delay construction of a new school for blacks after white parents complained that black and white students would be

taking the same roads to their respective schools. On another occasion, Carter supported buying new typewriters for white schools but
used typewriters for black schools. On the other side of the ledger,
Carter supported building a brand-new black elementary school in
Plains.[4] Glad concluded: "He does not seem ever to have taken a public stand for or against compliance with federal integration guidelines
in the schools or other public facilities. Not did he provide the
behind-the-scenes leadership that others attempted in one way or
another."[5]

Carter rebuffed solicitations to join the local chapter of the newly
formed White Citizens Council. Local Council members included the
Plains police chief, the local railroad depot agent, and a Baptist
preacher; Carter was supposedly the only white man in Plains who
refused to join. He was threatened with a boycott of his peanut and
farm supply businesses. But the boycott never happened. Betty Glad
suggests that the threatened boycott may have been a Carter embell-
ishment; "Townspeople do not recall it," she wrote.

In 1965, when Carter was a state senator, his church, which had
been de facto but not formally segregated (blacks regularly attended
special events like weddings, funerals, and baptisms), decided to make
an official policy of barring blacks—physically if necessary—from
attending Sunday worship services. Carter was a deacon in the
church, but missed the meeting at which the vote was taken. (The
vote was unanimous, including the pastor.) Carter gives no account
of why he missed the meeting, and wrote in *Why Not the Best?* that
"I heard about this meeting later, after the vote, and it disturbed me
deeply." Perhaps so, yet it is hard to imagine that Carter had no fore-
knowledge of what the deacons were intending to do. He later spoke
in favor of getting the deacons' decision reversed. He failed, but
reported that many members of the congregation told him privately
they agreed with his views.

Carter offered an opaque reflection about these incidents in *Why
Not the Best?*: "The significance of these two incidents—my experience with the White Citizens' Council recruiting effort and in my

own church—are still hard for me to assess." One obvious explanation is that even if Carter was out of sympathy with Southern opinion on racial questions, it was necessary to conceal this in order to
maintain his political viability, a calculation that could never be
admitted even in retrospect. Betty Glad's summary judgment was
that "to avoid these conflicts to the extent that he did, he had to
define his responsibilities as a leader and citizen in restrictive, even
passive, terms."[6]

Jimmy Carter the Politician Emerges

If Carter seemed weak or vacillating on desegregation, his tough and
determined side emerged when he ran for the state Senate in 1962.
Friends had urged Carter to consider politics; his mother suggested
later that he was growing bored with the life of peanut farming and
hungered for new challenges. He entered the race on September 30,
1962, barely three weeks before the primary election day. Although
Carter was technically running against an old-line incumbent, Homer
Moore, the state Senate district had been hastily redrawn and a new
election called after the U.S. Supreme Court decision in *Baker v.
Carr*, which required all state legislative districts in the nation to
have equal population. Moore's old district had covered very little of
the area near Americus and Plains, where Carter was well known, so
it was for all intents and purposes an open seat. Carter avoided racial
issues and ran a campaign emphasizing his business and community
experience and his military record.

Carter ran well on primary day, October 16, except in Quitman
County, where the local Democratic Party boss (and occasional boot-
legger), Joe Hurst, openly stuffed the ballot box and manipulated votes
on behalf of Homer Moore: Dead men voted, 126 people voted in
alphabetical order, and more votes were cast than there were registered voters on the rolls. Carter himself turned up at the polling station in the afternoon and personally confronted Hurst. Not only were
Carter's protests ignored, but Hurst threatened one of Carter's poll
watchers: "I have put three men in that river out back for doing less

than you're doing."[7] Carter's attempts to bring the voting shenanigans to the attention of the local newspaper failed—the reporter assigned to the story was a pal of Hurst. Carter lost Quitman County by 224 votes, and lost the election by 139.

Rather than acquiesce to a stolen election, Carter decided to contest the result. He demanded a recount in Quitman County, and began collecting affidavits from voters whose ballots had been remarked by Hurst and his cronies. Carter enlisted the help of two prominent Atlanta lawyers who became Carter insiders on his long road to the White House, Griffin Bell and Charles Kirbo. When the *Atlanta Journal* broke the story, the state Democratic committee appointed a three-person subcommittee to investigate. Conveniently for Moore, the voting roll and ballot stubs were missing. The recount committee decided to throw out the entire Quitman County vote as tainted. So Carter was now ahead by sixty-five votes.

Carter still needed to be officially certified as the winner, which didn't happen until the Saturday night before the general election. Because most ballots had already been printed, Carter and several close friends spent much of Sunday changing ballots by hand, crossing out Moore's name with a magic marker and stamping Carter's name onto the ballots. Meanwhile, Moore filed his own legal appeals, and obtained a ruling that called for a new hearing on Monday, the day before the election. This temporarily halted Carter's efforts to remark the ballots. Carter went to court to get his own injunction. The judge in the Monday hearing ordered both Carter's and Moore's name removed from the ballot, and ordered that a write-in election be conducted instead. Carter and Moore spent election day blanketing the district with handbills and ads informing voters about the situation and giving instructions for casting a write-in vote. This time Carter beat Moore by 831 votes, although two counties in the district had defied the judge's order and left Carter's name on the ballot. Nonetheless, Moore finally conceded to Carter.[8]

The political animal in Carter had been awakened in this campaign and its aftermath. Betty Glad observed, "He pursued this senate seat

with an intensity and a single-mindedness that seemed dispropor-
tionate to the end he would obtain."[9] He lost eleven pounds during
the two-week ballot controversy, and was exhausted. But his ardor for
the job was inexhaustible. Carter wrote, "I made what later sometimes seemed an unfortunate pledge—to read every bill before I voted
on it." Like most state legislatures, Georgia's state house would see
as many as 2,500 bills proposed each year. And although less than half
of these would come to a vote, reading all of them is a poor use of a
legislator's time. The longer bills especially are filled with technical
implementing language that has little bearing on the policy matter at
hand. Nonetheless, Carter stuck to his pledge, and, having taken a
speed-reading course, later claimed to have kept his promise. "I
indeed became an expert in many unimportant subjects," he wrote.
It is one Carter boast that is easy to believe.

Carter quickly gained the reputation as the hardest-working senator.
He was typically the first senator to show up at the capitol early in the
morning, which might be partly attributable to his non-participation
in the well-lubricated nightlife of the state capital. While his colleagues
were out dining and drinking with lobbyists—the typical life of legislators in every state capital—he would head to his hotel room and read
all those proposed laws.

Another key aspect of Carter, that of bringing his engineering mentality to politics, began to manifest itself. In addition to reading all
the bills, Carter delved deeply into the administration of government,
with an eye toward reform and efficiency. "Organizational confusion
aggravates government inefficiency," is a typical Carter reflection. A
colleague from his senate days recalled, "Jimmy would sometimes
stay up all night studying, and the next day would go over and talk to
a department head to find out how that department functioned."[10] As
Carter himself put it, he sought "comprehensive approaches to school
finance and education laws, taxation of utilities, scholarship offerings,
overcrowded state mental hospitals, election laws, budgeting proce-
dures, and uniform salaries for state officials." As befit an engineer,
he helped establish the West Central Georgia Area Planning and

Development Commission, an early form of regional planning agency that became ubiquitous throughout the nation in the 1980s and 1990s. (Carter eventually became its permanent chairman.) He also became known as a penny-pinching fiscal conservative, who was, in his own words, "appalled" at the perfunctory way in which the legislature oversaw the state budget.

Carter passed his first year, 1963, in the senate quietly, as is expected of freshman legislators. He claims he did not make his maiden speech on the senate floor until his second year, 1964. (This claim cannot be verified, as few senate speeches were recorded.) His only piece of legislation enacted in 1963 was a bill to regulate the market for agricultural limestone. The Georgia legislature, like most state legislatures at the time, was an amateurish body that tended to pass unanimously or by large margins bills the governor wanted. Senator Carter viewed his colleagues with little regard, though he never openly said so and usually voted with the majority. Carter kept a low profile, but did earn a reputation as a nag on special interest (or "private") bills. He objected to enacting special laws to benefit narrow interests, and often attempted to block or amend such bills. "To the extent that he had a political ideology," biographer Peter Bourne wrote, "it was a perception of himself as David against Goliath."[11]

Race and Religion

Carter's first year in the senate was a time of racial unrest in Georgia. National civil rights organizations such as the Student Nonviolent Coordinating Committee (SNCC) organized marches in Americus and Sumter counties, in the heart of Carter's senate district. Police and "deputized" mobs beat the marchers, and hundreds of blacks were arrested and jailed. This sorry spectacle drew national attention and widespread comment—except from Carter. (Nor does he recall these events in his account of his senate days in *Why Not the Best?*) The silence of an intelligent public figure is always meaningful; Carter's silence can be interpreted as the deliberate concealment of his private sympathy with the civil rights movement, even as most other Georgia politicians were vociferous in their support for segregation. (The local leadership in Carter's district remained "implacably opposed to integration," according to Peter Bourne.) In 1964, Carter did speak out in favor of an amendment to an election reform act to abolish the "thirty questions" asked of voters, that is, the "literacy test" used to keep blacks from voting. However, the "questions" were kept in the final bill, which Carter did not oppose.

Carter also ran against the grain on a surprising issue: religion. The 1963–1964 session of the legislature decided to take up the revision of the Georgia state constitution, and one section of the proposed bill of rights read: "Every man has the natural and inalienable right to worship God according to the dictates of his own conscience." Carter objected to this clause, arguing that it amounted to "a requirement that God be worshipped." He offered an amendment that called for substituting the language of the Establishment Clause of the First Amendment to the U.S. Constitution: "No Law shall be passed respecting an establishment of religion or prohibiting the free exercise thereof." The senate initially accepted Carter's amendment, but later went back to the original version that had already passed the Georgia house. Carter then voted against the constitutional revisions—one of only four dissenting votes.

Movin' on Up

By 1966, the last year of his first term in the senate, Carter had gained a seat on the crucial appropriations committee, and was voted by his fellow legislators as one of the five most effective senators. He had, significantly, voted against a number of popular public works projects—a foreshadowing of the early months of his presidency, when he shocked Congress by vetoing a popular water project bill. Carter carefully cultivated the press, which gave him good notices. An easy reelection seemed assured, and Carter's political future looked bright. In early March of 1966, Carter announced he would run for the United States Congress. Barely three months later, he raised the stakes and announced that he would run for governor instead.

A measure of personal animosity seems to account for both of Carter's decisions. He initially wanted to run for Congress to unseat Bo Callaway, who in 1964 became the first Republican elected to Congress from Georgia since 1874. Carter developed a deep antipathy to Callaway because, according to Carter, Callaway had used his influence as a member of the state board of regents to block the elevation of Georgia Southwest College from a two- to a four-year institution. (Callaway denied Carter's charges.) Promoting Georgia Southwest had been one of Carter's main priorities as a member of the governor's commission to improve education in Georgia. As would become a trademark Jimmy Carter practice, he transformed a policy disagreement into a personal affront, and went after Callaway with populist relish. He called Callaway "a rich young Republican from Harris County," and said a local four-year college was necessary because most people in the region couldn't afford to send their children to the University of Georgia or Auburn, or Harvard or Yale. There was nothing subtle about Carter's line of attack. Carter later admitted in *Why Not the Best?*, "Although it is not especially admirable, one of the major reasons [for my decision to run] was a natural competitiveness with Bo Callaway."

After Carter had announced his intention to run against Callaway for Congress, Callaway announced that he was going to run for governor instead. It is unlikely that Carter chased Callaway from the House race; Callaway was the strong favorite for reelection, and had substantial backing from Democrats in his district. Callaway was attracted to the governor's race because of the sudden weakness of the Democratic field. Georgia's governors were limited to single, non-consecutive terms; in practice, the Georgia governorship tended to rotate among former governors. In the spring of 1966, former governor Ernest Vandiver seemed the heir apparent, but withdrew after suffering a heart attack. That left another former governor, Ellis Arnall, a liberal who had been in office from 1942 to 1946, and Lester Maddox, the flamboyant Atlanta restaurant owner who had kept blacks out of his eatery by threatening them with an axe handle (*New York Times* reporter James Wooten colorfully described Maddox as "a sort of second-string George Wallace on the all-American racist squad"). A handful of minor candidates rounded out the Democratic field.

The Georgia Democratic Party establishment feared that Arnall would be certain to lose against Callaway; Maddox's chances were discounted. Carter found himself in the middle of intrigues to find another strong candidate. When no plausible candidate emerged, Carter decided that he should run himself. It was a gutsy decision; with Callaway's withdrawal from the congressional seat, the way was wide open for Carter to move on to a Washington political career.

Carter prepared the way for his sudden shift through the creation of a "draft Carter" movement, which successfully planted stories in the *Atlanta Constitution* that he was being urged to consider the race. One story noted that "many think he resembles the late President John F. Kennedy." A newspaper story the year before had carried a photo of Carter and his family playing touch football in their back yard, "just like another public figure, the late President John F. Kennedy."

All Things to All People

Now that he was on a statewide stage, Carter began to establish a reputation for dodging and weaving and calculating, which would become the dominant characteristic of his political career. It consists of one part evasiveness and one part viciousness. Carter had described himself during his short-lived congressional campaign as a "Russell conservative," after Georgia's senior senator Richard Russell. Russell, however, was a die-hard segregationist—he was among the leaders of the Southern filibuster against the Civil Rights Act of 1964—and on the cusp of becoming an anachronism, though he still commanded wide popularity among rank and file Georgia Democrats. Carter wanted at once to claim an association with Russell, yet not alienate his liberal constituents. When asked whether he was a conservative, moderate, or liberal at his announcement press conference, Carter answered, "I believe I'm a more complicated person than that."

Both Senator Russell and Georgia's other Democratic senator, Herman Talmadge, declined to endorse any of the Democratic candidates for governor in the primary election. That did not stop Carter from trying to claim their mantle. Carter's campaign sent out mailers purporting to be from an independent group, signed "Concerned friends of Senator Richard B. Russell and Senator Herman Talmadge" endorsing Carter and attacking his main rival, Ellis Arnall. Carter denied knowledge of the mailing.

Despite Carter's media-savvy announcement and early campaigning, he trailed even the minor candidates in the polls. At the end of July, one poll found Arnall the front-runner at 35 percent, with Carter polling at 5 percent. If he was to have any chance of overtaking Arnall, Carter would have to go negative. He called the fifty-nine-year-old former governor "bald, squat, and old," and made vague accusations of political corruption against him, even though he had been out of government for eighteen years. "I am finding everywhere," Carter said in August, "that the people are embarrassed and nauseated over the frivolity and clownish stunts that Mr. Arnall and Mr. Maddox continually inject into the campaign." "Inject" became a favorite Carter pejorative.

Another signature trait of Carter's manifested itself in this first statewide campaign: his projection of a morally superior character. "If I ever let you down in my actions," Carter said in many speeches, "I want you to let me know about it and I'll correct it. I promise never to betray your trust in me." Betty Glad summarized what could be seen about Carter from this first statewide campaign:

> A number of themes that would resound in his candidacy
> for the presidency were now emerging: refusal to accept
> ideological labels; avoidance of controversy; emphasis on
> personality, morality, and integrity; preference for concrete
> proposals over broad political issues; ability to corral a net-
> work of talented and energetic supporters as well as a dis-
> ciplined, effective staff; and willingness to go for the

jugular of his opponents when the circumstances seemed
to demand it.[12]

On the campaign trail, Carter attracted the attention of a number
of people who would later form the inner circle of his presidential
years. A twenty-one-year-old student named Hamilton Jordan became
Carter's youth coordinator after he heard Carter speak at an Elks Club
lunch. The president of the First National Bank of Calhoun, Bert
Lance, was impressed with Carter at an appearance at Berry College
in the town of Rome, Georgia, and signed up to support him. A young
Atlanta advertising whiz named Gerald Rafshoon ingratiated himself
with Carter and began to produce his television spots.

Carter estimated that he shook hands with 250,000 Georgians in
the course of the campaign. He lost twenty-two pounds, and weighed
just 130 pounds on primary day in September. Carter finished third in
the Democratic primary behind Arnall and Maddox. Arnall finished
with 29.4 percent to Maddox's 23.5 percent; Carter pulled 20.9 percent. Carter had played the role of spoiler. Had he not been in the
field, Arnall might have received 50 percent of the vote and avoided
a runoff with Maddox. On the other hand, Carter's rise from less than
5 percent in early polls to 20 percent in the final vote reinforced a
basic if unpleasant rule of politics: Negative attacks work. For the rest
of his political career, Carter would attempt to take the high, middle,
and low road all at once.

In the Democratic runoff, conducted as an "open" primary two
weeks later (in which Carter had declined to make an endorsement, as
is customary in Georgia Democratic politics), Maddox beat Arnall partially on the strength of Republican crossover votes. Republicans
thought Maddox would be an easier opponent for Callaway to defeat.
They were right; in November, Callaway topped Maddox 49 to 48 percent, but under Georgia law at the time, unless a candidate received
more than 50 percent of the total votes cast, the Georgia house of representatives decided the winner. The Georgia house was heavily
Democratic, and predictably selected Maddox to be the next governor.

"Having Maddox as governor was the worst of all possible outcomes," Peter Bourne wrote, "and he [Carter] was responsible for it."[13]

On the surface, Carter seemed to take his defeat in stride, setting in motion almost immediately what would be a four-year campaign for governor in the 1970 election. He held his first fund-raiser, in fact, just a few days after the November election, and continued to frequent the halls of the state capitol even though he no longer held any office, openly telling anyone who would listen that he was going to run for governor again in 1970. As Hamilton Jordan later put it, Carter was "the world's worst loser." "I remembered the admonition, 'Show me a good loser and I will show you a loser,'" Carter wrote. "I did not intend to lose again."

In fact, Carter was "profoundly depressed," according to all accounts. One of his traits mentioned most often in the media coverage of the 1966 campaign was his supreme self-confidence. "Carter radiates an unmistakable aura of confidence," read a typical newspaper story. Carter's confidence was undoubtedly authentic; supreme self-confidence is a dominant trait shared by all the men who have ascended to the presidency. It is the flip side of that essential immodesty required to assert one's fitness to lead a great nation.

Hence, it is understandable that Carter's disappointment at losing cut deep into his soul, and helped propel him into the most interesting and obscure passage of his life. He became "born again."

CHAPTER FOUR

The Born-Again Governor

"Religion is more frequently a source of confusion than of light in the political realm."

—REINHOLD NIEBUHR

That Carter was a born-again Christian was perhaps the most prominently advertised feature of his character when he ran for president in 1976. This was an especially popular variety of Protestant evangelical Christianity in the 1960s and 1970s; according to one 1976 survey, a third of the nation claimed to have had a spiritual experience that could be described as being "born again." Being "born again" refers to a singular moment of spiritual regeneration, after the New Testament verse John 3:3, in which Jesus says, "Verily, verily, I say unto thee, except a man be born again, he cannot see the kingdom of God."[1]

The variety of born-again experience runs the range from making an affirmative intellectual commitment to recognize Jesus Christ as one's personal Lord and Savior, to something akin to a Pauline moment on the Damascus road, when one is struck forcibly by the grace of God, to even more dramatic "charismatic" encounters with the Holy Spirit that can result in glossalalia, that is, speaking in tongues. (Carter's sister Ruth Carter Stapleton, a faith healer of some prominence in Southern Baptist circles, admitted to reporters in 1976 that she engaged in speaking in tongues.) Carter's own born-again experience seems to have been of the first kind—making an affirmative commitment.

Carter had been a regular churchgoer (but a mere "church Christian," as he put it) and Sunday school teacher his entire adult life. According to his sister Ruth, she was walking with Jimmy in the woods near his Webster County peanut farm when he asked her, "You and I are both Baptists, but what is it that you have that I haven't got?" Ruth told him that she had had to "forget everything I was."

"What it amounts to in religious terms is total commitment," she said. "I belong to Jesus, everything I am."

"That's what I want," Carter allegedly said. Ruth says Jimmy then broke down in tears, though he would not recall doing so. One particular detail stands out in his recollection of this walk in the woods with Ruth: She asked him if he was willing to give up politics. "I thought for a long time and had to admit that I would not." [2]

Carter's own personal account is more cerebral. In *Why Not the Best?*, Carter said he found himself challenged by the title of a Sunday sermon in his church: "If you were arrested for being a Christian, would there be enough evidence to convict you?" This slogan had been an evangelical chestnut for years, which makes it surprising that Carter found it novel, though perhaps it had been slow to make its way to Plains. Carter doesn't recall the content of the sermon; instead, he was caught short by the reflection that if he were to be arrested, he felt sure he could talk his way out of it. "I began to read the Bible with a new interest and perspective, and to understand more clearly the admonitions about pride and self-satisfaction." For the first time, he added, "I saw that *I* was a Pharisee."

Even as Carter was laying the groundwork for another run at the governor's mansion in 1970, he undertook several domestic Christian missions on behalf of his church. In 1968, he went on a two-week mission to Lock Haven, Pennsylvania, along with another aspiring Georgia politician, Hoyt Robinson, with whom he discussed the political implications of their faith. Carter would later say, "I believe God wants me to be the best politician I can possibly be." Late in 1968, Carter went on a second mission, to Springfield, Massachusetts. On both missions, Carter went door-to-door evangelizing, greeting people with, "Hi, I'm Jimmy Carter, a peanut farmer. Do you accept Jesus Christ as your personal savior?" One of Carter's fellow missionaries reports more than a dozen new professions of faith. In Springfield, the police actually brought Carter and his fellow missionaries into the station on suspicion of soliciting without a license. (They were released, but made sure to leave several Bibles and tracts at the station house.)

Although door-to-door evangelical missions are a rarity of American religion (excepting, of course, the Jehovah's Witnesses), they are merely a version of the traditional evangelical "altar call" and as such are an oddity only to a secularized media that is fully estranged if not hostile to evangelicalism. It would have been a matter of immense wonder and bafflement had the *New York Times* ever pondered why Billy Graham was often found to be the most admired man in America in public opinion surveys in the 1960s and 1970s. Still, it is probably not an oversight that Carter downplays his missions in the accounts of his born-again experience in *Why Not the Best?*.

The major news media cannot help but condescend to religious believers, even when they try hard to avoid doing so. Consider *New York Times* reporter James Wooten's description of Carter's born-again faith in his otherwise favorable account of Carter's rise:

> It was the very crux of the religious thinking that permeated the early life of Jimmy Carter and *still survives* in the minds of millions of Americans, Southerners and otherwise, rural and urban. It is the descendant of the fiery-furnace, old-time revivalism that accompanied the settlement of the American

South in the nineteenth century, an approach to evange-
lism that combined Chautauqua, circus, and indefatigable
oratory in its efforts to bring salvation to the world.[3]
(Emphasis added.)

Evangelical Christianity was exploding in popularity in the mid-
1970s, which is why it is revealing that Wooten should use the phrase
"still survives" to describe the belief of tens of millions of Americans.
Wooten's characterization clearly implies that such belief is an out-
moded relic of an age that healed with leeches. Wooten gilds this
point with a passage laden with relief that Jimmy Carter wasn't a
knuckle-dragging Christer: "In the years since his baptism, Jimmy
had come to a more sophisticated world view. That theology was no
longer the light of his spiritual life. He had read a great deal of the
work of modern theologians whose emphases were on the social and
ethical impact of the gospel."[4]

Here it is necessary to look past Wooten's condescension, however,
as he has inadvertently brought one of Carter's key aspects to light.
Hamilton Jordan would pinpoint Carter's born-again Christianity as
the cornerstone of what he called Carter's "weirdness factor" in the
1976 presidential campaign. However, the real "weirdness" was not
Carter's conformity to "born-again" Protestant Christianity, but
where he fit on the spectrum of evangelical belief, especially in the
context of the Southern Baptist denomination. Since the 1970s,
Southern Baptists have been divided between "fundamentalists," who
believe in the inerrancy and "literal" interpretation of the Bible, and
"moderates"—few Southern Baptists want to be called "liberals"—
who believe the Bible should be susceptible to modern interpretive
techniques. The fundamentalists ended up on top in the 1980s and
1990s, and now dominate the Southern Baptist Convention.

Carter never openly took sides in this internecine controversy in
his pre-presidential years or even gave evidence that he was aware of
it, though after his presidency he was critical of the Southern Baptist
Convention when it passed socially conservative resolutions, includ-

ing one critical of homosexuality and another banning female pastors. His frustration with his lifelong denomination has occasionally spilled out, though. In an early 2003 *New York Times* op-ed that argued President Bush's preemptive war against Iraq violated Christian "just war" doctrine, Carter added this gratuitous observation: "This is an almost universal conviction of religious leaders, with the notable exception of the Southern Baptist Convention, who are greatly influenced by their commitment to Israel based on eschatological, or final days, theology."

"How would you like to be the pastor of a church with eighty thousand members?"

Carter is an evangelical outlier in several other ways. Within American Protestantism, the theological dichotomy between the spiritual world and the material world has led many Protestant evangelicals to have an aloof attitude toward politics. This is one reason why voter turnout and political participation among evangelicals has fluctuated wildly over the last several decades, but is generally much lower than other denominations. The Reverend Jerry Falwell or the Reverend Pat Robertson (son of a Democratic U.S. senator from Virginia, it is important to note) are the exceptions rather than the rule among evangelicals.

Carter attests to this problem in *Why Not the Best?*, but passes over it without much reflection on its deeper meaning in a recollection of an argument with his pastor over his plan to go into politics. "The pastor was surprised that I would consider going into politics, and strongly advised me not to become involved in such a discredited profession. We had a rather heated argument." But rather than offer a theological justification for pursuing a political life, Carter's rejoinder to his pastor was, "How would you like to be the pastor of a church with eighty thousand members?" (Eighty thousand was the number of constituents Carter would have as a state senator.)

During his presidential campaign, Carter dropped repeated hints at liberal theological leanings with his habit of quoting snippets from liberal and neo-orthodox theologians such as Reinhold Niebuhr, Karl

Barth, and Paul Tillich.[5] In his peanut warehouse office, Carter kept a small statue of Gandhi. Notably missing from his repertoire of religious references are conservative theologians or thinkers present or past, such as C. S. Lewis, Francis Schaeffer, Charles Spurgeon, or Jonathan Edwards. These loud signals went unnoticed by the millions of conservative evangelical Christians who thought Carter was "one of us" in the 1976 campaign.

In one sense, Carter's heterodoxy is not entirely surprising. Baptists have always rejected the hierarchical order and doctrine of the Catholic and Episcopal churches, and have emphasized the autonomy of individual congregations. The individualist orientation of Southern Baptists suited Carter very well; given his refusal to embrace an unchangeable orthodox doctrine, he would make a terrible Catholic bishop. Carter's professed interest in Niebuhr was potentially significant. Niebuhr wrestled with the problem of Christianity and politics. This was directly relevant to Carter's later presidential crusade on behalf of human rights. Niebuhr, a man of the anti-communist left, rejected the sentimental idealism of revolutionary socialism and reformist liberalism alike. Even before the apogee of totalitarian ideology and the arrival of the atomic bomb in the 1940s, Niebuhr had rejected Christian pacifism and had articulated a robust, though anguished, attitude of Christian realism that revived the ancient tradition of just war theory and embraced the necessity of nuclear deterrence.[6]

Yet Carter's politics, as we shall see, reflect little of Niebuhr's hardheaded realism. Niebuhr criticized "moralists" for "seek[ing] peace by the extension of reason and conscience," which is a perfect one-sentence description of Carter's foreign policy moralism. Instead of highlighting one of Niebuhr's many hardheaded aphorisms about the necessity of political realism, Carter's favorite quote from Niebuhr was, "The sad duty of politics is to establish justice in a sinful world." Why is establishing justice a "sad duty," unless there is an ineluctable understanding that in a sinful world, establishing perfect justice is impossible, and therefore that politics has inherent limits? Carter has never offered any extended reflections on this problem, which is central to the relation of religion and politics. Arthur Schlesinger, Jr., one of the deans of liberal intellectuals, wrote that "one wonders whether Mr. Carter can really have understood Niebuhr."[7]

Carter's Theological Liberalism

Schlesinger was not alone among liberal intellectuals in doubting Carter's depth. Garry Wills, a former Catholic seminarian, wrote of Carter that "his religious confidence has a narrow base.... For a bright and educated modern man, he shows an extraordinarily reined-in curiosity. It suggests a kind of willed narrowness of mastery. He moves quick and certain within a deliberately circumscribed territory."[8] Wills expressed surprise that a longtime Sunday school teacher was totally unfamiliar with current trends in biblical interpretation (which might say more about Wills than Carter, however). Years later, after Carter left the White House, Wills returned to this theme, writing that Carter's "narrow and repetitive intensity of his thought about religion...was one key to the personal narrowness that remains one's lasting impression of him in the presidency." Kenneth Morris recounts a friend of Carter's who tried to discuss the controversial theologian Thomas J. J. Altizer's "death of God" theme with Carter, to which Carter responded, "You can't read that thing and understand it." Carter's acquaintance, Morris says, "took [this] to mean that 'he couldn't read it and understand it.'"[9]

On the surface, Carter appeared as nondescript in his Christian theology as he was in his political ideology. But underneath the surface, he embraced theological liberalism. "A quotation from Tillich sticks in my mind," Carter wrote and said on many occasions. "'Religion is the *search* for the truth about man's existence, and relationship with God.' Maybe our search will be fruitful."[10] The emphasis is in the original. A hallmark of modern liberal theology is that the *search* for truth is more important than the truth itself. Searching for truth is an existential delight, and for a liberal, it saves you from having to take a firm position on anything. Betty Glad rightly noted that Carter was "a kind of existentialist Christian."[11]

Although Niebuhr and other neo-orthodox theologians rejected the "Social Gospel" movement that thought the Kingdom of God was possible on Earth through scientific socialism, Carter betrayed sympathy for this kind of politicized Christianity. In a 1973 speech at the Kiokee Baptist Church near Appling in east Georgia, Carter said that his liberal programs should be understood in terms of "Christ's ministry to the suffering."[12] Peter Bourne records Carter saying that his social programs were "an extension of the gospel, problem-solving combined with Christian charity."[13]

Jimmy the Fabricator Runs for Governor

Soon after his defeat in 1966, Carter began his four-year-long campaign to win the governor's office. Carter estimates he gave 1,800 speeches, (which would be more than one a day, 365 days a year), and shook hands with 600,000 people outside factories, shopping centers, and sporting events. It was an extraordinarily modern campaign, making heavy use of polls, color-coded charts and graphs, and even statistical regression analysis to determine where Carter would gain the most votes with personal campaign appearances. *New York Times* reporter James Wooten summarized what Carter learned from his polls and analysis of the Georgia electorate: "He discovered something he had not quite grasped in 1966. Georgians, on almost every single issue, were either slightly or substantially more conservative than he. He knew that was important to keep in mind as 1970 approached."[14] "I was never a liberal," Carter would tell some Georgia voters. "I am and have always been a conservative."[15]

He publicly supported Lyndon Johnson's and later Richard Nixon's Vietnam policy, and had declined to be a delegate to the 1968 Democratic National Convention in Chicago. "Conservative leadership," he said, "resides with bankers, businessmen, and state legislators." On another occasion, he said he was "basically a redneck."

But for all his relentless campaigning and trying to portray himself as a man of the people, early polls in the fall of 1969 showed Carter far behind his main rival for the Democratic nomination, Carl Sanders, who had been governor from January 1963 to January 1967. As early as 1968, according to one campaign memo the *Columbus Ledger-Enquirer* obtained, Carter planned to employ tough political and personal attacks on Sanders if he found himself behind. The strategy called for portraying Sanders as a liberal, by tying him to the national Democratic Party, and as a "nouveau riche" out of touch with the common man. With these and other strategies, Carter wrote in the memo, "we can start driving a wedge between him and me."[16] Above all, these lines of attack on Sanders would enable Carter to position himself as a "populist" without having to define clearly his ideology.

Carter nursed a grudge against Sanders because Sanders had backed Arnall in 1966. He deployed his attacks on Sanders with an un-Christian relish. Painting Sanders as too wealthy and too ambitious to be the people's governor, he took to calling Sanders "Cuff Link Carl," and reinforced the epithet with a television ad featuring a close-up shot of a gold cuff link. Bizarrely, he alleged that the registration number on Sanders's private airplane—6272 Victor—was a sign of his ambition beyond the governor's mansion. "1962 was the year he [Sanders] was elected governor, and 1972 is the year Senator Russell's term expires."[17] This expedition into Farrakhan-like numerology neglected to mention that the plane had been given its registration number before Sanders acquired it. Sanders responded by saying that Carter "is becoming known as Jimmy the Fabricator."

Carter portrayed Sanders as a liberal. Because Sanders's campaign button maker had also made buttons for Humphrey in 1968, Carter linked Sanders to Humphrey, who was deeply unpopular in Georgia because of his leadership on civil rights issues. Carter attacked Sanders for preventing George Wallace from speaking on Georgia state property: "I don't think it is right for Governor Sanders to try to please a group of ultra-liberals, particularly those in Washington, when it means stifling communications with another state." Carter said that he, of course, would invite Wallace to Georgia to discuss "mutual" concerns. No mystery whose votes Carter was trying to gain with this line of attack.

For weeks, Carter made broad accusations that Sanders was corrupt. The media pressed Carter for specific charges and evidence, and days before the primary election Carter finally produced documents showing that Sanders sat on the board of directors of a finance company whose CEO did substantial business with the state of Georgia. "These documented facts," Carter said, "show a consistent pattern of combining political and business interests on behalf of Mr. Sanders." While insinuating conflict of interest, Carter stopped short of alleging any specific illegality on Sanders's part. Even Peter Bourne, Carter's most sympathetic biographer, says, "The heavily hyped 'proof' was a major letdown."[18] Sanders replied bitterly that Carter was "the penny-antiest politician I've ever come across." The verbally dexterous Carter managed to flip these words around into a fresh populist attack on Sanders: "I've been accused by the rich candidate of running a penny-ante campaign. I have to plead guilty because I'm running a relatively low-budget campaign and I've tried to reach poor people who, like myself, have to make ends meet."[19]

Sanders fought back with a radio commercial calling Carter a "land baron," pointing out that Carter was hardly the humble pauper he had implied ("poor people who, *like myself.* . ."). This time Carter's reply went too far. "He is a sick man," Carter said of Sanders. When called out on this intemperate remark, Carter displayed his skill at rhetorical prevarication that would become a trademark method of retreating from personal attacks that went over the line. Carter said he had been attacking Sanders's advertising style, not Sanders personally. "I certainly don't think he is a sick man." But that is, of course, exactly what he said. Carter subtly reinforced his attack on Sanders's stability in his explanation of why he refused Sanders's invitation for a head-to-head debate. Carter: "I don't think in *his present frame of mind*, it would be right to engage in a personal name-calling exercise on television." (Emphasis added.)

Playing the Race Card

The most dubious Carter attack was an anonymous mailer sent to barbershops, country churches, and rural law enforcement officers containing a grainy photo of Sanders, part owner of the Atlanta Hawks NBA franchise, at an after-game locker room victory celebration. Two black players were pouring champagne over Sanders's head. The *Atlanta Constitution* noted, "In the context of the sports pages, it was a routine shot.... But in the context of this political campaign it was a dangerous smear that injected both race, alcohol, and high living into to campaign."[20] Carter's senior campaign aides Bill Pope, Hamilton Jordan, and Jerry Rafshoon were behind the mailing; Pope was even spotted passing out the flyers at a Ku Klux Klan rally. "There is nothing in the record," Peter Bourne wrote, "to suggest that Carter was aware of what Bill Pope, Hamilton Jordan, and others were doing," which is not the firmest of denials that Carter knew about the mailer. Perhaps Bourne is right, though it would have been out of character for the detail-oriented engineer-politician to be totally oblivious to what was going on. The Carter campaign also produced a leaflet noting that Sanders had paid tribute to Martin Luther King, Jr.

Carter's use of race should be contrasted with Ronald Reagan's behavior in the 1976 North Carolina primary. Reagan's back was against the wall in his battle with Gerald Ford for the Republican nomination for president. Yet Reagan refused to allow Jesse Helms's political organization to send out leaflets suggesting that Gerald Ford might pick a black running mate. Reagan ordered the already printed leaflets destroyed, saying he never wanted to win an election on a racial appeal.

The Sanders mailer was not the Carter campaign's only cynical use of race. The campaign paid for radio ads for a fringe black candidate, C. B. King, in an effort to siphon black votes away from Sanders. Then there was the radio commercial in which Carter said he would never be the tool of any "block" vote, slurring over the word "block" so that it could be mistaken for "black." In his 1976 presidential campaign, Carter used this same tactic, but for the reverse purpose, running an ad on black radio stations that said, "Jimmy Carter went to Iowa as a political black horse," instead of the usual term "dark horse."[21]

Carter refused to say whether he would vote for the black man (and Carter's future ambassador to the United Nations) Andrew Young, on the ballot in 1970 for an Atlanta congressional seat, saying that it was an issue for local voters to decide. Carter also implied that he met privately with the head of the States Rights Council, a white supremacist group, and campaigned in all-white private schools that were known as "segregation academies," where he promised that he would do "everything" to support their existence. "I have no trouble pitching for [George] Wallace [segregationist] votes and the black votes at the same time," Carter told a reporter. Carter also said to another reporter, "I can win this election without a single black vote."

He was right. On primary day, September 9, Carter came in first, with 48.6 percent of the vote to Sanders's 37.7 percent. The remaining votes were scattered among a few minor candidates. Carter had received only 5 percent of the black vote. Because Carter didn't win a clear majority, he now had to face Sanders head-to-head in a runoff two weeks later. Carter won easily, winning 60 percent of the vote, though his share of the black vote barely budged to 7 percent. In November, he rolled to an easy victory over a weak Republican opponent, television broadcaster Hal Suit, again scoring 60 percent of the vote.

Carter blamed the Atlanta media for his poor showing among black voters, and boasted, "Throughout the campaign I had established a standard practice of working with them on an equal basis with whites. I was the only candidate who visited all the communities in cities, and who spent a large part of my time within the predominantly black stores, restaurants, and street areas."[22] But he was also the only candidate to receive Lester Maddox's endorsement, after Carter had won the runoff over Sanders. Maddox said, "I believe the peanut farmer is the right man," and further praised Carter for never having been mixed up with Hubert Humphrey. Carter reciprocated, saying that "Lester Maddox is the embodiment of the Democratic Party.... He has brought a standard of forthright expression and personal honesty to the governor's office and I hope to measure up to this standard." Maddox was Carter's de facto running mate, as he was elected to the step-down position of lieutenant governor.

Peter Bourne records an appalling post-election anecdote: "Affecting a South Georgia accent and humorously mimicking his campaign colleagues, Rafshoon would say, 'We coulda won by a lot more if we'd bin able to stop Jimmah saying so many nahs things abaht nigguhs."[23] Carter's other senior campaign aide, Bill Pope, was even more blunt, telling the *Washington Post* that they had run a "nigger campaign."[24]

Sociologist Kenneth Morris, whose study *Jimmy Carter, American Moralist*, is generally favorable to Carter, observes that the "not-so-subtle racism" of Carter's 1970 campaign was "blatant...the chicanery had been more than accidental; it had been systematic." Even Carter's own campaign strategists used the word "vicious" to describe their tactics. Morris reflects: "Vicious? The judgment is a harsh one. Yet for a candidate to describe himself as 'basically a redneck' and present himself as the populist underdog only to be remembered for waging a 'modern media campaign' suggests a certain discrepancy, beneath which may lurk something akin to viciousness."[25]

In his 1992 book *Turning Point*, which described his entry into politics in the 1960s, Carter deplores "references to the threat of 'bloc voting,' the political treasure trove of racism [that] is still tapped by some candidates....Playing the race card seems to be a tactic that still wins political contests."[26] There is no acknowledgment of Carter's own use of such tactics. All of this disappeared down a memory hole. Instead, his book criticizes Ronald Reagan for using race for political purposes, giving but one example, which is incorrect.[27]

Carter would later deny that he had ever embraced George Wallace or his ideas. But one thing is unmistakable: Carter traveled the low road to the governor's mansion. Perhaps Carter the Christian kept his peace of mind with another of Reinhold Niebuhr's political aphorisms from *Moral Man and Immoral Society*: "It may be necessary at times to sacrifice a degree of moral purity for political effectiveness."[28] Certainly Carter wasn't going to let morality get in the way of winning an election.

The Closet Liberal Escapes

"Carter's polarization of the electorate," Kenneth Morris notes, "misled voters about which side he was really on." They found out on inauguration day in January 1971. The first odd sign of things to come was Carter's selection of an all-black choir, who sang "The Battle Hymn of the Republic," which fits a Georgia political observance about as well as "Dixie" would fit in Howard Dean's Vermont. Carter made it immediately clear, though, that he now wanted the world to look away from how he had obtained office. "The election is over," Carter opened his speech after the usual salutations and pleasantries, "and I realize that the test of a leader is not how well he campaigned but how effectively he meets the challenges and responsibilities of office." A few in the audience perked up; was Jimmy making an oblique apology for his campaign? Rumors later spread that a remorseful Carter had telephoned Sanders to apologize for his campaign tactics. Carter denied this, and given his public record of never admitting mistakes or flaws, his denial is believable.

Instead, Carter was coming out of the closet as a liberal after all. "This is a time for truth and frankness," he continued. The peroration that followed could have come straight from the pen of Richard Goodwin or any number of other LBJ-style, Great Society wordsmiths that Carter otherwise deplored and ridiculed during his campaign: "Our people are our most precious possession and we cannot afford to waste the talents and abilities given by God to one single Georgian. Every adult illiterate, every school dropout, every untrained retarded child is an indictment of us all. Our state pays a terrible and continuing human and financial price for these failures."

Now came the *coup de main*: "At the end of a long campaign, I believe I know our people as well as anyone. Based on this knowledge of Georgians—north and south, rural and urban, liberal and conservative—I say to you quite frankly that the time for racial discrimination is over. No poor, rural, weak, or black person should ever again have to bear the additional burden of being deprived of the opportunity for an education, a job, or simple justice."

There—he said it; words he would never have spoken during the campaign: *The time for racial discrimination is over.* There were, according to Peter Bourne, "stunned gasps from his audience." Reg

Murphy of the *Atlanta Constitution*, always one of Carter's leading critics in Georgia, wrote that Carter's inaugural "strained credibility," suggesting that Georgians "forget a summer of speaking favorably of George Wallace." Separately, the *Atlanta Constitution* said Carter's inaugural represented "an end-of-an-era statement." One of Carter's own campaign staff told Betty Glad, "I was not aware that Carter was far more liberal than the campaign we were waging."[29] The lone black member of the legislature, Senator Leroy Johnson, provided Carter with the cover and pretext he needed. Johnson told the *Atlanta Constitution*, "I understand why he ran that kind of ultra-conservative campaign. You have to do that to win. And that's the main thing. I don't believe you can win this state without being a racist."[30]

Kenneth Morris reports that shortly after Carter's inauguration, "the consensus was that Carter's popularity dropped sharply," while Peter Bourne acknowledged that Carter's inaugural speech "angered a significant segment of the electorate that had voted for him believing he shared their views on race and now felt betrayed." The fact that Georgia governors were limited to single terms was surely a factor in Carter's about-face. It is doubtful that Carter would have said this if he had had to face the voters again. In fact, Carter's own polls (he polled frequently while governor) found that his prospects for another statewide election—he dropped hints about running for the U.S. Senate—were not promising. Carter later made the correct calculation that while Georgia voters might not elect him to statewide office again, they *would* support him for national office out of a sense of regional pride. Just to be certain, though, Carter supported legislation to push back the date of the Georgia presidential primary in 1976 so he would head into his home state with the momentum of a string of early primary triumphs.

Although Carter's nine-minute inaugural speech may not have played well with many Georgians, it reverberated loudly with the national media, which was probably its intended audience. Carter's speech was covered on the front page of the *New York Times* the next day. James Wooten, who wrote the *Times* story, later embellished its effect in his book on Carter, *Dasher*: "It was lovely. In a few deft strokes on that January morning in 1971, he had, for all practical purposes, purged the 1970 campaign from the public perception and replaced it at once with a new image."

A Born-Again JFK for the New South?

A few months later, Carter appeared on the cover of *Time* magazine in a drawing that *Time* itself described as "looking eerily like John F. Kennedy." Carter was the focal point for *Time*'s story about the "New South." Carter's declaration that the time for racial discrimination was past bowled over the editors of *Time*, who led their feature with an excerpt from Carter's speech. "It heralded the end of that final Southern extravagance," *Time* wrote, "the classic rhetoric of 'never.'" It was a remarkable puff piece for Carter, giving a short biographical sketch of his whole life and returning over and over again to his transformative virtues. It read like a combination campaign mailer and chamber of commerce promotional flyer.

Two aspects of Carter's favorable news coverage deserve comment. First, once again the fine hand of his ambition was at work behind the scenes. *Time* had originally planned a general story about the whole crop of new moderate Southern governors elected in 1970, including Florida's Rubin Askew, Arkansas's Dale Bumpers, and South Carolina's John West. The magazine had intended to include all of these governors in the cover artwork. But as reporters were doing background research for the story, the president of the Atlanta-based Coca-Cola company, J. Paul Austin, telephoned the editor of *Time* magazine and lobbied hard for Carter to be the main focus of the story and to appear by himself on the cover. As a major advertiser in Time-Life publications, Austin was undoubtedly persuasive. "Stories in the *New York Times* and *Washington Post*," Hamilton Jordan wrote in a memo to Carter, "do not just happen but have to be carefully planned and planted."[31]

Second, it is interesting to compare the liberal and media double standard toward Carter and Richard Nixon. Liberals never forgave

Nixon for running a "red-baiting" campaign against Helen Gahagan Douglas in California in 1950, but instantly overlooked Carter's race-baiting campaign of 1970. *Time* glossed over Carter's campaign tactics with this anodyne sentence: "To get elected, it was necessary to make some gestures toward the past." Carter redeemed himself with liberals by repudiating his own campaign theme.

Governor Vs. Legislature

Governor Carter settled into a rigorous daily routine, arriving at his desk typically by 7 a.m. He took home a stack of paperwork—sometimes a foot thick—every night, often working as late as 1 a.m. His long work hours did not prevent him, however, from ordering the construction of a tennis court and swimming pool at the governor's mansion without any public notice. This led to minor embarrassment when it was first reported in the *Atlanta Constitution*.

Carter was determined to be an assertive, activist governor, which represented a marked shift from previous Georgia governors, who were content to let the balance of power reside predominantly with the state legislature as long as the governor could have his few favored bills pass, which the legislature almost always did. Carter's conflicts with a state legislature dominated by his own political party were a harbinger of how he would fare with a Democrat-dominated Congress when he reached the White House. It didn't help that, rather than wining and dining them, Carter served food to legislators on paper plates at the governor's mansion.

Gary Fink, author of the most thorough study of Carter's governorship, summarized that "Carter's political style was one source of difficulty [with the legislature]. Reluctant to wheel and deal in the traditional fashion, he had problems pacifying legislators and building coalitions of support for his programs.... At times the Governor could be absolutely ruthless. More than one Georgia legislator primly escorted influential constituents into the Governor's office only to be bitterly chastised for opposing administration measures in their presence."[32] Ben Fortson, Georgia's longtime secretary of state (he had served in the position since 1946), offered one of the most colorful descriptions of Carter in testimony before a state senate committee: "Don't pay any attention to that smile. That don't mean a thing. That man is made of steel, determination, and stubbornness. Carter reminds me of a South Georgia turtle. He doesn't go around a log. He just sticks his head in the middle and pushes and pushes until the log gives way."

Carter's difficult relations with the legislature began immediately over what became the main initiative of his governorship: a sweeping reorganization of the state government. Georgia's government comprised nearly three hundred departments, boards, and commissions, often with overlapping jurisdictions or duplicated functions. Carter had never mentioned this topic during his campaign. His general election opponent, Hal Suit, had made reorganization a centerpiece of his campaign. But it is exactly the kind of initiative one would expect from the hyper-organized engineer-farmer. Although government reorganization sounds sensible in the abstract, there are always entrenched interests that resist managerial reform and dozens of pressure points to derail a practical scheme. Still, reorganization had been accomplished before. In the 1930s, when Richard Russell was governor, a round of reforms had reduced the number of state agencies from 197 to eighteen. Now, with state agencies having grown back like kudzu vines, Georgia had almost three hundred.

Carter pressed the legislature for a special grant of authority that would allow him to craft a complete reorganization plan and submit it as a package to the legislature. The legislature would be allowed only fifteen days to veto, by majority vote, specific aspects of the plan. The legislature balked at surrendering its power to control any reorganization bill, but Carter made passage of this enabling legislation a test of his strength. *Atlanta Constitution* reporter Bill Shipp wrote that Carter "made a number of senators see the light by threatening to cancel pet projects, by calling some of their key constituents back home, and, on occasion, by simply berating them in front of friends."[33]

Carter narrowly won this struggle. In the process, he boosted his own self-regard and confirmed his negative prejudices about the legislature. Carter's contempt for the legislature might have been deserved; a national group, the Citizens Conference on State Legislatures, ranked the Georgia legislature forty-fifth out of the fifty states for overall effectiveness.[34] Unfortunately, Carter had this same attitude about Congress when he got to the White House.

Georgia Gets an Overhaul

Carter immediately set in motion a massive management review process that involved dozens of executives loaned from private sector businesses and the consulting services of Arthur Andersen. Carter's team generated a 2,500-page report recommending three hundred specific changes to the structure of the state government. Carter claimed the changes would save the state $55 million. He was actively involved throughout the process, meeting frequently with the various task forces and reading through all the reports and memos the review team produced. Knowing the plan would have to get through the legislature's gauntlet, Carter launched a public relations offensive (which his PR wizard Gerald Rafshoon oversaw) to promote the plan. Carter's ad hoc "Citizens Committee for Reorganization" mailed out more than 300,000 brochures to community leaders in the state; the effort even included an eleven-minute film. Carter hosted countless meetings with civic groups at the governor's mansion.

Even with Carter's strenuous effort, by the end of 1971, the conventional wisdom was that Carter's plan was in trouble. Reporter Bill Shipp wrote, "Unless [Carter] pulls off a political miracle by January, his government reorganization will be doomed in the regular session of the General Assembly." Leading legislators were complaining loudly that Carter's plan represented a "power grab." Carter viewed the fight with his trademark self-righteousness: "I am going to get it because it is right," he told a reporter.

Carter's plan passed in January 1972 with few changes, a testimony to his relentless determination and skill. He eventually acceded to politics as usual by wheeling and dealing with individual legislators to get their votes, using his discretionary contingency fund of $2 million to dole out favors such as sending a high school band to the Rose Bowl Parade in California, fixing athletic stadiums, and repairing local public works.

The plan as enacted consolidated 278 state agencies into just twenty-two new agencies. The new Department of Natural Resources, for example, folded thirty-six existing state agencies into its purview; the new Department of Administrative Services absorbed seventeen existing agencies. Carter described it as "a revolution in state government that reduced administrative costs by 50 percent." It is extremely difficult to evaluate whether Carter's reorganization scheme really achieved significant cost savings or new efficiency. The total number of state employees under Carter went up—by 24 percent—rather than down, and state spending increased 55 percent during Carter's four years in office. But these were years of rapid population growth and rising inflation; Governor Ronald Reagan's spending numbers in California during these same years are comparable to Carter's. While Carter claimed $55 million in savings, one study concludes the real savings were only about $5 million.[35] Still, this political success would lead Carter to promise during his 1976 presidential campaign to repeat this process in Washington, with the promise of cutting the number of federal agencies from 1,900 to two hundred. Which ones, and how, he could not specify.

Reorganization was not Carter's only managerial reform. He also embraced a technique known as "zero-based budgeting," which he imported from the private sector. As a state senator, Carter had been dismayed at the perfunctory way in which state spending was reviewed (if it was reviewed at all) each year, and as governor he was determined to reform the budget process. Carter required that each department compose its budget request as if starting from zero every year, ranking its activities and programs in order of priority, instead of merely asking for budget increases based on the previous year's spending level, as is typically done almost everywhere in the public sector. Program spending priorities and funding levels would be bundled into a "decision package" for review by higher levels of authority, culminating ultimately with the governor himself.

The trouble with zero-based budgeting is that agency bureaucrats are amply skilled at distorting the process for their own ends with a variation of the device known as the "Washington Monument strategy." Under this strategy, if the National Park Service is faced with a potential budget reduction, they announce that the Washington Monument will be the first thing that will have to be closed. Picking a popular program for a budget cut is almost invariably an effective way to stave off cuts. In the case of zero-based budgeting in Georgia, career budget directors, skilled at bureaucratic infighting, simply inverted spending priorities, listing low priority items as their top priorities, and downgrading popular spending categories that enjoyed considerably political support and therefore couldn't be cut. In this fashion, most departments got what they wanted from the budget process.

The system was too unwieldy for Carter to intervene effectively. His budget process produced as many as 11,000 "decision packages." Obviously, Carter could not review all of them with any serious care. Betty Glad's evaluation is that "zero-based budgeting caused few shifts in spending despite fluctuations in the budget. In fact, only two of thirteen Georgia department heads responding to one survey would go so far as to say that zero-based budgeting 'may have led' to a reallocation of resources."[36] Nonetheless, Carter swore by the procedure, and promised in his 1976 campaign to bring it with him to Washington, D.C. Near the end of his term as governor, he said, "Zero-based budgeting in itself has given me an extremely valuable method by which I can understand what happens deep in a department."

Despite Carter's innate stubbornness and carefully cultivated image of being a purist "above politics," he nonetheless conducted his governorship in a more conventionally political way than is commonly thought. Betty Glad concluded, "Carter used the traditional weapons of power—patronage appointments, dispersal of discretionary funds, attempts to maneuver his supporters into key legislative posts . . . in

short, Carter was very much a politician."[37] Among other time-hon-
ored practices, Carter's friends in the legislature received more highway funds for their districts than Carter's opponents.

Practicing for the Presidency

Carter continued his campaign practice of straddling issues. He told an
anti–Equal Right Amendment group that while he favored the amendment, his wife, Rosalynn, didn't, which wasn't true. When Georgia
native William Calley was convicted for war crimes for his role in
the 1968 My Lai massacre in Vietnam, Carter responded by declaring
"American Fighting Men's Day," during which Carter urged Georgians
to drive with their headlights on in protest of Calley's being made a
scapegoat, which was how the case was widely seen in Georgia.

Carter also kept up his racial two-step, notwithstanding his inaugural proclamation about the end of discrimination. The number of
blacks employed in state government grew by a third under Carter,
and he sponsored the placement of a portrait of Martin Luther King,
Jr. in the state capitol, but he also continued to associate himself with
George Wallace. He wrote to a constituent, "I have never had anything but the highest praise for Governor Wallace. . . . I think you will
find that . . . George Wallace and I are in agreement on most issues."[38]
Carter privately disdained Wallace, once testily telling Jody Powell,
"If you think George Wallace is fit to lead the American people, you
tell them. Not me."[39] He unsuccessfully sponsored an anti-busing resolution at the 1971 meeting of the National Governors Association,
and in 1972 urged the Georgia legislature to pass a resolution calling
for a constitutional convention to adopt an anti-busing amendment.
He also opposed the presidential nomination of George McGovern
in 1972. Carter supported the hawkish (and anti-busing) Senator
Henry Jackson instead, and gave a nominating speech on Jackson's
behalf at the Democratic National Convention in Miami.

Interestingly, by endorsing Jackson, Carter might have double-
crossed Wallace, who claims that he made a deal with Carter to stay
out of the Georgia primary in return for Carter's support at the con-

vention, including a nominating speech. Carter refuses to comment on Wallace's claim. But it raises an interesting question: Was Carter already looking ahead to 1976 and wanting to keep his distance from Wallace? Behind the scenes, the maneuvering was even more Machiavellian, with Carter's operatives lobbying for McGovern to pick Carter as his running mate to balance the ticket with a "moderate" Southern Democrat.

Carter's ambitions were also evident in his use of overseas trade missions. Most governors make trade missions on behalf of business interests in their states, but Carter had an extra dimension—the worldwide reach of Coca-Cola, which Carter referred to as "my own private State Department." Coca-Cola used its international clout to open doors with foreign leaders for Carter, allowing the Georgia governor to establish his foreign policy credentials. Carter made an extensive trade mission to Latin America in 1972, visiting Mexico, Brazil, Costa Rica, Argentina, and Colombia, and a second trade mission to Asia. In 1973, he went to England, Belgium, West Germany, and Israel. Carter met West German chancellor Helmut Schmidt and Israeli prime minister Golda Meir, to whom he would later refer on the campaign trail as "my good friend" based on this one encounter. Carter tried to ingratiate himself with the Democratic foreign policy establishment by cultivating Georgia native Dean Rusk, who had been secretary of state for Presidents Kennedy and Johnson.

While in London on his 1973 trade mission, Carter formed one of his most important connections in burnishing his foreign policy profile: He met David Rockefeller for the first time. Rockefeller was in the midst of assembling the Trilateral Commission as a platform to network business and political leaders from Europe, Asia, and the United States, and he wanted a governor from each party. Governor Dan Evans of Washington was invited to be the Republican member of the Commission, and Rockefeller sought a Democratic governor from the "New South." Carter won the nod after his London dinner with Rockefeller (Rockefeller's staff had already been down to Georgia to check out Carter).

Typically, Carter became a diligent and enthusiastic participant in the Commission's proceedings. Carter met a number of people through the Commission who would play important roles in his drive to the White House and his subsequent administration. One was Columbia University professor Zbigniew Brzezinski, who later became President Carter's national security advisor.[40]

The bookend to Carter's inaugural address occurred in May 1974. Carter was invited, almost as an afterthought, to give remarks at the University of Georgia's annual Law Day. The featured speaker was Senator Ted Kennedy, then widely considered the front-runner for the Democratic nomination in 1976, though he would later announce that he would not run.

It was assumed that Carter, speaking after Kennedy, would make some brief concluding remarks. Instead, Carter talked for more than thirty minutes in a speech that upstaged Kennedy. "Gonzo" journalist Hunter S. Thompson, who had come to Georgia to see Kennedy only to be bowled over by Carter, recorded the scene: "The audience laughed politely [at Carter's opening jokes], but after he'd been talking for fifteen minutes I noticed a general uneasiness in the atmosphere of the room, and nobody was laughing anymore." Ostensibly a speech about criminal justice, most of Carter's speech was actually about his favorite subject—himself. The personal pronoun "I" appears ninety-eight times in text of the speech.[41]

> I'm not qualified to talk to you about law, because in addition to being a peanut farmer, I'm an engineer and nuclear physicist, not a lawyer. . . . But I read a lot and I listen a lot. One of the sources for my understanding about the proper application of criminal justice and the system of equity is from reading Reinhold Niebuhr. . . . The other source of my understanding about what's right and wrong in this society is from a friend of mine, a poet named Bob Dylan. After listening to his records about "The Ballad of Hattie Carol" and "Like a Rolling Stone" and "The Times, They Are

a-Changing," I've learned to appreciate the dynamism of change in a modern society.

It was all there: the name-dropping, the résumé-recitation, and the boasting about his grand stewardship of Georgia. One is led to speculate, in light of Carter's later bad blood with Ted Kennedy, how deliberately Carter calculated this moment. Although Carter was publicly fond of John F. Kennedy, and indeed, as we have seen, attempted to appropriate some of JFK's imagery, he never liked rivals. Betty Glad's judgment is that "his motivation might best be understood in terms of the competitiveness that had led him to take on Bo Callaway in 1966.... Given the opportunity, Carter evidently could not resist competing with the favored man and outdoing him in some way."[42]

An additional move figured prominently into the jigsaw puzzle of Carter's national profile. Democratic National Committee chairman Robert Strauss was looking for someone to serve as the party's national campaign chairman for the 1974 election cycle, when Democrats, owing to the disastrous fallout Watergate was having on Republicans, expected to do very well. Strauss decided to offer the position to Carter.

The national campaign chairman had typically been seen as an honorary or symbolic position, but Carter saw it as an opportunity to travel the country laying the groundwork for his 1976 presidential campaign. The irony is that Strauss picked Carter partly because he thought Carter would not use the post to promote himself to party leaders around the country. Strauss admitted later that his appointment of Carter "let the Trojan Peanut into the National Committee encampment."[43] "I do not intend for it to be an honorary thing," Carter told Strauss, and he made good on his word, sending top aide Hamilton Jordan to the Democratic National Committee headquarters in Washington to coordinate Carter's extensive campaign efforts.

Carter barnstormed the nation on behalf of Democratic candidates, visiting more than thirty states. He campaigned for sixty-two House candidates, appeared at dozens of candidate training workshops, produced thirty-four issue position papers for candidates to use, and formed an advisory group of about one hundred policy experts as a resource for candidates to consult. He paid special attention to getting on the good side of Chicago mayor Richard Daley, and the effort paid off when Daley publicly endorsed Carter at a crucial moment in the 1976 primaries.

All of this activity was conducted with a low profile. Carter was more intent on making contacts for later use than in gaining publicity for himself at the moment—a shrewd judgment; any publicity he might have received would have come at the expense of the candidates he was supposed to be helping. He did not hold a single press conference on any of his campaign swings. On election night in 1974, Carter worked the phones in a back room, making congratulatory phone calls to the winners (and condolence calls to the few Democratic losers) while Strauss fielded media interviews.

Despite Carter's national profile and good-government emphasis in the Georgia statehouse, his own polls showed that he was not popular with Georgia voters. Betty Glad observed, "Carter's political base had deteriorated by 1974 to the point that most statewide politicians preferred not to be closely associated with him. In the scramble for the governorship that year, the candidates, rather than vying for his endorsement, tried to avoid any identification with him."[44]

Former governor Marvin Griffin said, "A lot of people down here who voted for Jimmy are just disgusted with his political philosophy." It didn't matter to Carter. He was building his *national* profile. His audacious design to run for president had begun from his inaugural speech. Carter's election as president in 1976 was not a fluke of the post-Watergate moment, however much he exploited it. As with his four-year campaign to become Georgia's governor, he mounted a five-year campaign to become president. Jimmy Carter was intent on movin' on up.

CHAPTER FIVE

Jimmy Who?

> "He should appear all mercy, all faith, all honesty, all humanity, all religion. And nothing is more necessary to appear to have than this last quality. Men in general judge more by their eyes than by their hands, because seeing is given to everyone, touching to a few. Everyone sees how you appear, few touch what you are."
>
> —NICCOLÒ MACHIAVELLI, *The Prince*

In his book about America's ten worst presidents, Nathan Miller wrote, "Electing Jimmy Carter president was as close as the American people have ever come to picking a name out of the phone book and giving him the job."[1] No, what Jimmy Carter did was conduct such an effective campaign that it rewrote the nominating process for both parties. His extraordinary stamina led political reporters to call him "the first bionic candidate." Sam Donaldson likened Carter to "an electronically guided self-correcting missile." "Jimmy Carter's creation of a national organization from scratch between 1974 and 1976 was a work of brilliance," is Chris Matthews's judgment.[2]

Carter's achievement is all the more remarkable because he was a Southerner. In the first edition of his classic book on the presidency, published in the late 1950s, Clinton Rossiter wrote that it was unthinkable that a Southerner—unless he was from Texas, which is as much Western as Southern—could be elected president. The last Southerner elected president was Zachary Taylor, in 1848. Carter demolished the prejudice against a Southern president and paved the way for the later successful presidential run of Bill Clinton.

Many of Carter's close friends and associates say, with the perfect clarity of hindsight, that they knew as early as 1966 that Carter would run for president. But while a resident of Plains put this in writing in 1967, Bert Lance was the first public figure to make an explicit mention of a possible Carter presidency. It came in 1971, on Carter's forty-seventh birthday. Lance, then Carter's highway director, presented Carter with a commemorative coin set of the fifty states. Lance said, "This gift represents your dominion over one state as governor, but from what I've seen, at some point in the future you will have dominion over all fifty states."[3]

The hints came openly after that, and in 1974, Carter raised the subject with the *New York Times* editorial board, which interviewed him about the 1974 general election campaign. As *Times* editors and reporters rose to end the interview, James Reston asked Carter what his plans were after the election. Carter matter-of-factly replied, "I plan to run for president." The interview immediately resumed and lasted for another hour.[4]

President of What?

In September 1972, after Carter had been spurned as a potential running mate for McGovern, Carter's young political aides Hamilton Jordan, Jody Powell, and Peter Bourne had approached Carter with their audacious plan to skip the stepping-stone job of vice president and run for the presidency in 1976. "I don't think we underestimated what a long shot it was," Jody Powell said, "but we saw how it could be done."[5] Jordan had worked out the nuts and bolts of how Carter could reach the nomination. First, Jordan wrote in a now-famous fifty-page campaign strategy memo, position yourself as the alternative to George Wallace on the right, and Ted Kennedy on the left. Second, run in every primary, which Jordan later likened to "running for sheriff in fifty states." Third, cultivate the national media. Above all, focus on personal character rather than particular issues. As Jordan put it, "Most voters would be inclined more favorably toward a candidate stressing personal qualities such as integrity and confidence than those emphasizing ideological stands on the issues."

The shrewdness of this calculation is most fully appreciated when one realizes that Jordan made it well *before* the Watergate scandal, which put a public spotlight on character and integrity. Betty Glad acutely observed, "Carter's real genius was in seeing that beneath the demoralization, Americans were still yearning for the good authority they thought they had had in the past."[6] Watergate badly damaged the Republican Party and saved the Democratic Party from its potential leftward slide into another McGovern-style defeat. Carter's ability to straddle and evade issues, his ability to appeal simultaneously to moderates and liberals, and his self-portrayal as a man of honest, small-town character, made him ideal. Still, his campaign was an extraordinary long shot. It was, veteran political reporter Jules Witcover wrote, a "seemingly ludicrous proposition that the country should put itself into the hands of a peanut-farming one-term former governor of a Deep South state."[7] Democratic Party elder statesman Averell Harriman is quoted as saying, upon being told in 1975 that Carter was running for president: "Jimmy Carter. *Jimmy Carter?* How can that be? I don't even know Jimmy Carter, and as far as I know, none of my friends know him either." "Unlikely" seemed like the kindest word that could be used to describe Carter's prospects.

When Carter told his family that he intended to run for president, his mother reportedly asked, "President of what?" Atlanta businessman Marvin Shoob recalls that when he went to a 1974 luncheon to discuss Governor Carter's intention to run for president, Shoob assumed Carter was aiming for the presidency of the Atlanta Chamber of Commerce.[8] Carter himself admitted that "we were at first embarrassed about the use of the word 'president.'" Carter's obscurity was confirmed when he appeared on the syndicated TV game show "What's My Line?" in 1973. He stumped the panel, which not only didn't recognize him, but failed to guess he was a state governor. When pollster George Gallup drew up a list of thirty-eight potential Democratic presidential candidates in 1975, Carter's name was not on the list. The *Washington Post*, in a 1972 story, didn't even get his name right, calling him "Governor Jimmy *Collins*."

The Born-Again Mystique

Carter's religious faith would turn out to be the crucial ingredient of his appeal and his success. (Carter's evangelicalism also represented a temporary interruption in the Democratic Party's long-term trend toward secularism and hostility toward religious faith.) It was this dimension of Carter's persona that provided him with the mystique that captured the public imagination in 1976, and almost certainly it was the votes of "born-again" Christians that made the margin of difference in a close election. Polls showed that Carter enjoyed a 25 percent margin over President Ford among evangelical voters, a truly extraordinary political reversal. Since the Civil War, evangelicals had never given the majority of their votes to a Democratic presidential candidate.

Typical of evangelical enthusiasm for Carter were the words of the Reverend Lou Sheldon, who became nationally famous in the 1980s for his right-wing Traditional Values Coalition: "God has his hand upon Jimmy Carter to run for president. Of course, he's wise enough not to be presumptuous with the will of God. But he's moving in the will of God."[9] And the Reverend Pat Robertson trekked to Carter's home in Plains, Georgia, to tape a laudatory segment for his fledgling TV show, *The 700 Club*.

Carter rode the rising wave of born-again evanglicalism. Pollster George Gallup labeled 1976 the "year of the evangelical," and a *Newsweek* cover story, titled "Born Again!", observed that "Carter's dramatic capture of the Presidential nomination has already focused national attention on the most significant—and overlooked—religious phenomenon of the '70s: the emergence of evangelical Christianity into a position of respect and power."[10] (This was perhaps the last time evangelical Christianity would be treated in a positive light by a major media organ.)

Just as he straddled issues, Carter straddled his religious faith. Carter was fond of saying "My religion is as natural to me as breathing," yet at one point in the 1976 campaign Carter said he was "concerned" that people were putting too much emphasis on his profession of faith. "I did not want to mix in religion and my duties as president," he told Peter Bourne before the fall campaign.[11] Yet Carter also told his fellow Baptists, "There's no doubt in my mind that my campaign for the presidency is what God wants me to do."[12] Then there was the studied ambiguity of Carter's signature theme in his stump speech: "If I had to sum up in one word what this campaign is about, that word would be *faith*. The American people want to have *faith* in their government." The invocation of "faith" was clearly a carefully thought out crossover word; it served as an explicit appeal to his co-religionists, and also to the non-believing masses who had lost confidence in government. Above all, it tacitly suggested that both believers and non-believers could have faith in Jimmy Carter. It laid the foundation for Carter's most grandiose promise: "I'll never lie to you." After Lyndon Johnson and Richard Nixon, after Vietnam and Watergate, the nation wanted a saint. Carter's religion allowed him to assert the requisite sainthood indirectly. His 1976 campaign speechwriter Patrick Anderson sensed that Carter's private belief was "that he had been 'born again' not only in a religious sense but in a political sense."[13] True to the last, Carter's post-presidential memoirs are titled *Keeping Faith*.

Jimmy the "Conservative" Outsider

Carter's religious faith provided a strong bulwark for his deliberate image as an outsider. However much Carter's campaign résumé may have made him seem like an outsider, by 1976 he had become a consummate insider of the American establishment, which is merely the parent company of the Washington establishment. Carter's political positioning was a parallel of the New Testament injunction that

Christians should be *in* but not *of* the world; with all of his carefully cultivated national connections (such as his membership in the Trilateral Commission), by 1976 Carter was *in* the establishment, but could claim he was not *of* it. Carter might have realized intuitively what has become conventional wisdom among political scientists over the last two decades: Non-Washington outsiders fare better with voters. This is one reason why governors have dominated presidential elections over the last thirty years. Four of the last five presidents (Carter, Reagan, Clinton, and George W. Bush) were governors. Carter began his early stump speeches: "I am not a lawyer, I am not a member of Congress, and I've never served in Washington." It took chutzpah for a Democrat to attack the capital city that Democrats had dominated for the last generation, but Carter carried it off with aplomb. It was not entirely an act. When he ventured to the House of Representatives chamber to deliver his first address to Congress in 1977, it was the first time he had ever been inside the U.S. Capitol.

In addition to running as an outsider, Carter also ran as a conservative—when it suited him. In the run-up to the 1976 campaign, Carter variously described his philosophy as "benevolent conservatism" or "enlightened conservatism." Even after he became president Carter would periodically proclaim, "I am a very conservative Southern businessman by heritage."[14] But most of the time he continued avoiding "labels," telling reporters in January 1976, "I never characterize myself as conservative, liberal, or moderate, and this is what distinguishes me." He told *Face the Nation* in March, "I don't think the voters are in doubt about what I say; they just feel that I'm the sort of person they can trust, and if they are liberal, I think I'm compatible with their views. If they are moderate, the same; and if the voter is conservative, I think they still feel that I'm a good president."[15] Carter was looking ahead confidently—he still had to win the nomination. But his strategy of being the "common-man outsider" was inspired and stripped voters from left, center, and right.

In fact, Carter's attacks on Washington were virtually indistinguishable from Ronald Reagan's own stump speeches of 1976.

Reagan:

> Our nation's capital has become the seat of a buddy system that functions for its own benefit—increasingly insensitive to the needs of the American worker who supports it with his taxes. Today it is difficult to find leaders who are independent of the forces that have brought us our problems— the Congress, the bureaucracy, the lobbyists, big business, and big labor.

Carter:

> The people of the country feel they've been betrayed.... The competence of government is not an accepted characteristic any more. No matter what a person hopes to do ultimately in life, no matter what his top hope or aspiration may be, he feels, generally, that Washington is an obstacle to the realization of that hope.... We know from bitter experience that we're not going to get the changes we need simply by shifting around the same group of Washington insiders.... Washington has become a huge, wasteful, unmanageable, insensitive, bloated bureaucratic mess."

Other Carter themes could have come straight from the speeches of Reagan. The income tax code, Carter said with a deliberate Southern drawl, "is a *dis*-grace to the human race." He promised welfare reform with a conservative tinge: "There ought to be a 'work incentive' aspect built in," and "we should remove from welfare those people who can work full time." "We should decentralize power," he added. "When there is a choice between government responsibility and private responsibility, we should always go with private responsibility." Reagan could hardly have put it differently, or better. Reagan and Carter even quoted the same Bible verse in their campaign announcement speeches: "If the trumpet give an uncertain sound, who shall prepare himself to the battle."

Showing His True Colors

Carter's presentation of himself as a pious outsider served to mitigate the weakness of his regional identity and his limited experience in public office, which consisted of a single term as a state senator and a single term as governor—surely one of the thinnest résumés of any modern American president. Yet a number of persistent traits seemed to belie his image of a straightforward, upright character. In 1979, he attracted public attention by remarking at a press luncheon that if Senator Ted Kennedy challenged him for the Democratic nomination in 1980, he would "whip his ass." This was old hat to journalists who had covered Carter in 1976, when "kiss my ass" was Carter's frequent and favorite epithet. "I'm glad I don't have to kiss his ass," Carter said of Ted Kennedy in May 1976, when Carter was closing in on the nomination. When a journalist asked Carter what would he do if a member of his Cabinet lied to Congress, Carter snapped, "I'd fire his ass."[16]

These departures from "born-again" piety were nothing compared to the cognitive dissonance his famous *Playboy* interview generated six weeks before the November election. It wasn't simply the oddity of Carter confessing to virtual adultery by having "lusted in his heart" after women—this was orthodox New Testament teaching for evangelicals and fundamentalists, even if the sophisticates of the media didn't recognize it. It was his deliberate use of crude language in discussing the subject:

> I've looked upon a lot of women with lust. I've committed adultery in my heart many times. This is something that God recognizes I will do—and I have done it—and God forgives me for it. But that doesn't mean I condemn someone who not only looks at women with lust but who leaves his wife and *shacks up* with somebody out of wedlock.

Christ says, "Don't consider yourself better than someone else because one guy *screws a whole bunch of women* while the other guy is loyal to his wife." (Emphasis added.)

"Screws a whole bunch of women" is not a common translation of the Gospel passage about adultery. It was language not far removed from the Nixon Watergate tapes. (ABC News debated all afternoon before deciding to allow anchorman Harry Reasoner to quote Carter's words directly on the evening news broadcast; Walter Cronkite did not quote Carter's words on CBS, but merely characterized them as "perhaps a little racy for Sunday school.")

At the same time the *Playboy* interview was out, Norman Mailer quoted Carter in the *New York Times Magazine*: " 'I don't care if people say _____,' and he actually said the famous four-letter word that the *Times* has not printed in the 125 years of its publishing life. He got it out without a backing up of phlegm or a hitch in his rhythm." Was Carter's language a deliberate attempt to appeal to the hip readership of *Playboy* and the secular readers of the *New York Times?* Was he trying to send them a signal, such as, "I'm not a freak?" (Speaking before the National Religious Broadcasters convention, Carter justified the *Playboy* interview as "an opportunity to witness.") Was he trying to ingratiate himself with the macho Mailer and *Playboy's* interviewer, the secular and very left-wing Robert Scheer?

Politicians at the highest levels typically choose their words carefully, and though all of them commit a "gaffe" from time to time, it is possible to see a pattern in Carter's gaffes that suggest his sense of political calculation and subtle advantage overrode his sincerity. (In an off-the-cuff remark to reporters in February 1976, Carter said, "I never do anything unintentionally, even if it looks unintentional."[17]) The biggest flap of his campaign occurred in April 1976, when, during questioning about integration issues, Carter blurted out: "I see nothing wrong with ethnic purity being maintained. I would not force a racial integration of a neighborhood by government action." The reporter conducting the interview, Sam Roberts of the *New York*

Daily News, buried the quote in a jump paragraph that appeared on page 134 of the paper.

Rather than disappearing, however, the phrase "ethnic purity" ignited a firestorm. Under fierce questioning four days later, Carter poured gasoline on the fire: "What I say is that the government ought not to take as a major purpose the intrusion of alien groups into a neighborhood simply to establish their intrusion." This catapulted the story onto the front page of the *New York Times* and onto the TV network news. "Ethnic purity" and "alien intrusion" were red flags to liberals and civil rights groups, and Carter had to work mightily to mend fences. With his usual light touch, Jesse Jackson said that Carter's comment was "a throwback to Hitlerian racism." Julian Bond echoed Jackson, saying the statement sounded like "Nazi Germany," and Georgia civil rights activist Hosea Williams said it proved that Carter was a "sophisticated racist."[18]

But was "ethnic purity" an unintentional slip? This flap arose after Carter had vanquished Wallace in the Florida primary, and on the eve of a series of crucial northern primaries in states where Wallace had done well previously. Careful observers noted that while Carter included Martin Luther King, Jr. on his roster of great Americans, he conveniently omitted King's name before audiences of Southerners or suburban whites. Carter knew that Democrats had been losing the votes of suburban voters in the north because of busing and integration. Carter's aides denied the implication when reporters pressed the question. Yet Patrick Anderson recalled, "Another time, at a rally in West Virginia, he told a dumb joke about some tourists in Miami who started yelling 'Hialeah!' (the race track) instead of 'Hallelujah!' in church. Reporters immediately asked me if he could possibly be unaware that a West Virginia audience might take that as 'a Jew joke,' since at certain levels of Southern humor all visitors to Miami are assumed to be Jews."[19]

Carter Perfects His Straddle

Then there was Carter's elusiveness on major issues. "On a range of issues," Jules Witcover wrote, "he showed all the elusiveness of a scatback."[20] Carter had a way of making a refusal to give a plain answer to a direct question an act of political morality. He could carry off the most audacious contradictions with a confidence bordering on belligerence. Betty Glad described his method as "sending out complex messages that various listeners could interpret according to their own predispositions," in other words, sophisticated pandering.[21] Despite his explicit attacks on Washington as a "bloated bureaucratic mess" and an "obstacle to hope," Carter asserted to a stunned press conference in Washington, "I'm not anti-Washington; I've never made an anti-Washington statement."[22]

Typical of Carter's ability to straddle was his handling of the abortion issue in the Iowa caucuses. The 1976 election was the first presidential election since *Roe v. Wade*, and the politics of the issue were still crystallizing. But there were over half a million Roman Catholics in Iowa, and Sargent Shriver, George McGovern's pro-life Catholic running mate in 1972, was the obvious candidate for Catholics to support.

So when Carter met with Catholic clergy he emphasized that he opposed abortion as a matter of personal conviction, and though he would not support a constitutional amendment banning abortion, he would support a "national statute" regulating abortion, whatever that meant. "I would prefer a stricter ruling" was his comment when asked about *Roe v. Wade*. This was good enough for pro-lifers in Iowa, some of whom spoke up from the pulpit that Carter was their man. No one knew that he had written a foreword to a book, *Women in Need*, that advocated abortion rights, or that he had encouraged the plaintiffs in *Doe v. Bolton*, the Georgia abortion rights case that had been the companion to *Roe v. Wade*, or that he had supported abortion as a part of Georgia family planning programs while governor.[23]

Carter also met with members of the National Organization for Women (NOW) in Iowa, reassuring them that he supported their intransigent pro-abortion stance. Jules Witcover summarized the incident: "Carter's handling of the abortion issue in Iowa was a signal of things to come. He would display a talent for being on two sides of an issue that both dismayed and frustrated his opponents. In a political society accustomed to having its leading figures neatly compartmentalized as liberals and conservatives, Carter defied such categorizing."[24] William F. Buckley, Jr. wrote, "Carter's position on abortion is more variously conjugated than French irregular verbs." Columnists Rowland Evans and Robert Novak concluded that pro-life Democratic voters, deceived by Carter's prevarications, provided his margin of victory in the Iowa caucuses. A Catholic priest in Iowa was later quoted as saying, "I think I've been sandbagged." (Later, after the Democratic convention, Carter sent up more smoke, saying the Democratic platform stance on abortion was "a little bit too liberal, too permissive.")

Carter's gauzy conservative-sounding views and his fuzziness on the issues generated massive distrust among Democratic Party liberals. "This independent stance of his," said Arizona congressman Mo Udall, his principal rival on the left during the primaries, "may just be a camouflage for a 'closet conservative.' "[25] Indiana senator Birch Bayh attacked Carter by saying "We don't need a Democrat running around the country peddling Republican principles." Mark Shields, then working as an advisor to Udall, complained that Carter "has more positions than the *Kama Sutra*." Senator Bob Dole, Gerald Ford's running mate, tried to pin Carter as a liberal, calling him "Southern-fried McGovern." "Carter's like Gatsby," a journalist told *National Review*, "I don't know where he comes from."[26] Figuring out the "real Carter," the *New Republic*'s Richard Strout wrote, became "the greatest manhunt in political history.... I have never seen a candidate like him. I don't know if the country is having a presidential election or a religious revival."[27] George Will observed, "Carter seems to believe that the way to keep knowledge pure is to keep it scarce."[28] A major labor union leader told the *Washington Post*'s David Broder, "I don't know who he is, where he's going, or where he's been."[29] Chris Matthews described Carter as "a country slicker."[30] Steven Brill summarized the growing unease of the press with his observation that "His is the most sincerely insincere, politically antipolitical, and slickly unslick campaign of the year."[31] Even Willie Sutton, of bank-robbing fame ("Because that's where the money is"), got in on the act, saying of Carter, "I've never seen a bigger confidence man in my life, and I've been around some of the best in the business."[32]

Jokes about Carter's fuzziness began appearing in the media. When his father asked him if he had chopped down the family's beloved peach tree, went one popular gag, Jimmy replied, "Well, perhaps." Comedian Pat Paulsen quipped, "They wanted to put Carter on Mount Rushmore, but they didn't have room for two more faces."

Promises, Promises

Yet it worked. It might not have worked had Carter not enjoyed the luxury of having the liberal opposition in the primaries divided among five candidates. He knocked off his rivals one by one, starting with George Wallace in the Florida primary, then Mo Udall in Wisconsin, and Scoop Jackson in Pennsylvania. Carter attacked Jackson in vintage fashion. Having sponsored anti-busing resolutions at the National Governors Association, Carter now attacked Jackson for opposing busing, implying that Jackson was a racist: "Senator Jackson ran a campaign around the busing issue, one that has racial or racist connotations." Always looking to have things both ways, Carter was quick to add, "I don't think he is a racist. I think he recognized an emotional issue and capitalized on it."[33] By the time California governor Jerry Brown joined the race late in the spring and smashed Carter in several June primaries, it was too late. Carter had discovered how to succeed at being all things to all people, at least for the moment.

Carter made more campaign promises than any successful presidential candidate in history (his staff counted more than two hundred; the complete list required 111 pages).[34] Exit polls in the primaries showed that even people who voted for Carter were unsure of his stands on the issues. A CBS/New York Times poll on the eve of the Democratic convention in July found that 52 percent of the public thought Carter was a conservative, while a Harris poll in late September found that Carter "comes across as more conservative to conservative voters, more middle-of-the-road to middle-of-the-roaders, and more liberal to liberals."[35] Carter's own pollster Pat Caddell found on the November election day that "fifty percent of the public still does not know where Carter stands on the issues."[36]

Some conservatives were hopeful that Carter represented a return to the older, more moderate liberalism of Harry Truman and John F. Kennedy. Even *National Review* thought Carter had some promise. Former Agnew speechwriter John Coyne wrote, "There are many things to recommend Carter. As a devout Christian, he is also a dedicated anti-Communist. As a firm believer in the afterlife, he can be counted upon not to attempt to build the perfect society here on earth."[37]

It is a mistake to dismiss Carter's performance as simply skillful wishy-washiness. Carter's straddling ability kept the Democratic Party's conservative Wallace wing from openly splitting from the liberal McGovern wing, and prevented a cataclysmic crisis in the party. Bridging the two wings of the party was a considerable achievement, which he accomplished by subsuming the liberal wing of the party beneath his campaign of character over issues. This presented a terrible problem for liberals and liberalism, for it enabled liberalism to postpone confronting its problems—its increasing divorce from the American public on policy issues—for another decade. Few liberals understood the truth of political scientist Walter Dean Burnham's judgment at the time: "Carter's nomination by the Democratic party will virtually certify that activist liberalism, as a national political force, is now in receivership."[38] Carter's reliance on liberals to staff his administration kept the liberal wing of the party failing to recognize its difficulties and consolidating its dominance over the Democratic Party, to the dismay of the future "Reagan Democrats" who would migrate to the Republicans.

Even though Carter had never topped 54 percent in any contested primary, did not win a single head-to-head race, and lost eight of the last fifteen primaries, he nevertheless went into the Democratic convention with a solid lock on the nomination. Sixty-four percent of delegates told an NBC survey that they had "reservations" about Carter, but it was too late; a series of "Stop Carter" movements among party liberals never gained traction. This weakness enabled Carter to maintain his studied distance from liberals; he turned down Ted Kennedy's offer to place Carter's name in nomination at the convention. He kept up his "just folks" image right into his nomination acceptance speech, which began, "My name is Jimmy Carter, and I'm still running for president." He enjoyed a seemingly insurmountable thirty-point lead in the polls over either Ford or Reagan (the Republican contest had not yet been decided at the time of the Democratic convention). Patrick Anderson commented, "If he had packed up that night and flown home to Plains and gone fishing until election day, he might have won by a landslide."

"Unfortunately," Anderson added, "he campaigned."[39]

On the Campaign Trail

Carter experienced the largest post-nomination decline in voter support of any candidate since opinion polling began in the 1930s. It was inevitable that a nominee whom 98 percent of the public had never heard of the year before would suffer erosion in the polls as election day neared. What was not inevitable was the many ways Carter found to squander his big lead. "Carter's course," *National Review* observed on October 1, "has resembled that of a football team which, after a dazzling string of pre-season victories, throws away the winning game plan and adopts an inferior one for the actual season."[40] "It may be that Jimmy Carter was overexposed," Ken Bode wrote in the *New Republic*, "that his message of love, trust, and goodness began to curdle among those voters given the largest doses."[41]

The vagueness on issues that had served Carter so well in the primaries began to plague him as the fall campaign unfolded. He was repeatedly asked for details of his proposal for "sweeping tax reform." He promised would it be forthcoming in the spring, "after the convention." After the convention, he dodged the issue. "I just can't answer that question because I haven't gone into it. . . . It is just not possible to do that on a campaign trail." Some sloppy phrasing about raising taxes on those above "the median income" seemed to imply

that Carter would raise taxes on more than half of American households, and was quickly disavowed. Carter was alternatively for
defense cuts, but also for military strength, for détente, but for being
tougher on the Soviets, against abortion, but against any effective
restrictions on abortion, for new social spending, but also for a bal-
anced budget and against tax increases, against "socialized medicine,"
but for mandatory comprehensive federal health insurance, which is
the same thing. More and more media accounts were starting to dwell
on Carter's "flip-flops." In the end, however, it must be judged that
Carter's plunging lead in the fall campaign coincided with voters
coming to see that he was not a conservative. (This was predicted by
Time magazine reporter Stanley Cloud in June 1976. Cloud wrote,
"Conservatives may feel deceived when they discover that Carter's
liberalism borders on populism.")

Carter made numerous tactical mistakes on the campaign trail. He
promised a "blanket pardon" (which he somehow distinguished from
amnesty) to Vietnam draft dodgers in a speech before the conservative
American Legion. The audience of fifteen thousand erupted in loud
boos, and Carter had to stop speaking until the Legion convention
chairman could gavel the audience into silence. The scene was the
lead story in the next day's news. In another speech, Carter said that
according to the teachings of his church, homosexuality was a sin. It
was one thing to say this in the Bible Belt states of Iowa or Alabama,
but Carter gave this speech in San Francisco. At the traditionally
lighthearted and strictly nonpartisan Al Smith dinner in New York in
October, Carter stepped over the line with brazenly partisan remarks.
"Carter Booed at Al Smith Dinner" was the lead headline of the next
day's news coverage. Carter worsened the bad impression he gave by
leaving after his own remarks, missing President Ford's speech.

Carter's biggest mistake was the *Playboy* interview, which cut into
his support among women and evangelicals. The Reverend W. A.
Criswell of Dallas, Texas, pastor of the largest Southern Baptist congregation in the nation, promptly endorsed Ford. Carter did display
one of his few flashes of humor over the *Playboy* episode, however.

When asked by a reporter for his reaction to the interview, Carter replied that he hadn't read it yet. "I looked at the other parts [of the magazine] first," he told the *New York Daily News*.

The sensational sex talk of the *Playboy* interview overshadowed a more significant political gaffe contained elsewhere in the same interview. At the very end of the interview, Carter had said, "I don't think I would ever take on the same frame of mind that Nixon or Johnson did—lying, cheating, and distorting the truth." Johnson might have been an unpopular figure among liberal Democrats, but to equate him with Nixon was stepping into a deep pile of trouble. Lady Bird Johnson was furious, and Carter was about to campaign in Texas. Arriving in Houston, Carter tried to suggest that *Playboy* had conjured up an unfortunate "paraphrase" or "summary" of his remarks. But the phrase was a verbatim quotation, captured on tape. Reporters were outraged. "The candidate who promised never to tell a lie had told a whopper," Patrick Anderson wrote. Carter later tried to suborn journalists by inviting them to a private off-the-record meeting with him in which he solicited their advice on how he could campaign better. The journalists who attended were offended anew.

Was his slur regarding Johnson another of Carter's Freudian slips, like "ethnic purity," or was this another subtle indication of Carter's above-it-all attitude, which had caused him to remain deliberately aloof from other Democrats throughout the campaign? In local campaign stops, Carter eschewed the familiar photo opportunity with the local Democratic congressional candidate, and seldom endorsed the local Democrat in his remarks to crowds. It was as if he was running as a virtual independent. Democrats around the country reciprocated Carter's aloofness. The *Washington Post* commented, "Even now, as Carter crisscrosses the country, the old-time Democratic politicians greet him more often than not like a naturalized Martian rather than as a fellow soldier." "It's not that Carter's a Southerner," one Democrat was quoted; "it's him; and he's a strange guy, and people seem to sense it too."[42] "If I have to take Carter I'll take him, but I'll have to swallow hard," Pennsylvania Democratic state senator Martin Murray said, "He scares the hell out of me."[43] "There is enough in the Carter record, as governor and campaigner, to make us apprehensive," the *New Republic* editorialized. The flagship magazine of mainstream intellectual liberalism endorsed Carter "with reservations."[44] Worried liberals consoled themselves with the thought that at least Walter Mondale was on the ticket. "With Mondale's designation," the *New Republic* reassured itself, "the slate is bonded 100 proof liberal."[45] The *New York Times* financial page certified this judgment with the headline: "Sag in Stocks Laid to Mondale: Democratic Ticket Regarded Warily on Wall Street."

More significant than his slips and deliberate aloofness from the Democratic Party was the reemergence of Carter's nastiness, which dismayed even his closest advisors. Hamilton Jordan tried to persuade Carter to stop attacking "the Nixon-Ford administration." "The phrase 'Nixon-Ford administration,'" Jordan told Carter in a memo,

> suggests a very conscious effort on your part to equate Ford, the man, with Nixon, the man. This does not and will not wash with the American people and I believe will be generally interpreted as a personal attack on the integrity of Gerald Ford. When I watched you say that on the news recently, it sounded out of character for you. It certainly did not sound like the man who wanted to put Watergate behind us and unite the country.[46]

But Carter didn't let up on this or other slashing attacks on Ford. "Richard Nixon was bad enough," Carter said on the stump in Indiana in late September, "It's been worse the last two years."[47] "There was an undercurrent of malice in the Carter world," Patrick Anderson observed, while Jules Witcover scored Carter's "extraordinary churlishness."

By October, the effect of Carter's smile was wearing off. He was losing about half a point per day in the polls. By mid-October, the race was a dead heat. Ford had even closed the gap in the South. The race,

National Review observed, was now between a crippled hare and a stumbling tortoise. Whoever made the last mistake would lose. Luckily for Carter, Ford made a bigger blunder than Carter's *Playboy* interview.

The Ford-Carter Debates

The Ford-Carter debates of 1976 were the first since the Nixon-Kennedy debates in 1960. Because of the legend and effect of the Nixon-Kennedy debates, where the superficiality of the candidates' appearances trumped the substance of the encounter, most candidates preferred not to debate. But Ford was far behind in the polls when he issued his debate challenge to Carter; he apparently had nothing to lose. And for the confident challenger, he felt stepping into the ring against the incumbent president would give him instant stature.

The first debate in late September had gone well enough for Ford, with Carter seeming stiff, nervous, and deferential. Post-debate polls judged Ford the winner, and his surge in popularity continued. The second debate, in San Francisco in early October, was dedicated to foreign policy issues, and on the surface figured to favor Ford as well. Yet it was a tricky moment for both candidates. Carter had called for defense cuts, which appeased liberals, but made him vulnerable to the traditional Republican charge that Democrats were weak on defense and soft on communism. Carter effectively blunted this charge by attacking détente from the right. In Texas, he even ran a television ad quoting Ronald Reagan, approvingly, on foreign policy.

The Democratic platform criticized Ford's détente as little more than "bad bargains, dramatic posturing, and the stress on general declarations....We must avoid assuming that the whole of American-Soviet relations is greater than the sum of its parts, that any agreement is superior to none, or that we can negotiate effectively as supplicants." Polls showed that a large majority of Americans thought we had been going too easy on the Soviet Union; a *Newsweek* poll at the time of the second Ford-Carter debate found 73 percent agreed with the statement that the U.S. had "made too many concessions to the Soviets." But the same poll found a majority approved of Henry

Kissinger's job performance—a reflection either of his powerful personality or the cognitive dissonance of American public opinion. Could Ford find a way to get some of Kissinger's popularity and mystique to rub off? Carter made a point of baiting Ford in the debate, charging, "As far as foreign policy goes, Mr. Kissinger has been the president of this country."

The full decay of détente became evident when, late in the debate, the *New York Times'* Max Frankel posed a question to President Ford about the effect of the 1975 Helsinki accord on human rights. It was in answer to this question that Ford delivered one of the all-time clunkers of American politics: "There is no Soviet domination of Eastern Europe, and there never will be under a Ford administration."

Say what? Could Ford really be saying that the "Captive Nations" were no longer captive? Frankel couldn't believe his ears. Up in the control booth, Ford's national security advisor, Brent Scowcroft, turned white as Ford apparently dismissed the more than thirty Soviet divisions stationed in Eastern Europe as an irrelevance.

Frankel asked a quick follow-up question to see if Ford had misspoken and wished to elaborate. "[D]id I understand you to say, sir, that the Russians are not using Eastern Europe as their own sphere of influence and occupying most of the countries there and making sure with their troops that it's a communist zone?" At this point, Ford should have heeded the maxim attributed to the British politician Denis Healey, which he called "Healey's First Law of Holes," i.e., if you're in one, stop digging. Ford didn't know Healey's First Law.

> I don't believe, Mr. Frankel, that the Yugoslavians consider themselves dominated by the Soviet Union. I don't believe that the Romanians consider themselves dominated by the Soviet Union. I don't believe that the Poles consider themselves dominated by the Soviet Union. Each of those countries is independent, autonomous; it has its own territorial integrity. And the United States does not concede that

those countries are under the domination of the Soviet Union.

Carter couldn't believe his good fortune, and pounced hard on Ford's gaffe. "I would like to see," Carter replied in a rapid-fire staccato, "Mr. Ford convince the Polish-Americans and the Czech-Americans and the Hungarian-Americans in this county that those countries don't live under the domination and supervision of the Soviet Union behind the Iron Curtain." Over the next few days, Carter compared Ford to George Romney, the former Republican governor of Michigan—Ford's home state—who had said he had been "brainwashed" into supporting the war in Vietnam. Carter conveyed the none-too-subtle double criticism that Ford was under the brainwashing of Kissinger, and was too dumb to know it. "It doesn't surprise me that Mr. Ford didn't know the condition of relatives of Americans in Eastern Europe," Carter said. But he went on to display his nasty side: "Mr. Ford doesn't know anything about Americans in America." Ford stubbornly refused for almost a week to admit his mistake, and by then the damage was done. Ford's surge in the polls promptly stalled, and Carter opened up some daylight again.

Jimmy Wins

On election day, Carter won just over half of the popular vote, 50.1 percent, to Ford's 48 percent, but it was even closer than that. Carter's large majority in the South pushed him past the 50 percent mark; outside the South, Carter lost the popular vote to Ford. A switch of eight thousand votes in Ohio and Hawaii would have given Ford a slim majority in the electoral college (and very likely a Florida 2000–style imbroglio). Ohio is home to a large population of Eastern European immigrants. Polls showed Ford was running well with these voters until his clunker in the second debate. Exit polls nationwide showed that a quarter of independent voters made up their minds in the last five days before the election.

Republicans fared poorly all the way down the ticket. They lost one House seat, on top of the forty-three they had lost in the post-Watergate election of 1974. The Democrats' House majority of 292–143 was nearly as large as it had been after Johnson's landslide over Goldwater in 1964. The Senate remained unchanged, with a 62–38 Democratic majority. Democrats outnumbered Republicans in state legislatures by more than two to one: 5,116 Democrats to 2,368 Republicans. The GOP held a majority in both houses of only four state legislatures—those of Colorado, Idaho, South Dakota, and Wyoming—down from twenty states in 1968, and held only twelve governorships, down from thirty-two in 1968. Only 24 percent of all voters were registered Republicans, the lowest since the party was formed in the 1850s. The election produced, in the words of Michael Barone, "Democratic [Party] government as far as the eye could see." Among the winners in 1976 were Albert Gore Jr., elected to the house of representatives in Tennessee, and Bill Clinton, elected attorney general in Arkansas. Clinton, who would eventually inherit Carter's mantle, supported Jerry Brown in the primaries.

National Review presciently observed shortly after the election: "When Carter has to face as President the policy decisions he could fudge during the campaign, the divided character of the Democratic Party will surface with a vengeance. The ingredients for internecine warfare remain only too obvious."[48] This is exactly what befell Carter, starting on Inauguration Day.

CHAPTER SIX

President Carter at Home

"The central idea of the Carter administration is Jimmy Carter himself."

—Carter speechwriter JAMES FALLOWS

Carter's presidency was one of the most politically disastrous in history. His campaign piety had become governing self-righteousness. He alienated Democratic liberals like Tip O'Neill and Democratic conservatives like Scoop Jackson, and shredded his Southern evangelical base just as he had shredded his popularity with Georgians as governor. Incredibly, Carter thought he could govern as he campaigned, on image rather than substance. After the election, Carter pollster and advisor Pat Caddell drafted a fifty-six-page memo recommending exactly that course for the early months of Carter's presidency.

Carter followed Caddell's advice closely. He chose to be inaugurated in a plain business suit instead of formal wear. He walked down Pennsylvania Avenue with his wife and daughter, eschewing the presidential limousine, much to the consternation of the Secret

Service. He sold the presidential yacht "Sequoia," and ordered two Cabinet members and their staffs to move from four-star hotels into cheaper accommodations during his first state visit to Europe. He ended the playing of "Hail to the Chief" when he entered banquet halls and speaking venues, and circulated a memo to government offices instructing "that the official presidential photograph be limited to those places where absolutely necessary," which was not especially helpful guidance. He chose to make do without a White House chief of staff, because he wanted everyone to have "direct access" to the Oval Office. He gave his first televised address wearing a cardigan sweater beside a White House fireplace, self-consciously recalling FDR's radio "fireside chats." George Will remarked on Carter's "pompous crusade against pomp," of "a President who, with a flourish, bans ruffles and flourishes."

One of Carter's most "down-to-Earth" gestures was agreeing to do a call-in radio broadcast with Walter Cronkite titled "Ask President Carter." The calls were obviously not carefully screened. The program produced such gems as:

> CALLER: Two questions: Would it be possible to eliminate the word "drug" from drug store advertising? Also, when new drugs are invented, they always use the word "drug." Why not use the terminology "medication?" Maybe it would discourage drug abusers. What do you think?
>
> THE PRESIDENT: I think that's a good idea. . .

* * *

> CALLER (Mrs. Dehart): Well, I really had more of a favor to make than a request . . . . I have been reading about vitamin B17, Laetrile. And I feel that the people in this country should be permitted to use this treatment in this country. I realize that the AMA says it's not been proved safe, but

for a terminal patient, who is not going to live and has a chance to live with it, I don't see how it could be dangerous. And hospital insurance does not cover treatment not authorized by the AMA, and most hardworking people in this country cannot afford treatment that's not paid under insurance benefits. And if a person has money available to leave the country for treatment in one of the seventeen countries where the cancer specialists use this successfully, they have a chance of recovery. And a lot of people even from my area have done this. What I want to say is that we need your help and the government's help in taking this vitamin out, that it's made available to the American people.

THE PRESIDENT: All right. Mrs. Dehart, I might let someone from the Department of HEW give you a call Monday and talk to you about it further. And you didn't ask me a question, but I have heard about the controversy. I know that in some of our neighboring countries, I think Mexico, you can buy the Laetrile and be treated with it.

CALLER: That's right.

THE PRESIDENT: Why don't you let me have someone call you Monday, if you don't mind. It wouldn't help much if I called you, because I'm not a medical doctor and I'm not familiar with it. Would that suit you okay?

CALLER: Yes, sir, it would. . .

* * *

CALLER (Mr. Went): The question, Mr. President, is, would it be possible for you to accept an invitation from the governor of Minnesota or Mayor Geller of Granite Falls to be the speaker on National President's Day?

THE PRESIDENT: Mr. Went, I doubt it. . .

* * *

CALLER (an eleven-year-old girl): Why doesn't Amy go to a private school?

THE PRESIDENT: She goes to the public school and did in Georgia when we lived there as well. She enjoys it very much, and I have a very strong commitment to the public school system and don't have anything against the private school system. But I think it helps the public schools in Washington, D.C., to have the president's daughter go there . . . I hope sometime perhaps, Michelle, you can come and visit with Amy. . .

Saturday Night Live deftly satirized this episode with Dan Akroyd portraying Carter talking down a drug-tripping caller.

President Vs. Congress

When the new Speaker of the House, Thomas P. "Tip" O'Neill, arrived for Carter's inaugural dinner on January 20, 1977, he was stunned to find himself and his guests seated at the farthest table in the balcony, far away from the new president. "The next morning," O'Neill wrote in his memoirs, "I called Hamilton Jordan and said, 'Listen, you son of a bitch. When a guy is Speaker of the House and his family gets the worst seats in the room, he figures there's a reason behind it. I have to believe that you did that deliberately.' 'If that's the way you feel about it,' he replied, 'we'll give you back the three hundred dollars.' 'Don't be a wise guy,' I said. 'I'll ream your ass before I'm through.'"[1] From that moment on, O'Neill referred to Carter's top aide as "Hannibal Jerkin."

O'Neill's bad seats were not an oversight; Jordan had put him in the back of the room on purpose, as an overt sign of his contempt for the Democratic establishment he and Carter's campaign had routed in the long march to the White House. (In 1979, Jordan offered O'Neill a groveling apology for his arrogance.) But a low opinion of Congress wasn't limited to Jordan; Carter himself had scant respect for Congress. At their first meeting, before Inauguration Day, Carter told Speaker O'Neill that when the Georgia state legislature had tried to block his gubernatorial initiatives, he went over its head to the people, and that he would not hesitate to take the same approach with Congress. "I can talk to your constituents easier than you can," Carter said.

O'Neill was shocked, asking Carter, "You don't mean to tell me you're comparing the House and Senate with the Georgia legislature? Hell, Mr. President, you're making a big mistake." As O'Neill put it in his memoirs, "I tried to explain how important it is for the president to work closely with the Congress. He didn't seem to understand." O'Neill tried to make it simple, pointing out to Carter that three-fourths of the members of the House had run *ahead* of Carter in their districts in the election, and would not hesitate to run *against* Carter in the future if necessary. It was to no avail. The stubbornness that had served Carter so well during the long drive to the White House would typify his relations with a Congress dominated by his own party.

Carter, political scientist Charles Jones observed, "was almost incapable of saying anything nice about members of Congress even as he traveled among their constituents."[2] Although Tip O'Neill wrote in his memoirs that Carter was the smartest public official he had ever known, his administration was "like a bad dream." Democratic senator Daniel Inouye of Hawaii echoed O'Neill's complaint: "There were very few happy moments between the Democratic leadership and Carter."[3]

In a chapter of Carter's own memoirs, titled, "My One-Week Honeymoon with Congress" (it is arguable that it lasted even a week), Carter failed to note his administration's incompetence at dealing with Congress. Instead, he blamed Congress for the trouble, noting that the majority of its House members had been elected within the last four years, and that most Democrats had never served under a Democratic president before. But the miscues were obvious to everyone else. In one celebrated example, Carter's staff neglected to invite California's Japanese-American congressman Norman Mineta to a White House dinner in honor of the Japanese prime minister because they thought Mineta was Italian.

Carter made a bad start even worse when, barely a month into his administration, he threatened to veto a public works bill unless nearly two dozen water projects were cancelled. Carter was correct that this was pork-barrel spending, but he announced his veto threat without consulting congressional leaders or attempting to compromise. Congress first learned of Carter's threat the same way the public did: in the morning newspaper. "I've never been so upset in my whole life," one House committee chairman sputtered. "I just read it in the paper."[4]

President Vs. His Own Party

These populist touches helped to obscure further Carter's ideological fuzziness. During the campaign, Carter had promised to balance the budget by the end of this first term, and said he would not approve new spending programs incompatible with this goal. But he also endorsed several expensive spending ideas during the campaign, mostly to placate the liberal wing of the party. *National Review* predicted shortly after the election that "because of fiscal realities, he will almost certainly have to draw back from most or all of his liberal social-spending commitments, and when he does, the liberal bloc in Congress and the liberals in the media and in the academy can be expected to turn against him."[5] This is exactly how the first weeks of Carter's presidency unfolded.

Liberals were certain that Carter would acquiesce to new activist government programs once in office, and were shocked to discover that Carter really meant it about balancing the budget. Democratic senator Alan Cranston of California leaked the liberal unhappiness over Carter's stinginess to the media. "Many liberals in his own party," wrote Robert Shogan of the *Los Angeles Times*, "complain that he is the most conservative Democratic President since Grover Cleveland."[6] Carter relished the discomfort he caused liberals with this pledge. "I wish you could have seen the stricken expressions on the faces of those Democratic leaders when I was talking about balancing the budget," he told biographer Peter Bourne.[7]

It wasn't just members of Congress whom Carter upset. Carter charged his secretary of Health, Education, and Welfare, Joseph Califano, with the task of coming up with a welfare reform plan. Califano didn't take seriously Carter's condition that any reform plan had to be accomplished at current funding levels. When Califano presented Carter a set of options that all cost billions more, Carter exploded. "Are you telling me that there is no way to improve upon the present system except by spending billions of dollars? In that case, to hell with it! We're wasting our time."[8] Carter eventually relented, sending a welfare reform plan to Congress that he said would cost an additional $2.8 billion a year. When the Senate Finance Committee estimated that Carter's plan would cost nearly $15 billion more—a 70 percent increase over the current cost—the plan quickly died.

What most upset liberals, especially Senator Ted Kennedy, was Carter's refusal to back a comprehensive national health insurance plan that would cost upwards of $100 billion a year. During the campaign Carter had endorsed national health insurance, but in office proposed a slow, piecemeal approach to the issue. The government "cannot afford to do everything," Carter said, postponing even the introduction of a bill until 1979. What Carter eventually proposed in 1979 was a hospital cost-containment measure that went nowhere.

Liberals were braying publicly against Carter barely four months into his first term. The AFL-CIO, the U.S. Conference of Mayors, and the Americans for Democratic Action (ADA) all charged Carter with betraying his campaign promises. Michael Harrington complained that the Carter administration was "opposed to the principles of the New Deal." House Speaker O'Neill said, "I didn't become Speaker to dismantle programs I've fought for all my life." Senator George McGovern attacked

Carter at the annual convention of the ADA for "trying to balance the budget on the backs of the poor and the jobless." (Ted Kennedy said the same thing.) ADA national director Leon Schull threatened that if Carter continued on his present course, "the liberal movement, with the ADA in the forefront, will go into the opposition" just as it had against LBJ. In 1978, an Oval Office meeting between Carter and members of the Congressional Black Caucus turned into a shouting match, as Carter rebuffed demands for more spending on urban programs. Senator Ted Kennedy warned, "the party that tore itself apart over Vietnam in the 1960s can tear itself apart today over budget cuts in basic social programs."[9]

Carter's professed fiscal conservatism, which would soon be jettisoned, was matched with a professed cultural conservatism, if not Puritanism. "For those of you living in sin," Carter told his staff, "I hope you'll get married. For those of you who've left your spouses, go back home." His most quixotic gesture was his criticism of *People* magazine for encouraging fixations on celebrity. The rhetorical centerpiece of his tax reform plan was the elimination of the deductibility of the "three-martini lunch," which prompted many a smile. The puritanical crusade had provoked one of Gerald Ford's few genuine witticisms: "The three-martini lunch is the epitome of American efficiency. Where else can you get an earful, a bellyful, and a snootful at the same time?" Barry Goldwater quipped, "None of us had a three-martini lunch until Carter was elected."

A CBS/*New York Times* poll found that whereas 32 percent of voters thought Carter a liberal before the election, only 20 percent thought him a liberal in April 1977. Another poll found that half of the voters who had voted for Ford approved of Carter. Carter's balanced-budget talk led House Republican leader John Rhodes to say, "The president sounds so Republican I'm overwhelmed."[10] Even Ronald Reagan seemed to think Carter might not work out too badly, writing a newspaper column titled "Let's Give Carter a Chance." *Congressional Quarterly* noted that at Carter's first State of the Union speech, his statements on limited government "were greeted numerous times by applause, but frequently that applause was led by the Republicans in the House chamber, who obviously found much in the speech that could be applauded."[11]

A study of network news and newspaper coverage during his first few months in office found that 85 percent of the media criticism of Carter was instigated by Democrats.[12] Arthur Schlesinger, Jr. complained bitterly, "He's a Republican. He has the temperament of a small businessman who happened to become president." The *New Republic* found that its pre-election reservations about Carter had been justified: "The administration has a remarkable record. Almost everything it proposes turns to ashes." Inside the White House, Vice President Mondale privately sympathized with the liberal dismay. Mondale said years later, "I never understood how Carter's political mind worked. Carter's got the coldest political nose of any politician I ever met."[13]

The Micromanager in Chief

As Carter's public approval ratings sagged and his political fortunes with his own party soured, Carter's fiscal discipline—though not his fiscal rhetoric—quickly went by the wayside. He began to acquiesce to larger spending increases in order to appease liberals. After holding the deficit to a comparatively small $40 billion in fiscal year 1979 (Ford's last deficit had been $53 billion, down from a staggering $73 billion in fiscal year 1976), in 1980 the deficit swelled back up to $73 billion.

Carter attempted to compensate for his stiff personal skills and bad relations with Congress by adopting a crushing routine, working up to eighty hours a week and reading as many as three hundred pages of paperwork every night. It took six months before he would give up personally reviewing all requests to use the White House tennis court.[14] (Carter denied supervising the White House tennis court at a 1979 press conference, though his denial confirmed the perception that he was the Micromanager in Chief: "I have never personally monitored who used or did not use the White House tennis court.

I have let my secretary, Susan Clough, receive requests from members of the White House staff who wanted to use the tennis court at certain times, so that more than one person would not want to use the same tennis court simultaneously, unless they were either on opposite sides of the net or engaged in a doubles contest.")

Between his work habits and his deliberate plain touch, it was remarked that the U.S. had elected its first national city manager, or, as one reporter put it, "McNamara with religion." Carter flooded Congress with ambitious legislative and reform programs: Tax reform, health care, welfare reform, campaign finance reform, urban aid, and other ideas poured forth from the White House. Even Ted Kennedy, the avatar of activist government, observed that "Carter's reforms are lined up bumper-to-bumper." There was no hierarchy or priority among Carter's initiatives. He rejected advice that his administration was overloading Congress and trying to do too much. "It's almost impossible for me to delay something that I see needs to be done," Carter wrote in his diary after his first week in office. This is another example of Carter's stubbornness born of idealism. Near the end of his first year as governor of Georgia, Carter admitted, "If I have made one mistake, it has been in undertaking too many things simultaneously."[15] Yet he seems to have learned nothing from this mistake. Carter's entire legislative program was, not surprisingly, ground to dust or stalled in Congress.

Inflation, Stagflation, and "Limits to Growth"

Beneath the surface of Carter's halfhearted and ineffectual fiscal conservatism, however, could be discerned the rapid decay of liberal economic ideology. Economics was one topic about which Carter never boasted of special or exemplary knowledge. His background in economics consisted of reading a standard textbook used at the University of Georgia, shortly before he began his presidential campaign. It wasn't enough. Over the course of his single term, Carter announced seven major economic programs, on average a new one almost every six months, that shifted course several times without ever communicating a sense of ultimate direction. Both the policies and their articulation were characterized by vacillation, indecision, inconsistency, and confusion.

In the early months of his administration, Carter was pushing for a tax rebate as a means to stimulate the economy. He abruptly dropped the idea, again without consulting congressional leaders. Congressional liberals, meanwhile, were pushing for a full employment act known as "Humphrey-Hawkins" because of its two chief sponsors, Senator Hubert Humphrey of Minnesota and Representative Augustus Hawkins of California. It set a goal of achieving 3 percent unemployment within four years through a coordination of government programs and a guaranteed federal job for each worker if the private economy failed to achieve the 3 percent goal. The original draft of Humphrey-Hawkins included a clause allowing a worker to sue the federal government if the government did not find or create a job for him or her.

This was too much even for the AFL-CIO, which declined to support Humphrey-Hawkins. Some liberals, such as investment banker Felix Rohatyn, saw Humphrey-Hawkins as "the first step toward state planning of the economy." A few orthodox liberal economists were worried about the inflationary potential of a full employment program along the lines of Humphrey-Hawkins, but others dismissed this concern. Walter Heller, President John F. Kennedy's chief economic advisor, said the bigger budget deficits necessary to bring about full employment wouldn't risk inflation because the new money would only be putting idle men and machines back to work. A much watered-down version of Humphrey-Hawkins finally passed in 1978; the crucial compromise was giving inflation an equal priority with unemployment.

Inflation was the blind spot of liberalism in the 1960s and 1970s. Since Carter didn't want to stimulate the economy with the old-fashioned Keynesnian elixir of more deficit spending (the existing deficit was thought to have pushed up interest rates), he instead encouraged the Federal Reserve to lower interest rates by expanding the money supply. The money supply had already been growing at the rate of about 11 percent a year by 1977—a rate of money growth that monetarist economists warned was too high—up from 7 or 8 percent in 1974–1975. A parade of liberal economists, along with the Joint Economic Committee of Congress, was trotted out to argue that the money supply wasn't growing fast enough. "We need faster monetary growth," said economist and Carter advisor Lawrence Klein. "Government programs to stimulate the economy do not need to contribute to inflation."[16] *Time* magazine had recommended that the Federal Reserve "should pump out as much money as might be needed to keep interest rates relatively stable." Carter's Fed chairman, G. William Miller, obliged. The result was accelerating inflation.

Taking note of this monetary indiscipline, *National Review* predicted in 1975: "Nobody is even talking, anymore, about getting inflation below 6 or 7 percent. Having established that level as a politically viable floor for inflation, the discussion now centers on how rapidly we should take off from that point toward double-digit rates—and, of course, another big recession."[17] Inflation rose from 7 percent in 1977 to 9 percent in 1978 and the dollar began to plunge in the international currency exchanges. Carter said that the 9 percent inflation rate was merely "a temporary aberration." Polls in 1978 found that Americans now rated inflation as the most important national problem.

Liberals appeared confused about inflation's source—an inflated money supply—because they supported the policies that caused it. True to form, Carter tried to explain inflation as a moral problem afflicting the people. "It is a myth that the government itself can stop inflation." Rather, inflation was a reflection of "unpleasant facts about ourselves," of "a preoccupation with self" that retards the willingness of Americans "to sacrifice for the common good."[18] The chairman of the White House Council on Wage and Price Stability, Barry Bosworth, echoed Carter in blaming inflation on the private sector: "If government has any part to play in fighting inflation, it must have a role in private wage and price decisions."[19]

At no time did Carter mention the money supply, or the government's role in running the treasury printing press. The Carter administration proceeded to fight inflation through "jawboning," which meant giving an official scowl to businesses and labor unions that sought price and wage increases. In 1979, inflation soared further to more than 12 percent. With the prime rate nearing 20 percent and signs that inflation might begin spiraling to Latin American levels, Carter was forced to dismiss Fed chairman Miller and replace him with Paul Volcker, who immediately jacked up interest rates to curb monetary growth.

Between Humphrey-Hawkins, the wistfulness for national economic planning, and ramping up the money supply to stimulate the economy, the Carter administration thought it was reviving the can-do "growth liberalism" of the 1960s. But by the time Carter took office, liberalism was rapidly coming to embrace its opposite: the "limits to growth." This was partly the influence of the rapidly growing environmental movement, which, in its early days, was much taken with the 1972 Club of Rome book *The Limits to Growth*. The book offered a gloomy argument that natural resource depletion and rising pollution threatened mankind's long-term future unless economic growth was slowed or stopped. *The Limits to Growth* had the benefit of fortuitously appearing at the same time that commodity shortages were becoming chronic. In 1973, *Newsweek* ran a cover picture of an empty horn of plenty with the ominous headline: "Running Out of Everything?"

This was all nonsense, but the idea of "limits to growth" remained a core concept of environmentalism nonetheless, and became the new visage of liberal guilt. For some varieties of the liberal mind, gloom is exhilarating, and "limits to growth" offered a large-scale sequel to the Vietnam War. Carter embraced the "limits to growth" view in his inaugural address, noting, "We have learned that 'more' is not necessarily 'better,' that even our great nation has its recognized limits." Liberalism is historically an optimistic creed, and having open doubts about growth was a disaster outside of the environmental issue. In the space of a decade, the central governing challenge of liberalism had transformed from allocating abundance to rationing scarcity. Liberalism's contradictory embrace of old-time government activism and "limits to growth" ideology was the central cause of the incoherence of the Carter administration's domestic policy.

Carter's economic policies produced a disaster—stagflation: an economy with stagnating job growth and rapid inflation, a combination that liberal economists had thought impossible. Stagflation was Carter's greatest domestic achievement—one that would become the benchmark for the harm that liberal Democrats and big government can do to the economy. He used activist government to try to stimulate the economy—and succeeded only in stimulating inflation. He blamed the sluggish economy not on high taxes on investment, not on government spending crowding out the private sector, but on the American people, who had to accept that they were entering a time of scarcity that had to be managed by a government bureaucracy.

The "limits to growth" mentality can be most clearly seen in Carter's attempts to fashion a new energy policy. It was another disaster. The omen that it would be came on Inauguration Day, when a solar-heated reviewing stand in front of the White House performed miserably, leaving most of its crowd visibly shivering. Carter decided that the troubled energy sector of the economy should be regarded as a national crisis of the highest order, verging on "national catastrophe" unless drastic steps were taken. In a televised address, he declared, "We must face the fact that the energy shortage is permanent," and described the imperative of an ambitious energy policy as the "moral equivalent of war," which yielded the unfortunate but highly symbolic acronym MEOW.

We Have Met the Enemy, and He Is Us

If the energy crisis was the "moral equivalent of war," just who was the moral equivalent of the enemy? For most ordinary Americans, it was the Arab oil sheiks and their OPEC cartel, but the conventional wisdom of liberalism in the 1970s held fast to Pogo's observation:

The American people were the enemy, because of our profligate, energy-wasting lifestyle.

Carter proceeded to commit the same mistake that President Bill Clinton committed with health care reform in 1993: He developed a massive plan behind closed doors with little or no outside input. Neither his top economic advisors nor members of the Cabinet were apprised of the details of the plan before its release. "The plan was conceived in secrecy by technicians," the *New York Times* reported, and it "reflected a detached, almost apolitical attitude." The architects of the energy plan "functioned as if they were a self-contained unit and their task was as hush-hush as the Manhattan Project."[20]

The energy plan Carter produced contained a contradictory and complex mixture of tax incentives for conservation along with tax incentives to develop new supplies of energy. The populist cornerstone of the plan was a "gas guzzler tax" on large automobiles, then as now a popular target of enlightened people, along with a rebate for "efficient" smaller cars. (In answer to objections that such a plan would boost sales of foreign cars, the Carter administration proposed import restrictions.) Carter opposed the simple option of deregulating the market for domestically produced oil and natural gas. For political reasons, he had straddled the issue of natural gas deregulation during the campaign, telling voters in Oklahoma and Texas that he supported it, while telling voters in the Northeast that he opposed it. After taking office, he opposed natural gas deregulation on the grounds that it would be "immoral and obscene." Instead, Carter instituted a whole new set of complicated price controls in a technocratic plan that went beyond the wildest imagination of a government-interventionist New Dealer.

Carter's energy plan required four phonebook-sized volumes to spell out. House Speaker Tip O'Neill "took one look at it and groaned" when the White House delivered it to his office. O'Neill managed to shepherd Carter's energy plan through the House, but it was dead on arrival in the Senate. The Senate emasculated Carter's plan, carving it into 113 separate bills and finally passing a shriveled compromise for Carter's signature in the fall of 1978, almost eighteen months after Carter had announced his plan. (The plan that finally passed included partial deregulation of the natural gas market.) By then, the energy markets had calmed down; inflation remained the public's chief concern. The most significant result of Carter's energy plan was the creation of the Cabinet-level Department of Energy, which quickly came to have a budget that rivaled the combined profits of the major oil companies, though it produced neither a single barrel of oil or kilowatt of electricity.

The *Global 2000* Study

Even though the last thirty years have proven that there is no intrinsic shortage of energy supplies or any other raw material, Carter never revised his "limits to growth" views. His last major initiative in this regard was a massive report he commissioned and released with great fanfare late in 1980, shortly before he left office, known as the *Global 2000* study. It was a doom-and-gloom treatise worthy of the Club of Rome report, containing all the greatest hits of environmental alarmism. The beauty of *Global 2000* is that it offered specific predictions for a date certain—the year 2000—which can now be tested against reality. The report's introduction provides a flavor:

> If present trends continue, the world in 2000 will be more crowded, more polluted, less stable ecologically, and more vulnerable to disruption than the world we live in now. Serious stresses involving population, resources, and environment are clearly visible ahead. Despite greater material output, the world's people will be poorer in many ways than they are today. For hundreds of millions of the desperately poor, the outlook for food and other necessities of life will be no better. For many it will be worse. Barring revolutionary advances in technology, life for most people on earth will be more precarious in 2000 than it is now.

Most of the major predictions of *Global 2000* turned out to be wildly wrong, in some cases by an order of magnitude. The report predicted that the world would face an oil shortage of twenty million barrels a day by the year 2000, and that the price of oil would reach $100 a barrel in real, inflation-adjusted 1980 dollars. Instead, one can see that oil prices recently "surged" ahead to $34.56 a barrel (for oil to be delivered in March 2004) in 2004 dollars—the price in 1980 dollars would be markedly lower, about $14.42. There is no oil shortage. *Global 2000* also predicted increasing commodity shortages and sharply higher prices; in fact, nearly all commodities are in greater supply than in 1980, and commodity price *deflation* was the significant resource trend of the 1990s. Between 1970 and 2000, *Global 2000* predicted, world per capita food supplies would increase by only 15 percent, arable cropland would only expand by 4 percent, and real prices for food would double. Instead, food production—and caloric intake in the developing world—has continued to grow substantially, while the inflation-adjusted price of nearly all commodities and raw materials has continued to fall, a sign of their increasing abundance.

Global 2000 sought increased government power to manage resources and markets on a global scale to alleviate these supposedly dire problems. But the world in the twenty-first century—especially its poorest parts (except for those countries that are despotically governed)—is getting wealthier, not poorer, through markets and trade. Environmentalists (and Carter himself) complained bitterly in the early 1980s that President Reagan was ignoring *Global 2000*, to which Americans can only say, "Thank God he did."

Tax Firestorms

Carter's final domestic policy humiliation was tax policy. Once again, he showed himself to have a tin ear for public opinion. During the 1976 campaign, Carter had said tax reform would be a major priority, but he wouldn't be specific about what changes he might seek. There were three exceptions to his usual studied vagueness, two of which were disastrous. At one point, Carter suggested he might raise income taxes on households who earned "above the median" income, which implied that he would raise taxes on half of all American households. Carter beat a hasty retreat after a firestorm erupted. He also casually suggested in an early primary that tax reform might entail closing "loopholes" such as the mortgage interest deduction for homeowners. Another firestorm, and another hasty retreat.

Carter did articulate one highly sensible idea during the campaign: ending the double-taxation of dividend income (an idea that President George W. Bush advanced in 2003). But when he finally proposed a tax reform package, he proposed increasing capital gains taxes. Carter wanted the tax code to be more steeply progressive than it already was—however dampening this was for productive investment—by raising taxes on middle- and higher-income groups and cutting tax rates for low-income groups.

Congressional Republicans countered Carter's plan with a new "supply-side" program of their own. In 1978, New York congressman Jack Kemp and Delaware senator William Roth proposed a 30 percent across-the-board cut in income tax rates. "Kemp-Roth" became a rallying cry for conservatives, and later the central economic plan for Ronald Reagan. The Kemp-Roth tax cut proved surprisingly popular in Congress in the months before the 1978 mid-term elections, so much so that Speaker Tip O'Neill had to resort to a parliamentary double-cross and party-line arm-twisting to kill its momentum.

But then a political earthquake struck: the passage, by a two-to-one landslide, of California's Proposition 13 in June, which signaled the beginning of the "tax revolt." Carter attacked Proposition 13 with the revealing prediction that "There's no doubt about the fact that unemployment will go up in California, as government workers are laid off because of stringent budget requirements." In fact, California's economy boomed in the aftermath of Proposition 13.

Even though a capital gains tax cut enjoyed growing bipartisan support in the aftermath of Proposition 13, Carter threatened to veto any tax cut and denounced it as "a plan that provides huge tax windfalls for millionaires and two bits for the average American.... The Steiger

amendment [as the bill was called] is the greatest hoax ever perpe-
trated on the American people." Treasury Secretary Michael
Blumenthal called it "the millionaires' relief act of 1978," because
supposedly 80 percent of its benefits would go to taxpayers with
incomes above $100,000. But the House of Representatives rejected
Carter's own tax proposal by a vote of 225–193, and a capital gains tax
cut bill passed 362–49 in mid-October 1978, three weeks before the
mid-term elections. With such a crushing margin, Carter dropped his
plan to veto the bill. The surprising result (to conventional thinkers—
not to the new supply-siders) was that capital gains tax receipts
immediately went up, and there was a fifteen-fold increase in capital
formation in the two years immediately after the rate cut.

The net result of Carter's erratic economic policies was high inflation, slow productivity growth, stagnant personal income, and persistent unemployment. But those were the least of Carter's troubles
as his term progressed. Carter oversaw a ruin in foreign policy to
match the ruin of the domestic economy. By 1980, America's worry
about the prospect of war would reach its highest level since the
Cuban missile crisis.

CHAPTER SEVEN

President Carter Abroad

> "The Sermon on the Mount is the last word in Christian ethics. Everyone respects the Quakers. Still, it is not on these terms that Ministers assume their responsibilities of guiding States."
>
> —WINSTON S. CHURCHILL, *The Gathering Storm*

I f Carter's domestic policy was disastrous in its results, his foreign policy was even more so, and it was foreign policy that would prove Carter's ultimate undoing. Before he was done, Carter achieved a trifecta, as Henry Kissinger would summarize it in 1980: "The Carter administration has managed the extraordinary feat of having, at one and the same time, the worst relations with our allies, the worst relations with our adversaries, and the most serious upheavals in the developing world since the end of the Second World War."[1]

Like his domestic policy, Carter's foreign policy gave off contradictory signals from the start. He began well enough, declaring with a flourish that "human rights" would be the centerpiece of his foreign policy. His inaugural address proclaimed, "Our commitment to human rights must be absolute." This pledge cheered conservatives and liberals alike, and seemed to represent a repudiation of Kissinger-style détente with the Soviet bloc.

Jeane Kirkpatrick, who in due course would become one of Carter's most lacerating critics, wrote, "For having recalled Americans (and others) to historic moral imperatives and for having placed individual rights back on the international agenda, President Carter wins my applause.... Carter's emphasis on these themes is rewarding to people sick to death of having their motives, characters, and policies excoriated."[2]

"McGovernism Without McGovern"

In his first meeting with Soviet ambassador Anatoly Dobrynin, Carter sternly warned, "We will not back down on the human rights issue." Carter showed that he meant it when he released a letter he sent to dissident Soviet physicist Andrei Sakharov. Carter also received Vladimir Bukovsky, a prominent dissident exile, in the Oval Office—a stark contrast to President Gerald Ford's shameful refusal to meet Aleksandr Solzhenitsyn in 1975. The Soviets were outraged. They were also alarmed. The KGB conducted a hurried assessment to determine whether the Soviet Union was vulnerable to an American-inspired uprising.[3]

It had been a tacit agreement of the Nixon-Kissinger détente with the Soviets that neither side would engage in public attacks on the internal affairs of the other. In practice, this was a one-way street, because Soviet propaganda never relented in its ideological attack on "bourgeois democracy." Nor did the Soviets cease their disinformation efforts in the Third World. Even *National Review* cheered Carter: "It was exhilarating to contemplate the new Administration's straightforward criticism of Soviet treatment of nuclear physicist and political dissident Andrei Sakharov."

Other signs suggested Carter was serious in his criticism of détente. For his national security advisor Carter chose Zbigniew Brzezinski of Columbia University, who had a reputation as a hard-liner. During the Cuban missile crisis in 1962, Brzezinski had sent a telegram to Arthur Schlesinger at the White House that read: "Any further delay in bombing missile sites fails to exploit Soviet uncertainty."[4] With his thick Polish accent and heavyweight academic background, Brzezinski was intended to be Carter's answer to Kissinger. Liberals were initially dismayed at both the human rights campaign and the Brzezinski appointment. Senator George McGovern complained, "the Carter [human rights] policy looks like a reincarnation of John Foster Dulles's attempt to bring Communism down by encouraging dissent and revolt in Eastern Europe."[5]

Before long, however, it became apparent that Carter's foreign policy was sentimental rather than hardheaded or principled, and laced with a heavy dose of liberal guilt. Jeane Kirkpatrick judged that "Carter was, *par excellence*, the kind of liberal most likely to confound revolution with idealism, change with progress, optimism with virtue." Brzezinski, on closer inspection, turned out to espouse an optimistic version of Kissinger's historical determinism. Brzezinski had characterized Carter's foreign policy in 1977 as the recognition that "the world is changing under *the influence of forces no government can control*." (Emphasis added.) Kirkpatrick noted that in practice, this meant "to encourage the view that events are manifestations of deep historical forces which cannot be controlled and that the best any government can do is to serve as a 'midwife' to history, helping events move where they are already headed."[6]

The embrace of human rights and the rejection of Cold War containment turned into a rolling confessional about America's postwar foreign policy. Carter quickly eased up on his complaints about human rights in the Soviet bloc (during his state visit to Poland, he said, "Our conception of human rights is preserved in Poland"), and began using human rights as a cudgel against traditional American allies. Michael Ledeen and William Lewis observed, "Implicit in the statements of Carter administration officials was the conviction that the U.S. had itself been the root cause of many problems of the recent past. And there was more than a hint that America would—and should—do a sort of penance for its presumed sins in Vietnam, Cuba, and other areas."[7] Veteran Democratic foreign policy expert Eugene Rostow said, "Carter was McGovernism without McGovern."[8] McGovern himself confirmed this, telling friends that, having calmed down from his first appraisal of Carter as Dulles redux, he regarded Carter's foreign policy appointments to be "excellent, quite close to those I would have made myself."[9]

Despite Carter's public attention to Soviet dissidents, the real orientation of human rights policy could be (and was) summarized in the phrase, "No more Pinochets," a reference to the Chilean colonel who ousted the Marxist president Salvador Allende in 1973, supposedly with the approval and assistance of the United States. Carter's grand strategy could be (and was) reduced to the phrase, "No more Vietnams." ("There is no more South Vietnam," skeptics pointed out.) Senator Henry "Scoop" Jackson complained, "For too many officials [in the Carter administration], the intensity of the struggle for human rights is inversely related to the power of the offender.... Thus it is that the Administration speaks more about the abuses of human rights in Chile, the Philippines, Argentine, and Guatemala, while speaking less about violations of human rights in the Soviet Union."[10]

Senator Daniel Patrick Moynihan criticized Carter more broadly for "trying to divert our attention from the central political struggle of our time—that between democracy and totalitarian communism."[11] As the administration regressed, Moynihan would step up his criticism, saying in 1980 that Carter was "unable to distinguish between our friends and our enemies, [and] he has adopted our enemies' view of the world."

Part of this adoption of "our enemies' view of the world" was the acceptance by Carter's foreign policy spokesmen of the Marxist argument that the "social" and "economic rights" (such as universally provided government jobs, housing, and health care) touted by socialist regimes were at least as important as "human rights" as they were understood in the West (as freedom) and defined in documents like the Declaration of Independence and the Bill of Rights. This sort of relativism was inherent in some of Carter's election campaign speeches. The Soviet Union, Carter said at one point during the campaign, "will continue to push for communism throughout the world and to probe for possibilities for expansion of their system, *which I think is a legitimate purpose for them.*"[12] (Emphasis added.)

In a speech on human rights in 1977, Carter's secretary of state, Cyrus Vance, made the administration's relativism about human rights plain when he endorsed the view that "there is a right to the fulfillment of such vital needs as food, shelter, health care, and education." Other administration spokesmen, like Andrew Young, took this position even further, explicitly endorsing the communist view on social and economic "rights." The human rights theme, which began with such promise, quickly became yet another manifestation of Western weakness, confusion, and lack of self-confidence.

The "Inordinate Fear of Communism"

Four months into his administration, Carter made explicit his departure from the postwar foreign policy consensus of containing the Soviet Union. In a commencement address at Notre Dame University on May 22, Carter declared:

Being confident of our own future, we are now free of that *inordinate fear of communism* which once led us to embrace any dictator who joined us in that fear.... For too many years, we've been willing to adopt the flawed and erroneous principles and tactics of our adversaries, sometimes abandoning our own values for theirs. We've fought fire with fire, never thinking that fire is better quenched with water. This approach failed, with Vietnam the best example of its intellectual and moral poverty....

Our policy during this period was guided by two principles: a belief that Soviet expansion was almost inevitable but that it must be contained, and the corresponding belief in the importance of an almost exclusive alliance among

non-communist nations on both sides of the Atlantic. That
system could not last forever unchanged. Historical trends
have weakened its foundation. The unifying threat of conflict with the Soviet Union has become less intensive....

We can no longer separate the traditional issues of war and
peace from the new global questions of justice, equity, and
human rights. (Above emphasis added.)

In this speech—written primarily by Anthony Lake, who would
later become President Clinton's national security advisor—Carter
unilaterally declared an end to the Cold War. Carter the critic of
détente went beyond détente by rejecting his predecessors' "inordinate fear of communism." The *New Republic's* John Osborne said
Carter's speech "may be seen in time to have been the most significant presidential statement of American foreign policy since Harry
Truman committed the United States in 1948 to resisting the spread
of Soviet power."[13] Senator Daniel Patrick Moynihan responded to
Carter a month later, asking in a commencement speech of his own:
"What was the evidence that our relation with our great totalitarian
adversary had changed, that the adversary had changed?" Carter's
good wishes for better relations with the Third World "must not be
allowed to divert us from the reality of the military and ideological
competition with the Soviet Union which continues and, if anything,
escalates."[14]

Carter's anti–Cold War stance was not mere rhetoric. Carter's initial foreign policy act, committed during his first twenty-four hours
in office, was to order the Joint Chiefs of Staff to arrange for the withdrawal of all U.S. nuclear weapons from South Korea. He would follow this up a few days later by announcing his intention to withdraw
U.S. ground forces from South Korea as well. Carter made these decisions without any consultation with the Pentagon, congressional
leaders, the South Koreans, or any other U.S. allies, most notably
Japan, which was shocked by Carter's decisions. Carter didn't even

attempt to use the withdrawals as an enticement for North Korea to negotiate a reduction in tensions.

The decision stunned military commanders. When the third-ranking Army officer in South Korea, General John K. Singlaub, commented that the removal of U.S. troops would lead to war, Carter relieved Singlaub. But following bipartisan reaction against the decision on Capitol Hill, Carter had to "defer" his decision, which was tantamount to abandoning it. Before the ink was dry on his plan to remove troops from Korea, Carter also signed an executive order granting amnesty to Vietnam-era draft evaders, which Barry Goldwater blasted as "the most disgraceful thing a president has ever done."

Carter's defense policy closely followed his diplomacy. He wanted, among other things, to reduce U.S. arms sales to other countries. He also wanted to reduce arms sales to the U.S. military. In his first month in office, Carter cut an already lean defense budget by another $6 billion. He abruptly cancelled the B-1 bomber in June 1977 (so abruptly that congressional leaders had about one hour's notice), and two months later he deferred the development of the "neutron bomb," a low-yield weapon designed for use in the European theater to counter the massive number of tanks the Warsaw Pact forces were deploying. He indicated his interest in scrapping the Trident nuclear submarine as well. Overall, he planned to cut $57 billion from the seven-year defense-spending plan he inherited from President Ford. These reductions in America's arms development were undertaken unilaterally, without any attempt to negotiate reciprocal arms restraint from the Soviet Union.

Carter and his foreign policy team believed that the classic Cold War grand strategy of containment was no longer necessary. "The old ideological labels have lost their meaning," Carter told an incredulous audience on his first trip to Eastern Europe. Despite his reputation as a hard-liner, Brzezinski mostly agreed. Carter's other key foreign policy appointments certainly did. In one of the more peculiar utterances of Carter's ascendancy, Hamilton Jordan had told *Playboy*'s Robert Scheer during the campaign that "this government is going to be run by people you've never heard of." About foreign policy personnel, Jordan said, "If Cyrus Vance were named Secretary of State and Zbigniew Brzezinski head of National Security in the Carter administration, then I would say we failed, and I would quit. But that's not going to happen."[15] But it did happen, and Jordan didn't quit.

Carter's Defense Doves

Vance, one of Robert McNamara's protégés in the Pentagon during Vietnam, was named secretary of state. Vance's appointment set off the first alarm bells for conservatives in both parties. Civil rights lawyer and longtime Democratic activist Morris Abrams commented that Vance was "the closest thing to a pacifist that the U.S. has ever had as secretary of state, with the possible exception of William Jennings Bryan." Vance would tell *Time* magazine in 1978 that "President Carter and President Brezhnev share similar dreams and aspirations about the most fundamental issues."[16] Vance's fellow Cabinet member Harold Brown, who served Carter as secretary of defense, said that Vance "was persuaded that anything that involved the risk of force was a mistake," a view that eventually required Vance's resignation in 1980.

Other appointments reinforced Vance's dovishness. Carter's nomination of Theodore Sorenson to head the CIA had to be withdrawn in the face of Senate opposition. The same fate nearly met Carter's controversial pick for chief arms control negotiator, Paul Warnke. Warnke, another denizen of the McNamara Pentagon, brought a reputation as a dovish opponent of nearly all proposed U.S. weapons systems, from ballistic missile defense to MIRV warheads. Warnke had long argued in favor of the theory that the U.S. and Soviet Union "aped" one another, so that U.S. "restraint" in arms would effectively end the arms race. In 1965, Warnke said, "The Soviets have decided that they have lost the quantitative race, and now they are not seeking to engage us in that contest." Subsequently, the Soviets indeed sought to race ahead of the U.S. in every category of quantifiable strategic strength. Still, Warnke's worldview didn't change.

"The chances are good," Warnke wrote in *Foreign Policy* magazine in 1975, "that highly advertised restraint on our part will be reciprocated. The Soviet Union, it may be said again, has only one superpower model to follow." From such droppings George Will concluded that Warnke's views were "almost engagingly childlike." Carter put his prestige behind Warnke, and associated himself fully with Warnke's views. The Senate confirmed Warnke by a margin of 58–40, with only one Republican senator, John Chafee of Rhode Island, voting for him, and Democratic senators Daniel Patrick Moynihan of New York and Sam Nunn of Georgia voting against.

Most of Carter's foreign policy appointments to the second-tier posts that the *New Republic* called "the junior varsity" were similarly dovish. "Some among this establishment junior varsity," the *New Republic* observed, "can and almost certainly will succeed to the highest positions in a future Democratic administration, whatever their record in the next few years."[17] They had in mind such thirty-somethings as Anthony Lake, Richard Holbrooke, and Jessica Tuchman, all of whom did indeed go on to senior posts in the Clinton administration during the 1990s. Still other mid-level foreign policy appointments were further to the left, especially Patricia Derian, whom Carter picked to be assistant secretary of state for human rights. Derian had come out of the civil rights movement, had traveled little overseas, and had no foreign policy credentials.

Members of the Coalition for a Democratic Majority, which represented the center-right of the Democratic Party, including Ben Wattenberg and Senator Moynihan, had met with Carter and asked that he select some foreign policy appointees and ambassadors from the center and labor wing of the party—the faction that had supported Scoop Jackson against Carter in the 1976 campaign. The CDM group presented Carter with a list of fifty-three qualified people they wished Carter to consider for appointments. One of the names on the list was Georgetown University professor Jeane Kirkpatrick, who CDM suggested would make a good ambassador to Israel. Liberals in the administration later boasted of blocking her appointment.

Carter gave his assurances that he would pick appointees from all wings of the Democratic Party, but the only appointment from the CDM group was the special trade negotiator to Micronesia. "Not even Macronesia, but Micronesia!" Moynihan complained. "A conservative governor came to town and the people he appointed regarded the ideas of the Coalition as far more a threat to the republic than the ideas of the Republican National Committee."[18]

Carter's pollster Pat Caddell dismissed the CDM as a significant force among Democrats: "It isn't a wing; it's a feather." "The Carter administration froze us out completely," observed Elliott Abrams, then serving as an aide to Senator Moynihan. "That demonstrated to all of us that the Democratic Party was a McGovernite party." "What we put forward as an appointments list," one CDM member reflected ruefully, "was treated as a purge list."

And then there was Andrew Young.

The American Ambassador for the Destruction of Western Civilization

Carter selected fellow Georgian Young, who was then serving as a member of the House of Representatives, to be United Nations ambassador. Young had risen to prominence in the civil rights movement in the 1960s and became a fixture of Atlanta politics in the 1970s. Beneath Young's impressive and moderate-sounding demeanor lurked a fashionably leftist anti-American sensibility. In 1970, Young had defended the Black Panthers on an ABC television show with the explanation that "it may take the destruction of Western civilization to allow the rest of the world to really emerge as a free and brotherly society, and if the white West is incapable of brotherhood with colored peoples, then this small body of colored peoples, black people within the white West, may be the revolutionary vanguard that God has ordained to destroy the whole thing."[19] The ABC interviewer followed up to see if Young was merely describing radical black sentiment, or associating himself with it. "Would you support the destruction of Western civilization if you were convinced that the rest of the world would thereby be liberated?" Young: "I probably would."

Young lived up to this sensibility early and often in his UN post. On his first trip to Africa, Young disembarked from the State Department aircraft giving the "black power" clenched-fist salute, to the bewilderment of his African hosts. He said that Cuban troops in Africa could be considered a "stabilizing" influence, because they were in Africa "opposing racism" and providing "technical assistance." (Young's attitude spilled over elsewhere in the State Department, which at one point in 1978 referred to pro-Soviet guerrillas in Africa as "liberation forces." Pat Moynihan referred to this kind of rhetoric as "semantic infiltration."[20]) "Cuba is in Africa," Young clarified, "because it has a shared sense of colonial oppression and domination."[21] Young was equally candid about whom he had in mind as the colonial oppressors. He denounced Britain as a "racist" nation; Britain, Young said, "almost invented racism." (Carter made Young send a written apology to Britain's UN ambassador for that remark.) Richard Nixon and Gerald Ford were both racists, Young told *Playboy* magazine, because "every American, black or white, is affected by racism." A reporter asked Young, "Would that include Abraham Lincoln?" "*Especially* Abraham Lincoln," he replied.

In 1978, Young defended the Soviet trial of dissident human rights activist Anatoly Shcharansky by asserting a moral equivalence between the U.S. and the USSR. The trial, Young said, was "a gesture of independence" on the part of the Soviets that should not affect détente. But then came the clincher: "After all, we also have hundreds, maybe thousands of people in our jails that I would categorize as political prisoners." Young had previously explained that the Soviet Union had "a completely different concept of human rights. For them, human rights are essentially not civil and political, but economic." Young made it clear that the Soviet conception of human rights compared favorably to America's. "We unfortunately have been very reluctant to accept the concept of economic responsibility for all of our citizens."[22] Carl Gershman, executive director of Social

Democrats USA, observed that Young seemed unconcerned about the fate of freedom in the Third World "so long as the regime in question calls itself 'progressive'.... Yet in his eagerness to demonstrate his solidarity with the new Marxist-Leninist elite of black Africa, Young finds himself not on the side of the oppressed but of the oppressors."

The State Department had to issue repeated "clarifications" (that is, repudiations) of Young's "open-mouth diplomacy," but Carter defended him publicly as "the best man I have ever known in public life." Young finally went too far when he violated explicit U.S. policy about having direct contact with the Palestine Liberation Organization's UN observer. Young had argued within the Carter administration for an opening to the Palestine Liberation Organization (PLO), and for the PLO's direct participation in Middle East peace talks (as eventually happened in the 1990s). But he apparently couldn't wait on events. In the summer of 1979, Young went to a secret meeting with the PLO United Nations observer at the apartment of Kuwait's UN ambassador to discuss a "procedural" matter related to a forthcoming UN vote. Young had told no one at the State Department of the meeting, but the Israelis got wind of it and complained to Washington. Young dissembled, telling the State Department that the meeting had been "inadvertent." When the truth dribbled out that the meeting had been anything but "inadvertent" and that he had misled the State Department, support for Young collapsed. He was forced to resign in September 1979.

The Panama Canal Giveaway

While Young's candor and imprudence cost him his job, he undoubtedly expressed the soul of Carter's foreign policy better than anyone else in the administration. This can be most clearly seen in the way Carter approached the Panama Canal negotiations. President Carter was determined to conclude a treaty that had been under negotiation for the previous four administrations. Unlike his predecessors, he wanted to sign an agreement on terms favorable to Panama in order to expiate American guilt. The current American ownership and

control of the canal, Carter said, "exemplified those morally questionable aspects of past American foreign policy which the United
States as a nation should humbly acknowledge in its striving for
higher moral ground."[23] Carter more directly said that giving back the
canal would "correct an injustice" and constitute "a gracious apology." Carter offered no apology to former president Ford, even though
he had attacked him during the 1976 campaign, promising that he,
unlike Ford, "would never give up full control of the Panama Canal."

At the time Carter submitted the treaties (the negotiations produced
two treaty instruments—one transferring legal title to Panama of the
American canal zone, and a second protocol declaring the right of the
U.S. to defend the canal's neutrality against "external" threats) to the
Senate for ratification in the fall of 1977, opinion polls showed the public opposed to the treaties by more than a two to one margin. Illinois
senator Adlai Stevenson III reported that he received 5,600 letters opposing the treaties, and only five in favor. The *St. Louis-Globe Democrat*
newspaper reported similar numbers: 2,289 letters against the treaties
versus twenty-nine in favor. Carter hoped for a quick and easy ratification, and revealed his naiveté once again by expressing surprise that the
Senate ratification process was going to take several months.

In the weeks before the treaties were formally submitted in
September 1977, forty senators signed a resolution opposing the
treaties—six more than necessary to defeat the two-thirds vote
required to approve the treaties. The White House had to employ a
full-scale public relations and arm-twisting campaign to achieve the
ratification. Although opinion polls never registered a majority of the
public in support of the treaties, the Senate ratified them by a one-
vote margin, 68–32, on April 18, 1978.

The Camp David Accords

"The wonder is not that [Carter's] foreign initiatives sometimes misfired," Michael Barone observed, "but that some of them turned out
so well."[24] The most famous of Carter's successes was the Camp
David accords between Israel and Egypt in 1978. Yet even his one

undeniable foreign policy triumph grew out of a near-catastrophic blunder. Henry Kissinger had developed an incremental strategy for the Middle East, believing that a lasting peace in the region could only come about through a slow, step-by-step process of confidence-building agreements, with the United States as the honest broker. Following Kissinger's guidance, Nixon and Ford had backed Israel's refusal to participate in an all-party conference at Geneva that would include both the Soviet Union and the PLO. The impatient Carter, however, thought he could get a comprehensive settlement all at once, and on October 1, 1977, the Carter administration released a joint U.S.-Soviet statement calling for resuming the all-party peace process in Geneva. Carter had once again proceeded with no consultation with any allies (including Israel) or anyone in the Jewish community in the U.S., including his own political advisor on Jewish affairs.

In Cairo, Egyptian president Anwar Sadat was alarmed. "I'd just spent two years throwing the Soviets out of the Middle East," Sadat reportedly said, "and now the United States is inviting them back in." Sadat decided to take matters into his own hands, and announced that he was ready to go to Jerusalem and negotiate directly with Israel. Israeli prime minister Menachem Begin graciously invited Sadat to address the Israeli Knesset. This ultimately led to the two weeks of hard bargaining at Camp David in September 1978, during which Carter used all of his force and persuasive skill (including convincing Sadat to keep going after he had begun packing his bags to leave halfway through) to produce exactly the kind of incremental agreement that Kissinger had foreseen. Israel agreed to withdraw from the Sinai Peninsula, which it had occupied since the 1967 Six-Day War. It is telling, however, that for all of Carter's strenuous effort, he was not able to get a single Arab nation to endorse Egypt's decision to make peace with Israel.

Iran, an "Island of Stability"

The Middle East was also the scene of the greatest shipwreck of Carter's foreign policy, and ultimately his presidency: Iran. Since the end of World War II, when President Harry Truman had bluntly told the Soviet Union that Iran was off-limits to their territorial ambitions, Iran had been the West's primary strategic bastion in the Middle East against the southern flank of the Soviet empire. Its central location between NATO member Turkey and pro-Western Pakistan made Iran the linchpin of the northern tier nations containing the Soviet Union. Over the years, Iran served as a primary escape route for Soviet defectors, and also provided important listening posts for the CIA to conduct electronic eavesdropping on the Soviets. In 1953, the CIA engineered a coup against a Soviet-leaning government that had taken power in Iran, thus restoring the monarchy of the Shah Reza Pahlavi. Throughout the 1960s and 1970s, the U.S. supplied Iran with as much advanced weaponry as the shah's oil revenues could pay for, and also provided training for Iran's army. For a time in the 1960s, a young U.S. Army colonel named Norman Schwarzkopf ran the U.S. military assistance program in Iran.[25]

Iran was also an asset in the balance of power between Israel and the Arab states. Iran sold oil to Israel, and throughout his rule Pahlavi regularly received secret visits from Israeli leaders—a fact not lost on the PLO when the Islamic revolution began to destabilize the shah's rule.

As a monarch, Pahlavi was easily stereotyped in the West as an unappealing and unimaginative autocrat, but in fact he was a relatively progressive ruler compared to nearly every other regime on the Asian subcontinent. Under Pahlavi the literacy rate doubled, and life expectancy increased from thirty-five to fifty-two. But this forced progress was a large part of his undoing. Walter Laqueur observed that "the oil boom turned out to be not a blessing but a curse."[26]

Many critics point to aspects of "modernization," such as opening schools and universities to women and abolishing the requirement that women wear the *chador* veil, which ran counter to the fundamentalist beliefs of the Shi'ite clergy, as the key source of the shah's undoing. Yet the more significant disruptions to the Iranian social fabric came from Pahlavi's attempts to modernize the economy through centralized means. Although the economy was awash with oil revenues, Iran was basically a backward command economy, and Pahlavi was attempting to prop up the merchant class with subsidies. "What is going on in Iran is a transformation," he proclaimed in 1974, "physical, mental, economic—on an epic scale."[27] He predicted that within the next generation Iran would take its place among the world's five mightiest powers, and was buying arms in vast quantities from the U.S. toward this goal. Pahlavi used the nation's surging oil revenues to subsidize public works and shore up the growing professional middle class. The economy grew by a staggering 35 percent in 1974, and by another 42 percent in 1975. Per capita income rose to nearly four times higher than next-door Turkey. Such rates of growth were clearly unsustainable.

Pahlavi also instituted a land reform program (following the advice of some of the same American aid workers who designed the disastrous land reform program of South Vietnam), removing land from the control of the "mullahs," the Islamic clergy, and placing it under royal control. Therein lay perhaps his largest mistaken effort at social engineering, because the Islamic clergy represented the most significant independent force in Iranian society. It was the purported "Westernization" of Iran that most offended the fundamentalist Islamic clergy. In addition to the socio-economic dislocations, Pahlavi's periodic lavish and self-indulgent celebrations of his rule succeeded in alienating the rising educated professional class.

To be sure, the shah maintained a security force known as SAVAK—the Farsi language acronym for "National Security and Information Organization"—whose domestic police activities fell woefully short of Western standards of due process, to put the matter delicately. Still, on balance Pahlavi was not a great oppressor. He wanted to be loved rather than feared. For all the notorious excesses of SAVAK, Pahlavi did not permit the full force of the security organization to be brought to bear on his enemies.

There was no reason to suppose that there was any risk of instability or that the shah's grip on the nation was less than rock solid. Pahlavi commanded considerable wealth along with a well-equipped army of more than 400,000 troops. So it was when President Carter went to Tehran in January 1978 and offered remarks that would become deeply embarrassing just a few months later: "Iran, because of the great leadership of the shah, is an island of stability in one of the more troubled areas of the world." Carter added, "The cause of human rights is one that is also shared deeply by our people and by the leaders of our two nations."

The unraveling of Pahlavi's rule might be said to have begun in 1974, when French doctors diagnosed him with a slow-moving form of cancer. Although it was treatable, it came as a heavy psychological blow. Like most potentates, Pahlavi often came across as a megalomaniac, but he was in fact a deeply insecure person; a CIA profile concluded that he had an inferiority complex. But what is most significant is that *neither American intelligence nor U.S. diplomats knew of Pahlavi's health condition until after he left the country in 1979.* Even as the shah began visibly to lose his grip, American diplomats failed to understand the seriousness and full extent of his withdrawal from effective rule. The single most important reason why revolutionary fervor came to fruition in Iran is easy to discern, but somehow eluded the Carter administration: The shah possessed a weak character, his health was failing, and he had neither the stomach for crushing his opposition nor the political skill necessary to generate a successor regime.

The shah's aversion to violence was powerfully abetted by the Carter administration's enthusiasm for human rights. He had received mixed signals from the U.S. throughout the ordeal; Brzezinski assured him that the U.S. would back "decisive action" fully and "without reservation," while other public and private statements from the State Department and President Carter himself emphasized the need to avoid violence and respect human rights. Pahlavi was uncertain what actions the U.S. would support and afraid to take action that would offend the Carter administration.

Pahlavi's policy of compromising with his enemies was undercutting the monarchy. In 1975, a year after Pahlavi's cancer diagnosis,

Iran reached a settlement with Iraq over Iraq's Kurdish minority, which the shah had been supporting as a means to harass the Iraqi government. The treaty included a stipulation allowing for ten thousand religious pilgrims a year to travel from Iran to Iraq. This proved an immense boon to the person most determined to bring down the shah—the Ayatollah Khomeini.

Khomeini had been exiled from Iran in 1963 for inciting riots, and had spent much of the next decade in Iraq brooding over how to foment an Iranian revolution. Khomeini organized the religious pilgrims who started coming through Iraq into a courier network that carried cassette tapes to Shi'ite mosques throughout Iran, spreading Khomeini's fundamentalist and insurrectionist views. An operation of this kind cost money, much of which came from the PLO (it is thought that Syria's Hafez Assad also provided significant support), which in turn got much of its funding from the Soviet Union. Khomeini provided a focal point for organizing a revolutionary opposition to Pahlavi.

A number of other factors started to go badly for Iran. The nation was undergoing steady demographic dislocation; its urbanized population was growing by 100,000 a year by the mid-1970s, putting a strain on the cities. Tehran, for example, didn't even have a sewage treatment system. Inflation was accelerating, outstripping the ability to maintain subsidies for shopkeepers and merchants. Agitators were fanning popular anger against the shah, which was rising. On August 19, 1978, a fire broke out at the Rex Cinema in the port city of Abadan. Four hundred seventy-seven people died. Some of the theater's exits were locked, raising suspicions that the fire had been set intentionally. The revolutionary clergy claimed that the fire had been the work of SAVAK, and noted that the fire brigades were slow to arrive with help. Three weeks later, on September 5, government troops fired on a religious rally in Jaleh Square in Tehran after the crowd of twenty thousand had refused an order to disperse. The government admitted to killing 122 in what became known as the "Jaleh Square Massacre;" other estimates put the figure at more than one thousand.

There was still no recognition in Washington that the situation in Iran was dangerous. The CIA concluded in August 1978 that "Iran is not in a revolutionary or even a 'pre-revolutionary' situation," while the Defense Intelligence Agency asserted in late September—after both the Rex Cinema fire and the Jaleh Square Massacre—that "the shah is expected to remain actively in power over the next ten years."[28] One reason the CIA and DIA offered such poor intelligence is that Congress, in the wake of Watergate, had put severe restrictions on the CIA and DIA, making it difficult for the U.S. to conduct covert intelligence operations in Iran or elsewhere in the Middle East. Covert penetration of opposition groups in Iran and elsewhere had been curtailed, and many covert CIA operatives had been purged from the agency. By the late 1970s, the CIA had only two analysts working full-time on Iran. "U.S. intelligence capability to track the Shah's domestic opposition," Gary Sick admitted, "had been allowed to deteriorate to the vanishing point."[29]

Other nations' intelligence services were not similarly handicapped, and reached more prescient findings. Israeli intelligence had concluded as early as June 1978 that the shah's days were numbered. The only open question, the Israelis concluded, was how long he would last. Tel Aviv was sufficiently alarmed that it warned Jews living in Iran to make plans to leave the country. French intelligence came to the same finding as the Israelis, concluding in the spring of 1978 that the Shah would be gone within a year. Above all, both the French and the Israelis worried about the Ayatollah Khomeini, and especially what his "clerical fascism" might do to Iran if he led a successful revolution.

U.S. diplomats and intelligence officials dismissed both the Israeli and French reports as "alarmist," and never passed along these warnings to the White House.[30] The CIA, it later turned out, not only hadn't read any of Khomeini's writings but didn't even have copies of them. When the revolution started in earnest, the CIA called up the *Washington Post* to ask to see their copies of Khomeini's works. "Whoever took religion seriously?" a State Department official later asked.

While American leaders failed to perceive the unfolding circumstances in Iran, other American acts inadvertently fueled the fires of revolution. The radicals in Iran famously declared the U.S. to be the "great Satan," and this was no mere piece of jingoistic rhetoric. To the populist conspiratorial mind in the Middle East, the United States was thought to be the shah's puppet master. As such, even a small or seemingly subtle incident could take on great significance. The oddest such episode occurred when Pahlavi visited President Carter at the White House in November 1977. Sixty thousand Iranian students and other nationals swarmed to Washington to protest the shah's visit. The Iranian embassy organized other nationals into pro-Pahlavi rallies. The factions clashed near the White House and had to be dispersed by the D.C. police. As President Carter and Pahlavi gave their welcoming remarks on the south lawn of the White House, tear gas wafted across the scene, causing the shah to choke on his speech and Carter to wipe tears out of his eyes. At the state dinner later in the day, Carter joked, "There is only one thing I can say about the shah—he knows how to draw a crowd."

Back in Iran, the opposition movement reached a very different interpretation of events, which Carter's national security assistant Gary Sick described in *All Fall Down: America's Tragic Encounter with Iran*: "When the dissidents learned of the tear gas incident on the White House lawn, they reasoned that such an event could have occurred only at the president's behest. Thus they quickly concluded that Carter had abandoned the Shah."[31] The number and intensity of protests in Iran immediately escalated. Still, as the conspiratorial mentality is usually accompanied by paranoia, the radical opposition thought that the U.S. must surely have some nefarious scheme in reserve to maintain the shah in power.

In an odd bit of symmetry, Pahlavi believed the same thing. There was really only one serious option for him to shore up his political position, and that was a firm crackdown on the opposition—probably through a declaration of martial law. Many leaders of the Iranian military expected this, and were certain that the U.S. would make sure such a plan succeeded. After all, had not the CIA engineered the coup that restored the shah to the throne in 1953? Pahlavi remained supine, believing the U.S. would somehow come to his rescue. Not until it was too late did he realize that the Carter administration would do nothing.

"The basic problem throughout the crisis," Michael Ledeen and Bernard Lewis wrote in *Debacle: The American Failure in Iran*, "was that the President was notable for his absence. Carter never took an active role in the discussion, never gave any clear indication of the kind of solution he favored, and never put the question of Iran into the general context that would have aided the policymakers at lower levels in formulating options."[32] In Iran, the full confusion and contradictions of Carter's foreign policy were on display. Although a few advisors close to President Carter realized that a crackdown by Pahlavi was necessary, most of the Carter foreign policy apparatus ruled this option out.

The human rights office of the State Department was a case in point, blocking the sale of tear gas to Iran before eventually relenting and drawing the line instead on rubber bullets, which Iran then had to buy from the British. American officials, especially National Security Advisor Brzezinski and the U.S. ambassador to Iran, William Sullivan, repeatedly assured Pahlavi that the U.S. backed him fully, but in fact this backing extended little beyond private verbal cheerleading.

One reason for the tepidness and indecision of Washington was that significant factions of the administration, especially in the State Department, viewed the shah as the problem in Iran, and not so secretly welcomed the prospect of his demise. Neither the State Department nor the intelligence community took Islamic fundamentalism seriously, while American scholars on Iran deprecated the idea that the clergy would participate directly in forming or running a government. William Miller, chief of staff to the Senate Select Committee on Intelligence, went so far as to recommend that the U.S. openly *support* Khomeini and the revolution, arguing that Khomeini would be a progressive force for human rights. Miller had ready access to Secretary Vance for his views.[33]

Typical of the self-delusion of American liberals was the case of Princeton University professor Richard Falk, who wrote that Khomeini's circle was "uniformly composed of moderate, progressive individuals" who shared "a notable record of concern for human rights." Falk argued that "Iran may yet provide us with a desperately-needed model of humane government for a third-world country."[34] Henry Precht, the country director for Iran in the State Department, wrote to Ambassador Sullivan in Tehran in mid-December that U.S. policy should be to find a way for the shah to make a "graceful exit" while allowing the U.S. to take credit.[35] A few human rights activists in the State Department compared Khomeini to Gandhi, arguing that, like Gandhi, Khomeini would turn out to be a moral leader who would leave actual administration to a democratically elected government. "Top American officials," Michael Ledeen and William Lewis noted, "believed that Khomeini was a social democrat in priest's clothing."[36] Andrew Young even suggested that Khomeini would someday be considered "some kind of saint."

While the shah and the U.S. dithered through the summer and fall of 1978, events began to accelerate. In October, Khomeini decided to leave Iraq for Paris. The French considered blocking his entry, but relented when Pahlavi said he had no objection. This was a major blunder on the shah's part. Whereas communications between Iraq and Iran were slow and inefficient, from Paris Khomeini could command a modern communications apparatus. Significantly, the one industry never disrupted during the series of anti-shah labor strikes that paralyzed Iran in 1978 and 1979 was the telephone system.

Ledeen and Lewis noted another advantage of Paris: its access to western media. "Khomeini discovered one of the secrets of the late twentieth century: the mass media of the bourgeois countries can easily become the tool of a revolutionary movement."[37] The media gave Khomeini's every move and utterance saturation coverage, and international broadcasts, especially by the BBC, found their way into Iran. Prior to his Paris exile, few Iranians even knew what Khomeini looked like, since the Iranian news media was prohibited from publishing his photo.

In mid-October, the most significant blow to date fell: Khomieni called on workers to go on strike in the Iranian oil fields. Within two weeks, Iranian oil production was virtually shut down. Student riots followed throughout Iran. As popular discontent grew, Iran's military started to fall apart; desertions ran between five hundred and one thousand a day. Officers joined the growing crowds of protestors. As Khomeini made a bid to establish himself as Iran's de facto ruler-in-exile, Pahlavi and the White House began to contemplate the extreme measures they had hitherto avoided—the declaration of martial law followed by the establishment of a military government.

In Tehran, Ambassador Sullivan reached the conclusion that the shah would have to go, and began quietly contacting some leaders of the opposition—without authorization from Washington. Meanwhile, the human rights office of the State Department sent a special emissary to Tehran to pressure Sullivan into reminding Pahlavi that the U.S. expected human rights to be upheld. Secretary of State Vance hoped that a coalition government of opposition figures could absorb Khomeini harmlessly into the mix. Undersecretary of State Henry Precht argued that once the shah was gone, moderate elements would reassert themselves and gradually establish a regime compatible with American interests.[38] Among Carter's senior aides, only Brzezinski continued to argue that the fall of the shah would have catastrophic effects. Brzezinski continued to favor a military solution—either a military government and/or a military takeover if necessary. But by January, it became apparent that even this extreme option was no longer possible. The Iranian military was powerless, and had not made even preliminary plans for seizing control of the government.

In the midst of this deteriorating situation, the Soviet Union decided to stir the pot. There were more than four thousand Soviet "technicians" employed in Iran, one thousand of whom—some identified as KGB and GRU officers—worked at Iran's major steel mill. The newspaper of the communist Tudeh Party in Iran was probably printed in the Soviet embassy in Tehran; it began to take a pro-Khomeini line in 1978.[39] Then, on November 19, Leonid Brezhnev issued a warning to the United States: "It must be clear that any interference, especially military interference in the affairs of Iran—a state which directly borders on the Soviet Union—would be regarded as a matter affecting security interests.... The events taking place in that country constitute purely internal affairs, and the questions involved should be decided by the Iranians themselves."[40] Vance issued a typically weak response: "The United States does not intend to interfere in the affairs of any other country."

In December 1978, as Pahlavi's ability to rule was collapsing, a reporter asked President Carter at a press conference if the U.S. expected the shah to prevail. Carter replied, "I don't know. I hope so. This is something in the hands of the people of Iran. We have never had any intention and don't have any intention of trying to intercede in the internal political affairs of Iran. We primarily want an absence of bloodshed, and stability. We personally prefer that the Shah maintain a major role in the government, but that's a decision for the Iranian people to make."

Carter's words fell with a thud in Iran and elsewhere in the Middle East, where they were interpreted to mean that the U.S. was dumping Pahlavi. No such decision had been made, because the policy of the Carter administration throughout the entire crisis was to make no decisions but simply hope for the best. Carter even reversed the one decision intended to send a signal of American resolve: He quietly ordered the aircraft carrier *Constellation* to sail from the Philippines to the Persian Gulf. State Department opponents of the move leaked it to the *New York Times*, which immediately printed the story, whereupon Carter rescinded the order. But the signal to the Iranian military and opposition was clear: The Americans were tentative; it was only a matter of time before the shah would collapse for good. When the *Constellation* story ran in the *New York Times* in late December, the shah began making plans to leave the country.

After making some last-ditch attempts to stitch together a coalition government, Pahlavi left Iran on January 16, 1979. Under the old constitution, the shah was succeeded by a Regency Council headed by a new prime minister, Shapour Bakhtiar. His government lasted less than a month. Bakhtiar sent word to Khomeini in Paris requesting a meeting. Khomeini replied that Bakhtiar was a puppet of Pahlavi, and must abdicate immediately. Khomeini returned in triumph to Iran on February 1, and appointed a rival government under the leadership of Medhi Bazargan. Khomeini's well-organized followers seized radio stations and military facilities. When the army declared its neutrality, the already thin support for Bakhtiar's government collapsed. The military attaché in the U.S. embassy in Tehran sent a terse message to Washington: "Army surrenders; Khomeini wins. Destroying all classified [documents]."[41] Khomeini proclaimed a fundamentalist Islamic republic. Sixty-nine former government officials were executed in one night in March; most of Iran's senior military commanders who didn't flee the country were put to death. Laws restricting polygamy and allowing divorce were revoked. Homosexuality became a capital offense, and executions were meted out. Khomeini's regime executed more people in its first year in power than the shah's SAVAK had allegedly killed in the previous twenty-five years.

On Valentine's Day, the U.S. embassy was attacked by a revolutionary mob. Ambassador Sullivan and his staff were taken hostage. (On this same day, the U.S. ambassador to Afghanistan, Adolph Dubs, was murdered in Kabul.) Bakhtiar, foreign minister Ibrahim Yazdi, and some of Khomeini's forces intervened and within twenty-four hours ended the siege. But a ragtag "revolutionary guard" was placed outside the embassy to ensure its security. The embassy shipped hundreds of boxes of sensitive material to the State Department. Amazingly, the boxes were shipped back to the embassy only a few weeks later, when it was decided the immediate crisis was past.

How far-reaching the consequences of the revolution in Iran would be was difficult to say, but American strategists feared the worst. America's allies in the Middle East, especially Saudi Arabia, were alarmed at the outcome of the Iranian revolution and America's pusillanimous response to the collapse of an ally. Once again, the lesson was that it was not necessarily advantageous to be too close to the United States. Walter Laqueur of Georgetown University warned in March 1979 that "U.S. foreign policy has written off not only Iran but a far wider area, and that the countries concerned would be therefore well advised to come to terms with the Soviet Union as best they can....It may also encourage the Russians to engage in a forward policy elsewhere, as the risks involved must now appear small or non-existent."[42] Laqueur would not have to wait long to see his prediction fulfilled.

(Non-) Intervention in Nicaragua

Iran was not an isolated example of the ruin of foreign policy under the Carter administration. At the same time Iran was collapsing, Central America began to unravel, despite the initiative of the Panama Canal treaties. The focus of the trouble was Nicaragua, which was run by a family dynasty that Carter's State Department regarded as even more unsavory than the Iranian shah. The president and patriarch of the current generation, Anastasio Somoza Debayle, had been educated at West Point, and ruled with the aid of a loyal national guard. Even before Carter took office, Washington was starting to turn up its nose at Somoza's corruption and autocratic governance. Somoza and his cronies lined their pockets with millions of dollars in international relief aid that flowed into the country after a disastrous earthquake in 1972 (which meant that he merely followed the practice of the rulers of about half the membership of the UN General Assembly). In 1975, columnist Jack Anderson blasted Somoza as "the world's greediest dictator," and Gerald Ford's State Department leveled strong criticism of Somoza's human rights violations in 1976.[43]

Nicaragua appeared to be a promising opportunity for the Carter administration's human rights policy. The Panama Canal treaties were generating goodwill for the U.S. in Latin America. Moreover, in Nicaragua itself there was a moderate democratic opposition to Somoza centered around *La Presna* newspaper publisher Pedro Chamorro. Most important, the CIA judged, there was not much of a threat from the far left. Somoza's national guard, the CIA thought, had successfully stamped out the Marxist Sandinista guerrillas, named after Augusto Sandino, an anti-American rebel of the 1920s. In 1976, the CIA estimated that there were not more than fifty Sandinista guerrillas remaining in Nicaragua. The CIA consistently underestimated the seriousness of the Sandinistas. As late as May 1979, within two months of the Sandinistas' triumph, the CIA would still be reporting that they thought there was little chance that the Sandinistas would succeed in taking power.[44]

The Carter administration, declaring itself committed to the principle of non-intervention, nevertheless undertook to instigate the removal of Somoza and his replacement by a genuine democratic government. What it got instead was a civil war that left forty thousand Nicaraguans dead, one hundred thousand homeless, and a Soviet-leaning totalitarian government in its place that became the impetus for further upheaval in the region for a decade to come. What the Nicaraguan experience showed was that Carter's human rights policy *was* a form of intervention. The Sandinistas would not have come to power in the absence of the Carter administration's human rights policy. As Robert Kagan observed, "With a few words and a suspension of loans, the United States had helped alter the political balance in Nicaragua in potentially revolutionary ways."[45] The Nicaragua experience confirmed the defects of Carter's foreign policy that had been apparent in its handling of Iran.

Like most Latin American nations, Nicaragua received both military and economic aid from the U.S., and the Carter administration decided to use aid as a lever to bolster its human rights policy. Deputy Secretary of State Warren Christopher decided to withhold aid to Nicaragua in 1977 pending an improvement in Somoza's human rights record. The Carter administration hoped to strengthen the moderate opposition and pressure Somoza into holding free elections, but the result was just the opposite: American pressure on Somoza reinvigorated the extreme left, which recognized that American opposition to the regime provided them with a golden opportunity to step up violent guerrilla action. The Sandinistas also gained on the propaganda front. *New York Times* reporter Alan Riding gave the Sandinistas legitimacy with his coverage of their "major drive" to "topple Somoza" and by reporting—inaccurately—that the Sandinistas had moderated and turned away from Marxism.

Once again, the State Department, like the *New York Times*, misjudged the political situation inside Nicaragua. In a hearing on the administration's aid cutoff proposal, House Appropriations Committee Chairman Clarence Long asked Undersecretary of State Lucy Benson the following question: "What would be the reaction of the State Department if this committee were to suspend all aid to Nicaragua, in view of some of the gross violations of human rights that have taken place there? What would be lost to the United States and would there be a violation of our security interests?" Benson answered: "I cannot think of a single thing."[46]

In late 1978, both the Nicaraguan crisis and the Iranian crisis began spinning out of control simultaneously. The Carter administration grossly underestimated the anti-American forces at work in two hemispheres where vital American interests were at stake. Never before had an administration so bungled American foreign policy on a global scale, from Latin America to the Middle East.

Somoza promised that he would step down by 1981 and hold free elections. That date fell conveniently after the next U.S. presidential election, after which Somoza might have been hoping for American assistance to keep power. He never got the chance. In January 1978, Pedro Chamorro was assassinated, which immediately radicalized the situation. No one knows who was behind Chamorro's killing, but it chiefly benefited the Sandinistas. With the most formidable political figure of the center eliminated, the radicals gained. A general strike followed, and Nicaragua's neighboring nations broke off diplomatic relations and joined the U.S. in pressuring for Somoza's demise.

The next major shock occurred in August, when two dozen Sandinista guerrillas captured the National Palace while the Nicaraguan congress was in session. With the entire congress held hostage, Somoza flinched. Rather than contemplate the bloodshed that would necessarily accompany a military attempt to end the hostage-taking, Somoza gave in to Sandinista demands for money, the release of Sandinista prisoners, the publication and broadcast of a Sandinista manifesto, and safe conduct out of Nicaragua for the guerrillas. (Most of the guerrillas went to Cuba.) Somoza's capitulation made him look weak and boosted the Sandinistas' prestige. Many within the national guard criticized Somoza's weakness, and Somoza, fearing a coup, jailed eighty-five guard officers. The Sandinistas stepped up the pace and scale of their guerrilla attacks, and the national guard reacted brutally and indiscriminately, using tanks, artillery, and aircraft in ways that killed civilians and destroyed poor neighborhoods.

The Carter administration now belatedly recognized that it had a disaster on its hands. Instead of a peaceful transition to genuine democratic rule, it faced the prospect not only of violent revolution but perhaps even of regional war, as Panama's General Torrijos had threatened to bomb Nicaragua's capital city, Managua. Carter's foreign policy team didn't know what to do. The *Washington Post* took note of the precariousness of the situation in an editorial:

> [W]hat the United States is really dealing with, or so we increasingly suspect, is a revolution. It is comforting to think that the aging dictator Somoza will somehow fade away and be replaced in the scheduled 1981 elections by moderate democrats friendly to the United States. Such is the polarization and violence now building, however, that President Somoza may be forced out in an explosion well before 1981 and replaced not by centrist democrats but by elements politically and ideologically beholden to the guerrillas of the Sandinista National Liberation Front. A "second Cuba" in Central America? It is not out of the question.[47]

The prospect that Nicaragua might become a "second Cuba" was apparent as Cuba supplied the Sandinistas with arms. Panama, Venezuela, and Costa Rica, sensing that it was in their self-interests to accommodate Cuban regional ambitions if America was retreating from Somoza (who was widely loathed in the region in any event), became willing conduits for Cuban weapons shipments. Carter not only discounted Cuba's malevolent influence in Latin America, but for a time hoped to normalize U.S. relations with Castro. Latin American nations took their cue from Carter's bearings accordingly. Costa Rican president Rodrigo Carazo went as far as to remark, "It is more important for Somoza to fall than to keep out the Cubans." For his part, Castro visited several Latin American nations, repeating the boast that "Somoza will soon be in the garbage can of history."

American intelligence was well informed of the quantity of Cuban arms flowing through Panama, because Panama's intelligence chief, Colonel Manuel Noriega, was on the CIA payroll. Noriega had met with Castro to help set up the arms pipeline, which included plane-loads (sometimes the planes were supplied by the Panamanian air force) of .50 caliber anti-aircraft guns, AK-47 rifles, and handheld mortars. Cuba also dispatched military advisors to Costa Rica to help manage the arms flow and advise the Sandinistas on military operations. The Carter administration resisted or downplayed evidence of Cuban influence and involvement with the Sandinistas. It directed CIA agents in Panama to pay less attention to the arms trade and tried to block previous CIA reports from reaching Congress (Congress leaked, naturally).

Just as Carter administration officials argued that America could reach an accord with Khomeini, a State Department faction argued that America should accept or even support a Sandinista victory, because the Sandinistas weren't truly committed Marxist revolutionaries and were open to moderation. In the words of Assistant Secretary of State Viron Vaky, the Sandinistas were "classic *caudillo* types, searching for an ideology to sustain their search for power." Warren Christopher agreed with Vaky, telling a congressional committee that the Sandinistas were "generally moderate and pluralistic." Brzezinski, again, was the one realist in an administration crippled by indecision.

Somoza's position steadily eroded throughout 1979. When Somoza didn't respond to American emissaries who told him to step aside and leave the country, President Carter publicly stated that the United States favored a new government in Nicaragua. The American-led arms embargo was expanded to include pressuring other nations to stop supplying arms to Somoza. The U.S. even forced Israel to turn around a freighter that was nearing a Nicaraguan port. Cut off from outside suppliers, the Nicaraguan national guard found itself at a disadvantage against the Sandinistas. Jeane Kirkpatrick commented bitterly that "for the second time in a decade an American ally ran out of gas and ammunition while confronting an opponent well armed by the Soviet bloc."[48]

In June 1979, the final public relations blow came: A national guardsman was caught by a television cameraman ordering ABC News correspondent Bill Stewart to kneel on the ground. Then the guardsman shot Stewart in the back of the head. Stewart's brutal televised killing caused outrage in the U.S., and destroyed Somoza's remaining support among conservatives in Congress. Secretary Vance called for Somoza's resignation the following day. With the national guard nearly out of arms and the Sandinistas gaining control of more cities, Somoza decided in July to leave the country. He flew to Miami on July 17, 1979. As the Sandinistas advanced on Managua, the national guard disintegrated. The Sandinistas took over the government in Managua two days after Somoza's departure. Although the Carter administration was preparing to send massive amounts of American aid to Nicaragua in an effort to befriend the Sandinistas, Brzezinski understood that "the baton is being passed from the United States to Cuba." The Sandinistas did not disagree. Humberto Ortega, a member of the ruling junta and brother of the new president, Daniel Ortega, forthrightly declared, "We wanted to copy in a mechanical way the model that we knew, which was Cuba, and we identified ourselves with it. We didn't want to follow the other models."

The Cubans were happy to oblige, sending planeloads of advisors (including senior officials of Castro's secret police) to Managua within days of the Sandinistas' triumph. Within a year, more than four thousand Cuban "advisors" were in place, helping to run the Nicaraguan revolution. The PLO, which had helped supply and train the Sandinistas, announced plans to open an embassy in Managua. Soon Nicaragua was voting in lockstep with the Soviet Union at the UN. In the U.S., the same confusion and double-talk that occurred over Cuba twenty years before was repeated.

Carter publicly denied that Nicaragua was becoming another Cuba, even though U.S. intelligence agencies were telling Carter that the Sandinista government would soon lurch to the extreme left. It was a mistake, Carter said, "to assume or to claim that every time an evolutionary change takes place in this hemisphere it's a result of a secret, massive Cuban intervention." The Sandinistas were only too happy to play along with this charade, because it kept American aid flowing into the country. But the communist direction of the Sandinistas soon became undeniable even to the Carter administration. The "moderates" within the Sandinista regime were either marginalized, driven from office, or shown to be radicals after all. The junta announced, among other steps, that there would be no elections before 1985 at the earliest. The Sandinistas adopted a new national anthem for Nicaragua that identified "the Yanqui" as "the enemy of mankind." The most troubling portent of the situation, U.S. intelligence thought, was that Nicaragua would now support the guerrilla movements in El Salvador, Guatemala, and Honduras. "The Cubans," a CIA report to Carter concluded, "can also be expected in the months ahead to begin using Nicaragua to support guerrillas from countries in the northern tier of Central America."[49]

  "The failure of the Carter administration's foreign policy is now clear to everyone except its architects," Jeane Kirkpatrick wrote in her famous fall 1979 *Commentary* article "Dictatorships and Double Standards." She was not alone in this harsh judgment. Robert Tucker of Johns Hopkins University wrote in *Foreign Affairs'* annual survey of the world: "After almost three years, it is reasonably clear that the Carter Administration's foreign policy has been a failure."[50] In the

New Republic, Tucker added that on foreign policy, Carter "is virtually unteachable." "The foreign policy of the Carter administration failed not for lack of good intentions," Kirkpatrick continued, "but for lack of realism about the nature of traditional versus revolutionary autocracies and the relation of each to the American national interest."[51]

She had no idea that the worst was yet to come for Carter's foreign policy.

CHAPTER EIGHT

President Malaise

"People who talk about an age of limits are really talking about their own limitations, not America's."

—RONALD REAGAN

Before the end of 1979, the bottom fell out of Carter's presidency. Khomeini's triumph in Iran turned out to be not the end, but the beginning, of America's agony in the Middle East—an agony that includes today's "war on terror." For Carter, the immediate effect of the debacle in Iran was that the administration's foreign and domestic policies were shown to be utterly bankrupt, with enemies triumphant abroad and an oil crisis aggravating stagflation at home.

In December 1978, Iran cut the world's oil supply by two million barrels a day, which gave the Organization of Petroleum Exporting Countries (OPEC) the excuse for a fresh round of price hikes. OPEC started with a 14.5 percent price hike in April, which rose to 50 percent by the summer. When the price hikes finally ended, the world price of oil had increased 1,000 percent since the end of the 1960s.

Economists estimated that the 1979 price hikes could cost one million American jobs, add 1 percent to the inflation rate, which was already running at 13 percent in the spring, and further depress slumping American auto sales, a harbinger of recession. The Carter "energy crisis" led directly to the *summa* of Carter's presidency, the infamous "malaise" speech in July.

How severe the oil disruption would be to the U.S. wasn't obvious at first. Total demand for oil in the U.S. was up only slightly from the year before, and inventories of crude oil seemed large enough to absorb a short-term shock. But Energy Secretary James Schlesinger warned in February that the looming energy shortfall was "prospectively more serious than the Arab oil embargo of 1973–1974," and Carter, who never wavered in his view that changing America's energy mix was the "moral equivalent of war," swung into action. Carter asked Congress for standby authority to impose gasoline rationing, and gave another televised address to the nation about energy—the fourth of his presidency. Americans were paying less and less attention to Carter's pronouncements on energy; eighty million people had tuned in for his first energy address in 1977, but only thirty million saw this one, even though gas lines were spreading across the country. Carter asked individual Americans to conserve energy by cutting their driving by fifteen miles a week and by obeying the fifty-five-mile-per-hour speed limit. He also sought tax credits for wood-burning stoves, promised to eliminate free parking for federal employees, and later decreed that thermostats in federal buildings would be set at 78 degrees in the summer and 65 degrees in the winter.

The House rejected Carter's request for standby authority to impose gasoline rationing—"a complete and total repudiation of the President by his own party," Democratic congressman Ed Markey observed—prompting Carter to say, "I was shocked and I was embarrassed for our nation's government." House Speaker Tip O'Neill responded, "The members [of the House] don't pay any attention to him." In fact, however, the government was already rationing gasoline in the form of federally directed supply allocations to regions and even individual gas stations, so that, practically speaking, gas was rationed by waiting periods rather than by price. It was this attempt at government control of the energy marketplace that turned a temporary squeeze into a national crisis. Energy Secretary Schlesinger admitted as much, saying at the height of the crisis in July, "There would be no [gas] lines if there were no price and allocation controls." Carter recognized that truth when he agreed to the long overdue decontrolling of domestic oil prices. Domestic oil production had fallen by eleven million barrels a day since 1972. The reason? Government-mandated low prices for domestic oil discouraged domestic exploration and production and effectively subsidized foreign oil sales and production. Carter, typically, mitigated the beneficial effects of decontrol by phasing it in over a two-year period and seeking to impose a "windfall profits tax" on oil companies. He opposed instant decontrol of oil prices because "that would in effect be rationing by price. I am not going to do that." Even the *New Republic* savaged Carter for his gradual, halfway approach to decontrol. "Carter has stared the energy problem in the face and blinked," the journal of mainstream liberalism editorialized. "His program is a failure, and a cowardly failure at that."[1] Oil companies swore opposition to Carter's proposed windfall profits tax, which appeared to be another congressional battle Carter would lose.

Line Up

The first lines at gas stations started in California in the spring. The situation rapidly turned into panic buying and hoarding. The average credit card purchase during this period was only three dollars—a clear sign of hoarding—and motorists topping off their half-full tanks threatened to exhaust monthly inventories before the month was half over. Buyers lined up at 5 a.m. at gas stations. In response, many stations turned off their pumps by 10 a.m. or otherwise limited the amount they would sell. The California shortage affected even President Carter. On a trip to California in early May, Carter's motorcade had to go twenty miles out of its way to find an open gas station. California governor Jerry Brown instituted an "odd-even" rationing system: Cars with license plates ending in odd numbers could buy gasoline only on odd days of the month, and vice versa for even-numbered plates. Between price hikes and tight supplies, driving in California declined 10 percent from its level the year before.

Gas lines skipped over the heartland of the country and began to appear on the East Coast, punctuated by occasional violence that culminated in a two-day riot in Levittown, Pennsylvania, during the first week in July. The riot began, appropriately, at an intersection with a gas station on each corner. Over the July 4 holiday weekend, 90 percent of the gas stations in New York City area were closed, while 80 percent of stations statewide were closed in Pennsylvania.

Carter's approval rating sank to 25 percent, lower even than President Nixon's on the eve of his resignation after Watergate. Congressional leaders who had rejected Carter's requests for gas rationing still demanded that he "do something" about the gas crisis. New York City mayor Ed Koch accompanied a congressional delegation to a stormy White House meeting with Vice President Mondale, and told *Time* magazine, "I haven't seen a delegation this hot since the Vietnam War." A new bumper sticker started to catch on: "Carter—Kiss My Gas." With winter fuel oil shortages looming in the northeast, a popular bumper sticker in oil-rich Texas read: "Drive Fast, Freeze a Yankee."

Carter was equally unpopular abroad, especially with West German chancellor Helmut Schmidt and French president Valery Giscard d'Estaing. Europe's leaders regarded the U.S., with its low-mileage "gas guzzler" cars, as a profligate energy waster, even after Carter pledged to cut U.S. oil imports by 5 percent to help ease pressures on the world market. In a scene of hypocrisy that only government can achieve, the motorcade transporting the heads of state and their staffs to the opening session of the G-7 summit in June 1979 at Tokyo's Akasaka Palace required 124 cars. The G-7 nations tried to craft a buyers' cartel to combat OPEC by sticking with a collective import quota—but cartels and quotas tend to break, and did, under market pressures.

Carter returned from the G-7 summit in Japan at the end of June and announced plans to give yet another nationally televised address about the energy crisis. But his administration's energy policy was in such disarray that Carter abruptly and without explanation canceled the speech with only a day's notice. Then he left town for Camp David, also without explanation.

"What Are You Up To, Mr. President?"

The abruptness and silence about Carter's retreat to Camp David ignited rumors that Carter had suffered a nervous breakdown, or was involved in some secret bold stratagem to revive his sagging fortunes. Reporters noticed that most of the senior political staff to the president (but not many policymakers) were being helicoptered up to Camp David. *Newsweek* characterized this as "the nearly total disappearance of the government with no clear accounting of what it was up to."[2] The dollar took a pounding in the international exchanges, as foreign governments wondered aloud about the president's political health. The *New York Post* ran a banner headline: "WHAT ARE YOU UP TO, MR. PRESIDENT?"

What he was up to was the most remarkable exercise in presidential navel-gazing in American history. "They got up there," a White House aide told a reporter, "and they didn't know how to get out. It was chaotic, to say the least." Over the following eight days, Carter invited 134 eminent Americans from various walks of life to participate in heart-to-heart conversations with him at Camp David. Some observers remarked on the inclusion of a Greek Orthodox archbishop, but the guest list was orthodox in another way: Carter's interlocutors were almost exclusively liberals or liberal intellectuals, including Jesse Jackson, Vernon Jordan, John Kenneth Galbraith, Clark Clifford, and numerous other labor leaders, academics, journalists, and Democratic politicians. Among the politicians was Arkansas's young governor, Bill Clinton, who bluntly told Carter that he was not leading the nation effectively. Only four Republicans were invited. What was most notable about the guest list, aside from its political and liberal cast, was the scarcity of expertise about energy. "The guest register," *Newsweek* observed, "invited the view that the politics of recovery preceded policy on the agenda." The *New Republic* said it looked like "a tableau from *Who's Who*."

Rather than serving as deliberations on a new course for energy policy, the discussions were devoted to Carter's "leadership style" and the mood of the nation. Some of these conversations lasted into the small hours of the morning, with Carter sitting cross-legged on the floor. Not content with the parade of notables to his mountain retreat, Carter organized a backyard visit with an ordinary family at the home of William Fisher in Carnegie, Pennsylvania. Fisher, a machinist and union member, had been selected at short notice by the local Democratic Party, which didn't know about his criminal record, which included arson and assault.

At Camp David, Carter expressed deep pessimism about the nation's prospects, telling one group of visitors, "I think it's inevitable that there will be a lower standard of living than what everybody had always anticipated, constant growth.... I think there's going to have to be a reorientation of what people value in their own lives. I believe that there has to be a more equitable sharing of what we have.... The only trend is downward. But it's been almost impossible to get people to face up to this."

What's Wrong with America

Carter's "mystifying secret summit" (as *Newsweek* called it) had the desired dramatic effect. Carter came down from Camp David on Sunday, July 15, and preempted *Moses—The Lawgiver* on CBS to deliver his own televised sermon before the largest audience of his presidency. The hiatus from public view had built up expectations. The *Washington Post* announced the speech with the banner headline: "Carter Seeking Oratory to Move an Entire Nation." The president tried to be equal to the occasion. The trademark Carter smile was gone; he delivered the speech with a grim expression, flashing his eyes and gesticulating with a clenched fist for an effect that looked awkward and contrived. These physical touches had been devised and rehearsed on the advice of his longtime image advisor, Gerald Rafshoon. But what he said qualifies as the most dubious piece of presidential rhetoric in American history. It deserves quotation at length:

> It's clear that the true problems of our nation are much deeper—deeper than gasoline lines or energy shortages, deeper even than inflation or recession. And I realize more than ever that as president I need your help. So, I decided to reach out and listen to the voices of America.
>
> I invited to Camp David people from almost every segment of our society—business and labor, teachers and preachers, governors, mayors, and private citizens. And then I left Camp David to listen to other Americans, men and women like you. It has been an extraordinary ten days, and I want to share with you what I've heard. . . .
>
> [A]fter listening to the American people I have been reminded again that all the legislation in the world can't fix what's wrong with America. So, I want to speak to you first tonight about a subject even more serious than energy or inflation. I want to talk to you right now about a fundamental threat to American democracy.
>
> I do not mean our political and civil liberties. They will endure. And I do not refer to the outward strength of America, a nation that is at peace tonight everywhere in the world, with unmatched economic power and military might.
>
> The threat is nearly invisible in ordinary ways. It is a crisis of confidence. It is a crisis that strikes at the very heart and

soul and spirit of our national will. We can see this crisis in the growing doubt about the meaning of our own lives and in the loss of a unity of purpose for our nation.

The erosion of our confidence in the future is threatening to destroy the social and the political fabric of America. The confidence that we have always had as a people is not simply some romantic dream or a proverb in a dusty book that we read just on the Fourth of July. It is the idea which founded our nation and has guided our development as a people. Confidence in the future has supported everything else—public institutions and private enterprise, our own families, and the very Constitution of the United States. Confidence has defined our course and has served as a link between generations. We've always believed in something called progress. We've always had a faith that the days of our children would be better than our own.

Our people are losing that faith, not only in government itself but in the ability as citizens to serve as the ultimate rulers and shapers of our democracy. As a people we know our past and we are proud of it. Our progress has been part of the living history of America, even the world. We always believed that we were part of a great movement of humanity itself called democracy, involved in the search for freedom, and that belief has always strengthened us in our purpose. But just as we are losing our confidence in the future, we are also beginning to close the door on our past....

In a nation that was proud of hard work, strong families, close-knit communities, and our faith in God, too many of us now tend to worship self-indulgence and consumption. Human identity is no longer defined by what one does, but by what one owns. But we've discovered that owning things and consuming things does not satisfy our longing for meaning. We've learned that piling up material goods cannot fill the emptiness of lives which have no confidence or purpose.

The symptoms of this crisis of the American spirit are all around us. For the first time in the history of our country, a majority of our people believe that the next five years will be worse than the past five years. Two-thirds of our people do not even vote. The productivity of American workers is actually dropping, and the willingness of Americans to save for the future has fallen below that of all other people in the Western world.

As you know, there is a growing disrespect for government and for churches and for schools, the news media, and other institutions. This is not a message of happiness or reassurance, but it is the truth and it is a warning.

This stunning peroration about America's spiritual condition broke off halfway through the speech, however, and Carter then pivoted back to the conventional policy ideas and hortatory themes he had been propounding for the previous three years. In other words, there were no new real policies in the speech. However, the little personal steps Carter had been urging people to adopt took on a grandiose patriotic tone:

And I'm asking you for your good and for your nation's security to take no unnecessary trips, to use carpools or public transportation whenever you can, to park your car one extra day per week, to obey the speed limit, and to set your thermostats to save fuel. Every act of energy conservation like this is more than just common sense—I tell you it is an act of patriotism....

So, the solution of our energy crisis can also help us to conquer the crisis of the spirit in our country. It can rekindle our sense of unity, our confidence in the future, and give our nation and all of us individually a new sense of purpose.

Finally, Carter exhorted his audience, "Whenever you have a chance, say something good about our country."

The first thing to notice about the speech is that Carter did not use the word "malaise." Carter's pollster Pat Caddell used the term afterward in a press briefing. From then on the label stuck (though it should be noted that Carter's notes from his Camp David meetings do use the term "general malaise" to describe America's mood), and ever after, "malaise" is how most people recall the speech. It was even lampooned in a 1990 episode of the television show *The Simpsons*, in which a statue of Carter in the mythical town of Springfield bore the legend "Malaise Forever!"

The public initially responded favorably, with Carter's approval rating jumping from 25 to 37 percent in the days immediately after the speech; 86 percent of respondents, according to one poll, agreed with Carter's central theme about the "crisis of confidence." But the critical reaction was overwhelmingly negative. *National Review* called it "obfuscation and Elmer Gantryism," and offered a no-nonsense reflection: "The U.S. Government has nothing to do with spiritual crises or the meaning of our lives.... The last time we looked, God was not a member of the Carter Cabinet."[3] The *New Republic* was more savage, calling the speech "pop sociology stew" filled with "servile flatteries." "Carter seems to think that teaching us to sing 'Let a Smile Be Your Umbrella' can be a substitute for leading us in out of the rain. Fortunately, he utterly lacks the rhetorical skill for such a con job."[4]

This represented a striking turnabout for the *New Republic*. When Carter first declared the energy crisis to be the "moral equivalent of war" in the spring of 1977, the *New Republic* editorialized, in a vein that anticipated the Carter of July 1979, "To us, whatever contraction of affluence this country may suffer over the next few years appears no more than a byproduct of the contraction of the spirit we are already suffering."[5] A labor leader who had supported Carter in 1976 complained, "The fault is his, not ours, and asking us to say something nice about America is like Gerald Ford telling us to pin on little lapel buttons and 'Whip Inflation Now.'" Naturally, Carter's message rubbed Ronald Reagan the wrong way: "People who talk about an age of limits," Reagan said, "are really talking about their own limitations, not America's."

Foreign reaction was equally pungent. A high-ranking West German official was quoted in the press asking, "Is this serious, or is this just a great religious exercise for the soul?" In Britain, the *Economist* called Carter's act "amateurism," while the *Daily Mail* newspaper was bewildered: "From this side of the Atlantic, Jimmy Carter's frenzied efforts to revive his personal standing with voters before the next presidential election look more like a narcissistic crusade than a national crusade." Even Swedes found Carter's exercise odd; a Stockholm newspaper observed, "As a document of the emotional climate of the late 1970s, [Carter's] speech should be historic. It is also historic in its lack of concrete means of effecting a cure."[6]

Carter is said to have been influenced by Christopher Lasch's bestselling book, *The Culture of Narcissism: American Life in an Age of Diminishing Expectations.*[7] The very first page of Lasch's book used both "crisis of confidence" and "malaise" to describe the American outlook. Some of Lasch's language closely tracks Carter's speech. "[T]he impending exhaustion of natural resources," Lasch wrote, "[has] produced a mood of pessimism in higher circles, which spreads through the rest of society as people lose faith in their leaders." Despite being a man of the left, Lasch's cultural conservatism and critical appraisal of political liberalism led some conservatives to embrace his book.

While Lasch's *Culture of Narcissism* can be read as the background text for Carter's speech (according to some accounts, it was Carter's favorite book at the time), the real motivating force behind the speech was Pat Caddell, Carter's *wunderkind* pollster, who brought Lasch's book to Carter's attention. "Caddell," Elizabeth Drew wrote, "is an excitable young man with what many people consider a brilliant mind (some think him a genius) whose brow is often folded in worry."[8]

Since January, Caddell had been pressing the "crisis of confidence" thesis on Carter, backing it up with poll data demonstrating the nation's pessimistic mood. One statistic in Caddell's poll alarmed Carter: For the first time, a majority of Americans thought their children's lives would be worse than their own. "America is a nation deep in crisis," Caddell wrote to Carter in a monster 107-page memo titled "Of Crisis and Opportunity." It was a crisis "marked by a dwindling faith in the future." Caddell recommended that Carter undertake "consultations" with a cross-section of Americans to get his bearings—exactly the process Carter would go through at Camp David.

Carter was hooked on the idea, but much of his staff was not. Caddell's critics inside the White House dismissed the paper as the "Apocalypse Now" memo. The most strenuous objection came from Vice President Mondale, who was so upset with Carter's drift that he considered resigning. Mondale thought Caddell was the Rasputin of the White House, and that Carter was exhibiting catastrophic weakness. "Everything in me told me that this was wrong," Mondale said later. "I was morose about it because I thought it would destroy Carter and me with him."[9] Caddell's craziest suggestion, Mondale thought, was that President Carter should call for a constitutional convention (an idea that was discussed and finally rejected at Camp David). Mondale and other conventional political thinkers in the administration preferred a no-nonsense presidential policy speech, not criticism of the American mood. At one point during the Camp David retreat, Mondale bluntly told Carter that a speech based on Caddell's ideas would be "political suicide," and that he doubted he would be able to defend it. "You can't castigate the American people," Mondale told Carter, "or they will turn you off once and for all."[10]

Mondale was right. Carter had run for office on the promise of "a government as good as the people." Carter was now saying, in effect, that the people were no good.

"The most thoroughgoing, and puzzling, purge in the history of the U.S. presidency"

After the speech, Carter demanded the pro forma resignation of his entire Cabinet, along with twenty-three other senior White House staff. Carter accepted five of the resignations—Treasury Secretary Michael Blumenthal, Energy Secretary James Schlesinger, Transportation Secretary Brock Adams, Attorney General Griffin Bell, and Health, Education, and Welfare Secretary Joseph Califano. Bell had wanted to leave for some time. Schlesinger was dismissed for being ineffectual. The other three were dismissed for being "disloyal"—Califano, in particular, had close ties to Ted Kennedy. In addition, Califano's aggressive anti-smoking campaign had caused Carter political heartburn in tobacco-growing states such as North Carolina and had led to one of Carter's more embarrassing moments—a speech in North Carolina where he said the federal government's efforts would make cigarette smoking "even safer than it is today." Califano got in a subtle dig at Carter's resistance to activist liberal social policy when he remarked, "It has been a deeply enjoyable experience to administer so many of the programs enacted into law under President Lyndon Johnson."

Carter thought wielding his axe would bolster the image he had tried to create in his "malaise" speech of a decisive leader setting a bold new course for the nation. The effect was just the opposite. The biggest Cabinet upheaval since 1841 (*Time* described it as "the most thoroughgoing, and puzzling, purge in the history of the U.S. presidency") sent the dollar into a new tailspin, and the price of gold shot up to over $300 an ounce for the first time. Califano and Adams had been well respected in Washington, while some of the Cabinet members Carter retained (such as HUD Secretary Patricia Harris) were not.

Along with the Cabinet sackings, Carter announced he was officially elevating Hamilton Jordan—who was heartily disliked in Washington—to chief of staff, a position that Carter had ostentatiously pledged on taking office that he would not fill.

This was too much for Capitol Hill. Democratic congressman Charles Wilson of Texas complained, "Good grief! They're cutting down the biggest trees and keeping the monkeys." *Time* judged that "the housecleaning...provoked new doubts about Carter's understanding of the Federal Government and about his own leadership ability."[11] Ken Bode wrote "It's Over for Jimmy" in the *New Republic*:

> The past two weeks will be remembered as the period when President Carter packed it in, put the finishing touches on a failed presidency....It's over for Jimmy Carter. He needed a new image, so he took the advice of his pollster, his ad man, and his wife, and wound up immobilizing his own government, imperiling the American dollar on the international market, and looking more than ever like a crude, erratic, unstable amateur....The Carter administration has simply imploded, collapsed inwardly under the weight of its own incompetence.[12]

The quick bump in Carter's poll the day after the speech proved evanescent; by the end of the week, his approval rating had fallen back to the pre–malaise speech 25 percent. As Carter was botching the energy situation and sacking his Cabinet, a number of personal pratfalls added to Americans' impression of his incompetence. Some observers worried whether Carter's problem was not his competence, but his state of mind. A few of these worries were spoken openly. Republican senator Ted Stevens (one of the few Republicans who had been invited to the Camp David affair) wondered aloud on the Senate floor and again on television, "Some of us are seriously worried that he might be approaching some kind of mental problem. He ought to take a rest."

Killer Rabbits and SALT II

A truly bizarre episode concerned an incredible account of Carter fending off an attack from a ferocious...*rabbit*. While fishing on a pond on his Georgia farm, the story went, a frenzied "swamp rabbit" had attempted to climb into Carter's boat. Carter counterattacked with his paddle, but with the intent of driving off the beast rather than striking it. Carter related the story to his press secretary, Jody Powell, who made the mistake of passing the story along to Associated Press reporter Brooks Jackson. Jackson filed a "human interest" story about the episode, which the *Washington Post* ran on the front page beneath the headline, "President Attacked by Rabbit." "A 'killer rabbit' attacked President Carter on a recent trip to Plains, Georgia," Jackson's story read. "The rabbit...was hissing menacingly, its teeth flashing and nostrils flared, and making straight for the President." All three television networks carried the story, which seemed straight out of a Monty Python skit, on their national news broadcasts. (The *New York Times* had the sense to run the story on page twelve.)

Comedians had a field day: "I didn't think Carter had a paddle," Mark Russell quipped on PBS. The story took on symbolic significance far out of proportion to its merits. Beyond the sheer incredulity of the image itself ("killer rabbit?"), the assertion that Carter did not strike the rabbit with the intent to kill it was transformed into a metaphor for his weakness in office. A grainy color photo by a White House photographer of the incident existed, but Powell refused to release it because it would have caused "the rabbit controversy" to continue. Later in the summer, Carter, an occasional jogger (he had run on the cross-country team at the Naval Academy in the 1940s), decided to enter a ten-kilometer road race in suburban Maryland. He collapsed halfway through the race, a victim of the late summer heat and humidity. A photo of a faltering Carter being propped up by Secret Service agents ran on the front page of most newspapers—another unflattering symbol of weakness in the commander in chief. Carter's symbolic answer to charges of weakness, according to Hamilton Jordan, was his refusal to use an umbrella in the rain when he traveled to Vienna to meet with Soviet leader Leonid Brezhnev, for fear it would summon images of Neville Chamberlain's appeasement.[13]

That trip to Vienna in June 1979 was to sign the SALT II arms control treaty with the Soviet Union. Carter's ebullience for the treaty led him to give Brezhnev a hug and kiss on the cheek, a step that startled the feeble Soviet boss and nauseated American conservatives. Carter no doubt thought the prestige of achieving a new arms treaty with the Soviet Union would provide him with a political lift sufficient to fend off the expected challenge from Ted Kennedy for the Democratic Party's presidential nomination in 1980. Carter assumed that SALT II would ease Cold War tensions and reinvigorate détente. It had just the opposite effect: SALT II touched off the most ferocious and fundamental foreign policy debate since the beginning of the Cold War. And if that weren't enough, the Ayatollah Khomeini's Iran was about to hand Carter a full-scale disaster.

CHAPTER NINE

Carter Held Hostage

"Fuck the Shah."

—PRESIDENT CARTER, fall 1979[1]

The final details of the SALT II treaty required a circuitous negotiating process, stemming chiefly from yet another Carter blunder
early in his administration. President Gerald Ford and Secretary
of State Henry Kissinger had reached a basic framework for a SALT II
treaty at the summit meeting in Vladivostok in 1975. The core of their
provisional arms deal was an agreement that each side would have the
same number of inter-continental ballistic missiles (ICBMs), which
was thought would remedy a chief defect of the first SALT treaty that
Nixon had signed in 1972. After hard bargaining with Kissinger in
1975, the Soviets finally agreed to an equal number of "launchers"
(launchers being the more inclusive term for aircraft, submarines, and
silos that could serve as platforms for delivering nuclear warheads).

Had Carter concluded SALT II swiftly on Ford's and Kissinger's
terms in 1977, the treaty likely would have been ratified. Yet Carter's

negotiators didn't get final agreement on SALT II until the spring of 1979, two years later, by which time the political climate had changed substantially. Once again, the odd and contradictory nature of Carter's character generated a snafu. On one hand, Carter had criticized Ford and Kissinger for not being tough enough with the Soviets; on the other, Carter's pacifist sympathies led him to call for "real arms control"—that is, deep *reductions* in nuclear weapons (a goal he shared, incidentally, with Ronald Reagan). Yet both SALT I and the prospective Vladivostok framework for SALT II allowed the number of nuclear warheads to go up. Carter and his foreign policy team decided to try for a better deal.

Carter blundered, however, in going public with the idea rather than proposing it privately to the Soviets over the negotiating table; his early human rights rhetoric had already offended them. He announced his general intention to cut nuclear weapons in a speech to the United Nations, then followed up with a letter to Brezhnev proposing deep cuts in existing Soviet missile forces, but with little or no reduction in U.S. missile forces. The only American concession would be to slow down new weapon systems on the drawing board. Then, at a press conference, Carter dug a deeper diplomatic hole by declaring variously, "We will be taking new proposals to the Soviet Union," "We're not abandoning the agreements made," and, "If we're disappointed—which is a possibility—then we'll try to modify our stance." To the Soviets, Carter's public statements sounded provocative, weak, vacillating, and a deliberate attempt to sour relations all at once.

When Secretary of State Cyrus Vance arrived in Moscow in late March to formally present Carter's arms cut proposals, the Soviets snubbed him and canceled the negotiating sessions. Anatoly Dobrynin, the Soviet ambassador to the U.S., said, "The members of the politburo were outraged" by Carter's high-handed diplomacy.[2] Foreign Minister Andrei Gromyko called a rare press conference in Moscow, blasting the U.S. for a "cheap and shady maneuver" designed to give the U.S. a "unilateral advantage" in nuclear weapons.

Carter's arms control plan thus, in the words of Strobe Talbott, degenerated "into an inter-continental shouting match."[3] Robert Gates, who served in Carter's National Security Council (and later became CIA director under President George H. W. Bush), wrote later that "relations between the Soviet Union and the United States were more consistently sour and antagonistic during the Carter administration than was (or would be) the case under any other President of the Cold War except Harry Truman—including Ronald Reagan."[4]

Conservatives were initially buoyed by this turn of events, thinking that Carter would indeed be tougher with the Soviet Union. George Will celebrated that the period of "détente drunkenness" had finally ended. Only two months later, however, Carter's "inordinate fear of communism" speech made clear that Carter suffered from a lingering détente hangover, if not a form of *delirium tremens*.

Over the next two years, Carter's negotiators closed the breach, apologized for Carter's proposal (just as Carter avoided all mention of human rights when he met with Ambassador Dobrynin in early 1979), and produced a treaty that built closely upon the framework that Kissinger and Ford had worked out in 1975. However, they weakened it significantly. By 1979, Carter was so desperate for an arms agreement and a U.S.-Soviet summit that his negotiating team made concession after concession to the Soviets—so many concessions that both Kissinger and Ford criticized the treaty. To be sure, the central feature of SALT II was equal numbers of "launchers" for both sides (2,400 apiece), but there were a number of what experts called "asymmetries" in the treaty. While the Soviets' largest missiles could carry up to ten warheads, American missiles carried only three warheads, which meant that despite having an equal number of "launchers," the Soviets had a great advantage in "throw-weight." At the time SALT II was signed in 1979, the Soviets had increased the number of warheads in their ICBM force to nearly 6,500, while the U.S. had only 2,154.

There were other problems with the three-hundred-page treaty. The U.S. agreed to include its bomber forces, consisting of aging B-52s and

F-111s stationed in England, within its quota of "launchers," while the Soviet Union's new-generation "Backfire" bomber was not included. The Soviets assured the U.S. that the Backfire was not an inter-continental bomber, even though it could fly a one-way mission against the U.S. and land in Cuba, or be refueled in-flight—a capability the American military had already observed. This concession in SALT II was especially troubling, as the U.S. had no serious air defense, no surface-to-air missiles, and only 309 active fighter-interceptor aircraft—"a derisory force by any estimate," commented defense analyst Edward Luttwak. The Soviets, on the other hand, took air defense seriously, with more than 2,500 fighter-interceptor aircraft and 12,000 surface-to-air missiles, vastly complicating any bombing missions by B-52s.

The U.S. trump card for these vulnerabilities was the cruise missile. These small, highly accurate missiles were the ideal deterrent weapon, because they could be deployed by a variety of mobile means: from submarines, surface ships, aircraft, and even on ordinary trucks based in Europe. That the cruise missile could be launched from American aircraft flying outside Soviet borders extended the life and credible threat of the 1950s-era B-52s. Edward Luttwak observed: "Since they are so small and versatile in deployment, CM [cruise missile] forces are inherently very stable indeed: not even the most optimistic counter-force planner could hope to target a diversified CM force distributed among ships, submarines, aircraft of various kinds, and small ground vehicles."[5] The Soviets had nothing like the cruise missile in prospect in their own arms development program.

But the SALT II treaty included a protocol allowing long-range cruise missiles launched from heavy bombers only, and limiting the range of all other cruise missiles to six hundred kilometers (less than four hundred miles). This effectively removed their strategic deployment on ships and submarines. The protocol was set to expire in 1985, after which the U.S. would theoretically be allowed to deploy long-range cruise missiles in any mode it chose. Yet the momentum of arms control (a SALT III treaty was expected by 1985) was such that it was plausible to expect that the Soviets might well demand that the cruise missile limits be made permanent. The Carter administration insisted that it would never agree to any permanent limit on cruise missiles "which were not in the interests of the U.S. and its allies," but this assurance rang hollow, as did its statement that "The Soviets have agreed to furnish specific assurances concerning the Backfire" as an inter-continental threat.

Carter knew all along that getting a two-thirds vote in the Senate would be difficult, so much so that at one point during the negotiations he considered making SALT II an "executive agreement" (similar to the North American Free Trade Agreement) rather than a formal treaty. This meant that it would require only a majority vote of both houses of Congress, instead of a two-thirds vote in the Senate. The Senate signaled its displeasure with this trial balloon, and Carter had to abandon the idea. Now he had to trust that Senate Majority Leader Robert Byrd could bring the treaty to a successful ratification vote.

But by the fall of 1979, Carter had a more immediate foreign policy problem. The shah of Iran wanted to come to the United States.

The Hostage Crisis

When Pahlavi had left Iran in January, he had gone first to Egypt and then to Morocco. In the back of his mind, he had harbored thoughts that the U.S. or the Iranian military would find a way to restore his throne, as had been done for his father in 1953. Hence he wanted to stay close to the Middle East. Once it became clear by late February that a restoration was beyond hope, he wanted to come to the U.S. Carter reacted angrily to the idea. "Fuck the Shah," he was reported as saying.[6] His senior foreign policy advisors were no warmer to the idea, and stalled for time. Carter worried that Pahlavi's entry into the U.S. might provoke retaliation in Iran, perhaps even the taking of hostages. Vance agreed, though Vice President Mondale argued that it would look bad for America to turn its back on a longtime ally. David Rockefeller and Henry Kissinger both pressured the administration to admit Pahlavi—Kissinger attacked Carter for treating the shah "like a Flying Dutchman looking for a port of call"—and suggested having

Pahlavi go to the Bahamas. Over the summer the shah moved again, this time to Mexico.

It was not until October 18, 1979—four years after it was first diagnosed—that American intelligence realized that Pahlavi had cancer. With this discovery, Secretary Vance told Carter that the U.S. could not in good conscience refuse the shah entrance to the U.S. for medical treatment. Carter was still reluctant. "Does somebody here have the answer as to what we do if the diplomats in our embassy are taken hostage?" Carter asked. When no one answered, Carter said, "I gather not. On that day we will all sit here with long, drawn, white faces and realize we've been had."[7]

The shah was finally admitted on a tourist visa for medical treatment in New York City. He arrived on October 22. There were street protests by Iranian students in New York, and protests in Iran, but the U.S. had received an assurance from Iran that there would be no reprisals. The first sign of trouble came on October 31, when Iran sent the U.S. a formal note of protest declaring that Iran "did not accept the American government's excuses for granting entry permission to the deposed Shah."

Four days later, a mob of Iranian "students" stormed the U.S. embassy, taking sixty-seven Americans hostage. (Fourteen black hostages were released a few weeks later in a ham-handed attempt to stir up racial animosity in the U.S.) The State Department was taken by surprise and unsure what to do, while some of the hostage-takers have testified that the embassy occupation would have ended at the first credible threat of American military action. They were startled that Carter quickly and publicly disavowed the use of force (though Carter did send a private warning to Iran threatening severe but unspecified consequences if the hostages were harmed).

With military force ruled out, it was clear the crisis would drag on for months. The PLO offered to intervene, but Khomeini bluntly refused them. Carter turned to his brother Billy and Libya's Mohammar Qaddafi for help, asking his brother—who had accepted a $200,000 "loan" from Libya that would become an embarrassment to Carter in the summer of 1980—to intercede with the anti-American tyrant of Tripoli. Khomeini was not impressed. Carter then decided to send former attorney general Ramsey Clark—an ambulance-chasing advocate of American guilt who had already offered the Iranians advice on how to seek damages for the "criminal and wrongful acts committed by the shah"—as an envoy to Iran. Khomeini spurned him. Even freezing billions of dollars of Iranian assets in the U.S. and packing the shah off to Panama did nothing to break the siege.

Invasion

Before the end of the year, the other shoe dropped. On December 13, a story in the *Washington Post* noted in passing: "Within the past several days, U.S. intelligence had picked up the movement of one or two Soviet battalions, organized and armed for combat, to the vicinity of the Afghan capital of Kabul. These 400 to 800 Soviet troops were an addition to 3,500 to 4,000 Soviet military personnel already in the country." Deputy Secretary of State Warren Christopher summoned the deputy Soviet ambassador to lodge an official U.S. protest. On December 23, an ominous headline appeared on page eight of the *Washington Post*: "U.S. Worries About Possibility of Soviet Dominance in Afghanistan."

On that same day, Soviet "advisors" in Afghanistan persuaded two armored divisions in the Afghan army to turn over their ammunition for "inventory"—a convenient way of disarming them. Two days later—Christmas Day—the Soviet Union invaded Afghanistan. Transport planes with crack Soviet airborne troops landed at a rate of one every ten minutes at airfields throughout the country. There were forty thousand Soviet troops on the ground in Afghanistan in the first few days; within a few weeks the total number of troops swelled to eighty-five thousand. Soviet forces immediately swarmed the capital city of Kabul; a KGB team disguised as Afghan soldiers stormed the presidential palace and murdered Prime Minister Hafizullah Amin, making hash of the Soviet claim that Amin had "invited" them into the country. Radio Kabul announced that a coup had taken place, resulting in the restoration of a previously ousted ruler, Babrak Karmal. But U.S. intelligence quickly figured out that the "Radio Kabul" transmissions were originating from a location just across the Afghan border in the Soviet Union.

The invasion should not have been a surprise. The Soviets had been constructing highways from the Soviet Union into Afghanistan for years, U.S. intelligence had noted Soviet troops mobilizing near the Afghan border in early December, and Carter had been warned as early as July that the Soviets might intervene in the country. But the full-scale invasion and occupation took Carter completely by surprise.

Control of Afghanistan put the Soviets within 350 miles of the Arabian Gulf, and in position to preempt any American moves against Iran. The CIA discovered that the Soviet General Staff had a contingency plan to occupy the northern tier of Iran.[8] Unrest among the Kurds, Azerbaijanis, and Baluchis could provide a pretext for "restoring order" along the Soviet Union's central Asian border, with an eventual strategic goal of reaching farther south and acquiring a warm-water port, a long-standing Russian ambition. The CIA concluded: "The possibility that Afghanistan represents a qualitative turn in Soviet foreign policy in the region and toward the third world cannot be ruled out."[9]

Brezhnev told Carter over the hotline that the Soviets had taken this step to protect Afghanistan from outside aggression. Carter was furious for being treated as a fool—and being made to appear one as well, having hugged and kissed Brezhnev six months earlier. On New Year's Eve, Carter told Frank Reynolds of ABC News that "this action of the Soviets has made a more dramatic change in my own opinion of what the Soviets' ultimate goals are than anything they've done in the previous time I've been in office," which raised questions about what Carter hitherto thought about the character of the Soviet Union. He went on to describe the invasion as "the most serious threat to world peace since World War II.... It is even more serious than Hungary or Czechoslovakia."

Carter now decided to take a harder line with the Soviets. He recalled the U.S. ambassador to Moscow, cancelled sales of technology, imposed an embargo on grain sales (but only on grain intended for livestock, not people, Carter hastened to point out), and decided that the U.S. would boycott the Moscow Olympics (thirty-six other nations joined the U.S.-led boycott). He also approved covert aid to the Afghan resistance.

In his State of the Union speech to Congress in January, he announced the "Carter Doctrine": "An attempt by any outside force to gain control of the Persian Gulf region will be regarded as an assault on the vital interests of the United States of America, and such an assault will be repelled by any means necessary, including military force." True to form, Vance urged Carter not to make this declaration, but Brzezinski fought successfully to keep it in the speech. "The Soviet invasion was a body blow to Vance," NSC aide Gary Sick wrote, "and he seemed to age visibly under the impact."[10]

The only problem with Carter's threat of war was that the U.S. lacked the capacity to make good its threat. As if to underscore the problem, Carter dispatched a squadron of F-15 fighters to the Middle East as a token show of force—token, because they were sent unarmed. Nonetheless, war fever was in the air. The *Bulletin of Atomic Scientists* in San Francisco moved their "doomsday clock" from nine to seven minutes to midnight—midnight being the onset of nuclear war. American public opinion quickly abandoned the neo-isolationism that had been evident after the fall of Saigon five years earlier. A Harris poll found that 75 percent of Americans would support military intervention against the Soviets in the Persian Gulf; only 18 percent were opposed.[11]

To show he was serious, Carter acceded to the Senate's demand for 5 percent increases in defense spending over the next several years, up from the 3 percent increase he had promised America's European allies. Senate Majority Leader Robert Byrd told Carter that the already dim prospects for SALT II were dead, and that Carter should shelve the treaty. This Carter did.

The Soviets were said to be surprised at the vehemence of Carter's reaction, but they could also note that behind Carter's anger lay his typical vacillation. Carter called his shelving of SALT II a "postponement" instead of a withdrawal—he was hoping that it might yet be ratified early in his second term in 1981—and said that the U.S. would abide by the terms of SALT II anyway. That the Soviets had already calculated that the chances for SALT II ratification were dim might have been a factor in their decision to invade Afghanistan. Robert Tucker observed in *Foreign Affairs*: "Given the American record of recent years, Moscow has reason to believe that once Afghanistan is reduced, we will not spurn yet another détente. Moreover, Soviet leaders have the history of 1968 to consider, when outrage in the West over the Russian invasion of Czechoslovakia soon gave way to détente in Western Europe. If Western Europe did not permit Czechoslovakia to stand in the way of détente, why should it permit Afghanistan to do so?"[12] A State Department analyst told much the same thing to the *Washington Post:* "The Soviets clearly asked themselves what of value they stood to lose with the United States by going into Afghanistan and concluded the answer was: not much."[13] Carter's own dovish advisor on Soviet affairs, Marshall Shulman, predicted that the Soviets would soon launch "an old-style agitprop peace offensive."

Conservative critics once again hoped that Carter might drop détente and confront the Soviets. "Carter's more vigorous response to the invasion of Afghanistan had raised the hopes," Jeane Kirkpatrick recalled, "that he had a new realism in his assessment of the Soviet Union."[14] Senator Daniel Patrick Moynihan wrote that Carter's new toughness "at the very least means bringing into his administration people who share the views he now propounds.... New policies must to some extent mean new people."[15]

Wishing for Reagan

A group of conservative Democrats were invited to the White House on January 31, 1980, at the behest of Vice President Mondale. The group included Jeane Kirkpatrick, Norman Podhoretz, Midge Decter,

Ben Wattenberg, Elliott Abrams, Max Kampelman, retired admiral Elmo Zumwalt, Austin Ranney, and Penn Kemble. Carter had spurned these conservatives before. At the meeting he spurned them again.

Austin Ranney, speaking for the group, told Carter they were encouraged by the change in his view of the Soviet Union, and hoped he would now appoint officials who were in harmony with a tougher policy. Carter cut Ranney off: "Your analysis is not true. There has been no change in my policy. I have always held a consistent view of the Soviet Union. For the record, I did not say that I have learned more about the Soviet Union since the invasion of Afghanistan, as is alleged in the press. My policy is my policy. It has not changed, and will not change."[16]

Admiral Zumwalt told Carter that existing U.S. Navy forces were incapable of defending the Persian Gulf and Indian Ocean oil routes. Carter responded with what was described as "a stare that in a less democratic society would've meant he was destined for a firing squad." Maybe, Carter went on to suggest when the topic moved to human rights, this group could help with human rights in Uruguay.

The meeting was the last straw for these "neoconservative" Democrats, despite Vice President Mondale's efforts to repair the damage. Mondale knew the meeting had been a disaster, and asked the group to stay after Carter left. It was to no avail. Carter, Jeane Kirkpatrick told Morton Kondrake after the meeting, "threw cold water on whatever hopes we had that Iran and Afghanistan would have a broad effect on the president's foreign policy orientation."[17] Elliott Abrams was so discouraged with Carter that he wrote a memo to his boss, Senator Moynihan, making the case that Moynihan would make a good running mate—for Ronald Reagan.[18] In subsequent months, Carter's public statements began to erode the tough line he took in January. When Congress decided in May to add an additional $3.2 billion to the defense appropriation above what Carter requested, the president complained that the defense increase "severely restrains programs for jobs, for cities, for training, for education." The increase "is more than we actually need."

In the short run, both the hostage crisis and the Soviet invasion of Afghanistan provided a major political boost for Carter. Polls before the crisis showed him badly trailing Senator Ted Kennedy among Democrats for the 1980 Democratic nomination. Kennedy suffered the bad fortune of having scheduled the formal announcement of his candidacy two days after the hostages were taken in Iran. The sudden onset of the hostage crisis provided a jump in Carter's public approval ratings, as the public rallied to their leader as Americans always do in time of crisis. Pollster George Gallup called Carter's turnabout "stunning," adding that the jump in Carter's approval rating was "the largest increase in presidential popularity recorded in the four decades of the Gallup Poll."[19] This dealt a blow to Kennedy, who was already suffering from several self-inflicted wounds. Although Kennedy's challenge was not over and would deal Carter several setbacks over the next six months, the most formidable challenge to Carter was clearly going to come from Republicans.

The two Republicans Carter's political team feared most were moderate conservatives: Senator Howard Baker and former director of Central Intelligence George H. W. Bush. Their favorite opponent: the right-wing Ronald Reagan. Handling the sixty-nine-year-old ex-movie actor would be an easy piece of work, they thought, especially now that the issue of war and peace would be on center stage of the 1980 campaign. "The American people," Hamilton Jordan said, "are not going to elect a seventy-year-old, right-wing, ex-movie actor to be president." The polls supported Jordan's confidence. In mid-December, a Gallup poll showed Carter leading Reagan by a whopping 60 to 36 percent in a head-to-head matchup. Pat Caddell was confident of Reagan's weaknesses. "There's so much to work with, when you look at the data you just salivate."[20]

On November 13, ten days after the hostage crisis began, Ronald Reagan announced his candidacy for the White House in a nationally televised address in New York City. He was the clear front-runner for the Republican nomination in every poll. It appeared Carter might get his wish.

CHAPTER TEN

Reelect President Vicious

> "I want to be the next president. But that doesn't mean that I have to take my political success from personal hatred and attacks on the character or ability of my opponent."
>
> —Candidate JIMMY CARTER, 1976
>
> "The Carter campaign is as mean-spirited as any you'll see in American politics. Where this meanness comes from is obvious to anyone who has watched Carter's rise to the Presidency and the attempts to keep him there—it comes from the top, from Jimmy Carter."
>
> —Journalist RICHARD REEVES, 1980

In the aftermath of Carter's dreadful "crisis of confidence" speech, a parade of Democratic politicians trooped through Kennedy's office, begging him to save the party by taking Carter out. Among Kennedy's supporters were senators Pat Moynihan and Scoop Jackson, both of whom described themselves as "comprehensively disillusioned" with Carter. At that point, polls showed Kennedy leading Carter among Democrats by as much as thirty-eight points. The biggest strategic concern of Kennedy's advisors was how and when they would approach Carter to ask him to step aside.

Kennedy privately informed Carter in September 1979 that he intended to challenge him for the Democratic Party nomination in 1980. Kennedy had to delay the public launch of his campaign, however, when Carter shrewdly agreed to attend the dedication of the John F. Kennedy Library in Boston in late October. By the time Kennedy was ready for his formal announcement in early November, the hostages had been seized in Iran. Carter now surged ahead of Kennedy in the polls, and won by large margins in both the Iowa caucuses (59 to 31 percent) and New Hampshire primary (49 to 38 percent). Kennedy lost five more primaries to Carter (including Illinois), and polls showed that Kennedy would lose to Ronald Reagan, at a time when Reagan still trailed Carter. Kennedy couldn't even retain a majority of the Catholic vote. Though Carter's popularity ebbed as the hostage crisis showed no signs of resolution, it appeared that he would coast to a landslide victory in the New York primary on March 25. Kennedy's campaign would start looking to bow out gracefully. But then one of Carter's most boneheaded blunders caught up with him.

On Saturday, March 2, the U.S. cast a "yes" vote on a UN Security Council resolution condemning new Israeli settlements on the West Bank, the Gaza strip, and Jerusalem. Anti-Israel resolutions were perennially passing through the UN. But on previous similar resolutions, the U.S. had abstained. This time, Secretary of State Vance persuaded Carter of the wisdom of voting with the majority. The resolution passed unanimously, and all hell broke loose. An angry Robert Strauss, Carter's campaign chairman, told Carter, "Either this vote is reversed or you can kiss New York goodbye."[1] Invoking a parliamentary technicality, the U.S. managed to get a revote on the resolution the next day, and changed its vote from "yes" to "abstain."

Carter attempted to explain the "mistake" by claiming that the inclusion of settlements in Jerusalem was supposed to have been struck from the resolution, and said that the U.S. vote resulted from a "failure of communication." Whatever the truth of the matter, the administration was either politically or diplomatically incompetent. Vance didn't help matters by defending the original "yes" vote to the

Senate Foreign Relations Committee four days before the New York
primary. Jewish voters, who had never been enthusiastic about the
Southern Baptist president anyway, were outraged. Jewish communities in New York and Connecticut voted for Kennedy by margins of
four or five to one over Carter, and Kennedy racked up his first primary wins (excepting his home state of Massachusetts), beating
Carter by sixteen points in New York and eighteen points in Connecticut. Kennedy finally had something to cheer about; his concession and withdrawal speeches were thrown away. No one paid close
attention to the exit polls, which revealed that a large proportion of
the vote was anti-Carter rather than pro-Kennedy. Four out of ten
Kennedy voters in New York said they would not vote for him in
November if he won the nomination.

The depth of anti-Carter sentiment in New York alarmed the
White House. Though the delegate numbers still favored Carter, his
strategists knew they were losing momentum, and that the nomination was not securely in their grip. Kennedy now campaigned with
the vigor and effectiveness his supporters had always expected.
Kennedy hit hard on Carter's weak leadership. In his best booming
oratory, Kennedy said, "I reject the counsel of the voices, no matter
how high in government, that talk about a *malaaaaaise* of the spirit."

The April Fool's Day Announcement

The next primary showdown was a week later, in Wisconsin—liberal
territory. Kennedy territory. Just before the polls opened, word came
from Tehran that Iranian president Abolhassan Bani-Sadr was arrang-
ing for the Revolutionary Council to vote on an order requiring the
"students" to turn over the hostages to the "government," which the
Carter administration seized upon as a possible first step in gaining
their release. Carter decided to call a live press conference to announce
the news, at 7:13 a.m. Eastern Standard Time (EST). As voters awoke
in the Midwest to head to the polls (Kansas was holding its primary
on the same day as Wisconsin), they saw Carter on the morning news
announcing that a "positive development" was under way in the

hostage crisis. This "positive step" meant that the U.S. would not have to impose additional sanctions against Iran. Although Carter didn't directly say that the end of the crisis was at hand, he implied that the endgame was near. A reporter asked, "Well, do you know when they'll be actually released, I mean, brought home?" Carter: "I presume that we will know more about that as the circumstances develop. *We do not know the exact time schedule at this moment.*" (Emphasis added.)

It was April 1—April Fool's Day—and there were many candidates for the biggest fool of the day, starting with Carter. Even the ostensible transfer of the hostages from the "students" to the "government" hardly represented a breakthrough, so Carter's exploitation of the moment bred deep cynicism that would come back to haunt him in the fall. Carter was made to look an even bigger fool when it soon became evident that Bani-Sadr couldn't deliver on his promise of a Revolutionary Council measure to transfer control of the hostages.

Still, Carter's morning announcement on April 1 was followed by his win over Kennedy in Wisconsin and Kansas. Pat Caddell thought the announcement affected a significant number of voters; Carter's other political advisors scurried to deny it, sensing political disaster when Iran reversed course. A week after this dramatic breakthrough announcement, Carter reluctantly imposed additional sanctions on Iran and broke diplomatic relations. Two weeks later, Kennedy beat Carter in Pennsylvania—the state where Carter had made his breakthrough in 1976—and Michigan.

Once again, Carter's presidency seemed to be falling apart. For the first time, polls showed Reagan pulling ahead of Carter. Carter had said he would not leave the White House until the crisis was resolved, which gave him a convenient excuse to avoid debating Kennedy, as he had previously agreed to do. But the crisis, which had elevated his role as commander in chief and given him a political boost, was a rapidly depreciating asset, and finally a liability. Carter needed a "long bomb" to reverse his fortunes. He was about to attempt one. It blew up in his face.

Disaster in the Desert

Within days of the hostage taking in November, Carter had ordered the Joint Chiefs of Staff to begin exploring options and making plans for a military rescue. The sheer difficulty and improbability of a rescue are what encouraged the Pentagon to believe a surprise raid could be done. The U.S. had an intelligence agent inside the embassy compound, an Iranian cook who regularly relayed information to other U.S. agents in Tehran about the number and disposition of guards on the scene. By the spring, the number of armed guards had dropped to about twenty—a number that could be easily overcome by highly trained American special forces.

Carter cautioned the mission planners that he did not want "wanton killing" of Iranians, but aside from inquiring whether the hostage takers could be disabled with "sleeping gas," he did not hobble the mission with any restrictions on the amount or kind of force used. The commander of the mission, Colonel Charlie Beckwith, did, however, recall a general squeamishness about the whole enterprise. Secretary of State Vance opposed the plan entirely, telling Carter that he would resign after the operation whether it succeeded or not. Vance had said to Vice President Mondale, "I'll guarantee you something will go wrong. It never works the way they say it's going to work. There's a good chance disaster could occur here."[2] Vance's deputy, Warren Christopher (later destined to become Bill Clinton's first secretary of state), struck an odder pose. When Beckwith informed Carter and his senior aides that American forces intended to shoot any Iranian holding a hostage "right between the eyes," Christopher asked, "You mean you can do that?" Yes, Beckwith said, "We work very hard to do that." Christopher then followed up with, "Well, would you consider shooting them in the leg, or in the ankle, or the shoulder?"[3] Christopher, like Vance, wanted to try more diplomacy, such as increasing the pressure on Iran through United Nations resolutions and economic sanctions.

Beckwith and his team never got the chance to kill or disable any of the hostage takers, as the mission ended in a fiasco in the Iranian

desert when three of the eight helicopters developed mechanical problems. One of the helicopters crashed into a tanker plane as the mission was being aborted, killing eight American soldiers. "The
planning and execution were too incompetent to believe," an Israeli
officer told *Newsweek*. Military analyst Richard A. Gabriel argued
that the hostage rescue mission "was an operation so poorly planned
and executed that failure was almost guaranteed."[4] Beyond the military second-guessing, the political fallout was swift and severe. The
New Republic dubbed it "The Jimmy Carter Desert Classic," saying
the failed mission was yet another example of Carter's "incompetence." Carter's own reaction was vintage doublespeak; he called the
failed mission "an incomplete success," and, because he defined it as
a "humanitarian mission," he would persist in his proud boast of
being "the first American president in fifty years who has never sent
troops into combat," and that no American soldiers had died "in combat" during his administration.

Secretary of State Vance carried through on his threat to resign over
the mission; it was Vance's fourth resignation threat.

"Hubert Horatio Hornblower"

Carter now realized he had to emerge from his self-imposed Rose Garden internment to campaign. In a press conference five days after the
rescue mission, Carter justified his newfound willingness to travel by
saying that "a lot of the responsibilities that have been on my shoul-
ders in the past few months have now been *alleviated to some
degree*....None of these challenges are completely removed, but I
believe they are *manageable enough* now for me to leave the White
House for a limited travel schedule, including some campaigning if I
choose to do so...." (Emphasis added.) In the wake of the failed rescue mission, the Iranian hostage crisis could hardly have been said to
be more "manageable," nor were the nation's economic problems
"alleviated."

Carter might as well have stayed with his Rose Garden strategy.
Kennedy won five of the last eight primaries held on June 3. Even

though Carter had accumulated enough delegates to assure himself of winning renomination, Kennedy refused to drop out of the race, and several prominent Democrats were calling for an "open convention." Kennedy dominated the writing of the party platform, skewing it far to the left of what Carter wanted. Kennedy's rousing speech to the convention—"The dream will never die!"—assured that Carter's acceptance speech would be anticlimactic. Kennedy's speech, Jack Germond and Jules Witcover wrote, "seemed to touch every liberal nerve and revive every liberal memory on the floor."

Carter's speech, in contrast, became famous not for its passion, but for its blooper. In a litany of Democratic worthies from the past, Carter came to Hubert Humphrey's place on the list. Out of his mouth came: "Hubert Horatio *Hornblower*—er, Humphrey!" It was exceeded as a low moment only by the closing tableau of the convention, when Carter literally chased Kennedy around the stage hoping to get him in the traditional linked-arms victory clasp.

Despite this near-disastrous convention, Carter received a substantial "bounce." Pre-convention polls found Reagan leading Carter by as much as twenty points. In early August, Carter's approval rating fell to a new low of 21 percent—lower than Truman at his worst point, lower even than Nixon on the eve of his resignation. A Reagan landslide appeared probable. But Reagan committed a series of campaign blunders in the late summer that, combined with Carter's convention bounce, suddenly made the race a statistical dead heat.

If the economy were the sole focus of the election, Reagan would win handily. Carter did Reagan the favor of opposing tax cuts. He pledged to veto any tax cut that reached his desk: "I reject the easy promise that massive tax cuts and arbitrary roll-backs of government programs are the answer. Such facile, quick fixes should be recognized as political double-talk and ideological nonsense." Carter rejected "The Reagan-Kemp-Roth plan" as "perhaps the most inflationary piece of legislation ever to be seriously considered by the U.S. Congress."

What the Carter campaign called "the Tolstoy issue"—war and peace—was Reagan's single greatest vulnerability. One of Richard

Wirthlin's polls late in the summer found that 44 percent of voters considered Reagan "dangerous," or agreed with the statement "He is most likely to get us into an unnecessary war."[5] On the other hand, polls also showed that voters considered Reagan to be a stronger leader than Carter. A Yankelovich, Skelly and White poll in mid-September found that voters by a 59–28 margin favored Reagan over Carter for "keeping our defenses strong" and by 57–25 for "standing up to the Russians." Still, the survey found that by a margin of 50–29 voters thought Carter less likely to overreact in a crisis, and by a 41–16 margin trusted Carter more than Reagan to keep the nation out of war.[6]

The poll numbers showing nervousness about Reagan's views on war and peace, combined with Carter's nasty streak, ended up turning the election. Carter and his campaign attempted to portray Reagan as a mad bomber. But Carter wasn't content with just this attack. He and his campaign decided to call Reagan a racist as well. Reagan inadvertently goaded Carter with a campaign mistake. On September 1, Carter was opening his fall campaign in Tuscumbia, Alabama, while Reagan was appearing at the Michigan State Fair outside Detroit. A woman wearing a Carter mask walked near the stage, heckling Reagan. Reagan usually responded deftly to hecklers, but this time he misfired. "I thought you were in Alabama today," Reagan said, addressing the woman as though she were Carter. "You know, I kind of like the contrast, though. I'm happy to be here, where you're dealing at first hand with the economic problems that have been committed, and he's opening his campaign down in the city that gave birth to and is the parent body of the Ku Klux Klan." A gasp went up from the crowd, and Reagan immediately regretted the remark. For one thing, he had his facts wrong again; Tuscumbia was not the founding city of the Klan. Someone in his campaign entourage had mentioned before the event that Tuscumbia was a "center" of Klan activity (in fact on the day of Carter's appearance forty robed Klansmen paraded through town), and the thought tumbled out of Reagan's head in the heat of the moment.

Carter reacted with righteous indignation: "Anybody who resorts to slurs and innuendoes against a whole region of the country based on a false statement, a false premise, is not doing the South or our nation a good service." It was especially embarrassing for Reagan because the largest Klan chapter in the nation, based in New Orleans, publicly endorsed Reagan shortly after the GOP convention. The Republican platform, the KKK said, "reads as if it were written by a Klansman." Reagan promptly repudiated the endorsement: "I have no tolerance whatsoever for what the Klan represents. Indeed I resent them using my name."

Playing the Race Card Again

This sideshow over the Klan led Carter into a series of gaffes of his own, which became the second key turning point of the fall campaign. Using a playbook that has become depressingly familiar in national elections since 1980, Democrats dealt the race card from the bottom of the deck. Carter's campaign was probably hoping to provoke Reagan into some kind of undignified outburst, knowing from their opposition research that this was the one charge about which Reagan was most sensitive. Reagan's impolitic remark about the Klan on September 1 was probably a reaction to criticism he received over the Klan endorsement. Carter's tacticians no doubt hoped to goad him into more missteps.

Patricia Harris, Carter's secretary of Health and Human Services, told a steelworkers' union conference in early August, "I will not attempt to explain why the KKK found the Republican candidate and the Republican platform compatible with the philosophy and guiding principles of that notorious organization." But, she added, when Reagan speaks before black audiences (Reagan was scheduled to speak to the National Urban League in New York and meet with Jesse Jackson in Chicago), many blacks "will see the specter of a white sheet behind him." Andrew Young went even further, saying that Reagan's remarks seemed "like a code word to me that it's going to be all right to kill niggers when he's president." Coretta Scott King managed to top Young: "I am scared that if Ronald Reagan gets into office, we are going to see more of the Ku Klux Klan and a resurgence of the Nazi Party." Maryland congressman Parren Mitchell, a leader of the Congressional Black Caucus, said, "Reagan represents a distinct danger to black Americans." Garry Wills wrote in *Esquire*, "Reagan croons, in love accents, his permission to indulge a functional hatred of poor people and blacks."[7]

Not only were these charges outrageous on their face, but Reagan, it should be noted, received the endorsement of several black leaders who were fed up with Carter, including the Reverend Ralph David Abernathy, Martin Luther King, Jr.'s successor as head of the Southern Christian Leadership Conference, and the Reverend Hosea Williams, another prominent cleric from the civil rights movement. Ben Hooks, president of the NAACP, had spoken at the Republican convention.

It is one thing for campaign surrogates to engage in the lowest hyperbole in the service of firing up constituency groups. The candidates themselves, especially incumbent presidents, usually find a way to stay above the fray. Right after the Democratic convention in August, journalist Richard Reeves offered a prescient observation: "The Carter campaign is as mean-spirited as any you'll see in American politics. Where this meanness comes from is obvious to anyone who has watched Carter's rise to the Presidency and the attempts to keep him there—it comes from the top, from Jimmy Carter."[8] Carter was about to prove Reeves correct by joining in the chorus of race-baiting himself. Speaking at Martin Luther King, Jr.'s Ebenezer Baptist Church in Atlanta on September 15, Carter said, "You've seen in this campaign the *stirrings of hate* and *the rebirth of code words like 'states' rights'* in a speech in Mississippi, in a campaign reference to the Ku Klux Klan relating to the South. . . . Obviously the Ku Klux Klan is an obnoxious blight on the American scene and anyone who injected it into the campaign made a serious mistake. . . . Hatred has no place in this country." (Emphasis added.)

Carter and the Democrats perhaps believed that the media would amplify their caricature of Reagan in much the same way they had for

Lyndon Johnson against Barry Goldwater in 1964. They were wrong. The media was harsh on Carter for his indulgence of race-baiting. The *New Republic* wrote: "President Carter has made a grave moral error in trying to portray Ronald Reagan as a racist," and that Carter's statements were "frightful distortions, bordering on outright lies."[9] *Boston Globe* columnist Curtis Wilkie wrote, "Just as surely as the werewolf grows long fangs and facial hair on a full moon, the darker side of President Carter emerges in election years." The Associated Press sent out a wire story noting that Carter's followers (Patricia Harris, et al.), not Reagan, had first "injected" the Klan into the campaign. *Washington Post* reporter Richard Harwood wrote, "There is nothing in Reagan's record to support the charge that he was 'racist.'" The editorial page of the *Post* was biting:

> Mr. Carter has abandoned all dignity in his round-the-clock attack on Mr. Reagan's character and standing, jumping (in a most sanctimonious tone of voice) for "offenses" similar to many Mr. Carter himself has committed, and, most recently, concluding from all this that Mr. Reagan is a "racist" and a purveyor of "hatred." This description doesn't fit Mr. Reagan. What it fits, or more precisely, fits into, is Jimmy Carter's miserable record of personally savaging political opponents (Hubert Humphrey, Edward Kennedy) whenever the going got rough. . . . Jimmy Carter, as before, seems to have few limits beyond which he will not go in the abuse of opponents and reconstruction of history.[10]

The "meanness" issue, first spotted by Carter's own staff in the 1976 campaign, now took on major importance in the campaign. He immediately backed down, claiming that he was not saying or implying that Reagan was a racist. "I am not blaming Governor Reagan," Carter said to the amazement of reporters. "That's exactly the point. The press seems to be obsessed with this issue. I am not blaming

Governor Reagan....I do not indulge in attacking personally the integrity of my opponents and I hope that I never shall."

But he did, several times. At first Carter repaired to the warmonger theme, telling a Los Angeles audience that the election "will determine what kind of life you and your families have, whether this nation will make progress or go backward, and *whether we have peace or war*." (Emphasis added.) Carter may have thought his comment was merely raising the "war and peace" issue in stark terms that would focus voters' minds on Reagan's views, but it backfired. Media stories dwelled on the harshness of Carter's charge—the "meanness" issue again—and Reagan's reaction rang true. "I think to accuse that anyone would deliberately want a war is beneath decency," Reagan said. The media started asking Carter directly about "the meanness issue." Carter had to back down again, telling the *Detroit News*, "I'm not accusing Reagan of wanting a war."

A week later, in Chicago, Carter let fly with his most self-destructive comment of the campaign. Appearing in a backyard setting on October 6, Carter said, "You'll determine whether or not this America will be unified or, if I lose the election, *whether Americans might be separated, black from white, Jew from Christian, North from South, rural from urban*." (Emphasis added.) Reporters in the press pool couldn't believe it, and the comment was the lead sound bite on all the network news broadcasts that night, along with Reagan's sorrowful response: "I just have to say this. I can't be angry. I'm saddened that anyone, particularly someone who has held that position, could intimate such a thing. I'm not asking for an apology from him. I know who I have to account to for my actions. But I think he owes the country an apology."

Carter tried lamely the next day to wiggle out in an interview with Barbara Walters. Walters's first question put him on the spot: "Mr. President, in recent days you have been characterized as mean, vindictive, hysterical, and on the point of desperation." Carter replied, "There is enough blame to go around" and "I don't intend to apologize for that statement, except to say that I did not insinuate and do not claim that Governor Reagan would deliberately try to set one American against another." But the very next day, Carter let out a new rip: "Reagan is not a good man to trust with the affairs of this nation."

The network news spin was devastating to Carter. NBC's Chris Wallace said Carter's comment "showed Mr. Carter as mean and unpresidential, Reagan as caring and mature." ABC's Sam Donaldson said, "Carter campaign officials are deeply worried tonight that the president's reelection is slipping away." New polls showed that the number of people who agreed with the statement "President Carter is not a man of high integrity" had doubled from the year before.

The Reagan campaign thought so, too. Richard Wirthlin later said, "[Carter] came close to handing us the election that night." Carter had squandered his largest remaining asset with voters, the view that he was a decent and honorable person. Three days later, in a "town meeting" at the Grand Ole Opry in Nashville, a high school student from Winston-Salem, North Carolina, delivered a roundhouse: "Sir, why is it that if you are the right man for the job, that you and your staff have to lower yourself to the extent of slinging mud and making slanderous statements with [sic] your rival, Ronald Reagan?" The audience erupted in applause.

Carter to Soviets: Help Me Beat Reagan

Carter secretly undertook other desperate measures that seemed to make American foreign policy negotiable on the basis of what might help Carter's polling numbers. The industrialist billionaire Armand Hammer, whose longtime good relations with leaders of the Kremlin going back to Lenin were a source of deep suspicion in the American intelligence community, approached Soviet ambassador Anatoly Dobrynin on Carter's behalf in early October. Hammer suggested that a Soviet move to ease Jewish emigration would help Carter's election prospects. Hammer allegedly assured Dobrynin, "Carter won't forget that service if he is reelected."[11] Moscow, fed up with Carter, did not respond. Then, two weeks before the election, National Security Advisor Brzezinski tried again with Dobrynin, dangling the promise of several key concessions to the Soviets on Afghanistan, arms control, and Central America—concessions they would never get from Reagan—if Carter was reelected. Brzezinski was more skilled in the indirect language of diplomacy; Dobrynin wrote, "It was hard to say whether it was aimed at obtaining some positive gestures from Moscow on the eve of the poll." But, Dobrynin concluded, "his message was clear: Moscow should not do anything to diminish Carter's chances in the election race and might even help a bit."[12]

It is hard to escape the conclusion that Carter was willing to throw over his foreign policy to stay in office. It was not without precedent in his past. In fact, the Hammer mission was a reprise of a similar mission in 1976 that Averill Harriman had undertaken for Carter. According to a Soviet deputy foreign minister, Georgii Kornienko, Harriman bore the message that Carter was eager to make deals with the Soviet Union and would be more agreeable to them than President Ford.[13] In June 1980, Harriman pleaded with the Soviets to make some gesture in Afghanistan that would relieve political pressure on Carter.[14]

Despite the damage they inflicted on the president himself, Carter's personal attacks proved the effectiveness of negative campaigning. Reagan's pollster Richard Wirthlin was stunned when the campaign's daily tracking polls showed the governor's slim lead slipping away. "For five or six days, from October 4 to about October 9 or 10, our support collapsed." On October 14, Wirthlin's polls found Carter ahead by two points. Other public polls were reporting the same thing; a CBS/*New York Times* poll gave Carter a one-point edge, while a Gallup poll put Carter ahead by three. Most worrisome to the Republicans was the finding that the number of voters who thought Reagan "does not understand the complicated problems a president has to deal with" was rising. Equally alarming to both campaigns was the high number of undecided voters. In 1976, only 6 percent of voters had described themselves as "undecided" in mid-October, but now 20 percent of voters were undecided. This suggested that a large proportion of independent and swing voters were unhappy with Carter but uncomfortable with Reagan. "For the first time," Democratic pollster Peter Hart said in mid-October, "I feel the election may be starting to elude Ronald Reagan's grasp."[15]

Adding to the anxiety of the Reagan campaign was the fear of an "October surprise" in the Iranian hostage situation. If Carter could contrive to bring the hostages home on election eve, it would probably swing the close contest. Carter's announcement about "progress" in the hostage crisis the morning of the Wisconsin primary was in the back of everyone's minds. However, some poll data suggested that the public remembered this, too, and might react cynically to another hostage ploy close to election day.

On October 15, the *Washington Post* reported that a breakthrough in the hostage crisis might come in the next two weeks, and on October 19, columnist Joseph Kraft wrote, "The Carter Administration has embarked on an all-out effort to win release of the American hostages.... The present scheme bears all the marks of a mad electoral maneuver."[16] Washington was thick with rumors that a deal was all but done. Jack Anderson produced a breathless column asserting that Carter was preparing an election-eve invasion of Iran, but the *Post* refused to print the piece.

Reagan's campaign prepared contingency radio and TV ads, and lined up Kissinger and Ford to hit the television talk shows to respond to any Carter moves. The Reagan campaign even had its own intelligence operation. Though Reagan received regular State Department and National Security Council briefings (a routine courtesy for presidential candidates), his campaign had a network of people watching Air Force bases for signals of an imminent move to bring the hostages home. This fed wild speculation years later that the Reagan campaign, specifically George H. W. Bush and Bill Casey, had intervened to prevent the Iranians releasing the hostages before the election. Repeated investigations have failed to substantiate these rumors.

"There You Go Again"

The erratic polls and the fear of an "October surprise" led to the final turning point of the election campaign: Reagan agreed to debate Carter. The debate was scheduled for Tuesday, October 28—exactly one week before election day. Carter was eager, thinking he could easily dispose of this Hollywood lightweight. Several of his senior advisors disagreed with him. Pat Caddell warned Carter in a prescient memo that "the risks outweigh the possible advantages.... There is a 75% chance that Carter will 'lose' the debate even if he 'wins' on points."[17]

The debate was announced on October 18, which had the effect of freezing the campaigns for the ten days leading up to it. Carter and his closest aides retreated to Camp David for rehearsal, and Reagan repaired to a rented house in the Virginia countryside for the same purpose. Political scientist Samuel Popkin served as Reagan's stand-in at Carter's Camp David debate rehearsals; in Virginia, thirty-three-year-old congressman David Stockman of Michigan served as Carter's stand-in, while George Will and Jeane Kirkpatrick played the role of the media panel asking questions. Reagan professed to be startled at how well Stockman portrayed Carter in their mock debates. "After Stockman," Reagan said, "Carter was easy." Perhaps that's because Stockman was privy to Carter's debate briefing book.

The day of the actual debate, Stockman kept an appointment to speak to an Optimist Club luncheon in his Michigan congressional district. There he regaled the lunch audience with tales of his work helping Reagan to prepare—remarks that were reported the next day in a local newspaper, the *Elkhart Truth*, based in the nearby Indiana town of Elkhart. On page fifteen, the newspaper story mentioned that Stockman had used a "pilfered copy of the briefing book Carter was going to use.... Stockman outlined the 'white lies' Carter was going to center on in the debate. Apparently the Reagan camp's 'pilfered' goods were correct, as several times both candidates said almost word for word what Stockman predicted."

The story never went beyond the pages of the *Elkhart Truth* until 1983, when Laurence Barrett's book about Reagan, *Gambling with History*, repeated the story, touching off a full-scale scandal that became known as "Debategate." It could never be determined how up to seven hundred pages of Carter's preliminary debate materials had found their way to the Reagan campaign. A receptionist later told the FBI that a "clean-cut young man" brought a large stack of documents into the Reagan campaign headquarters in Arlington, Virginia, in mid-October. Speculation eventually turned to a Democratic political consultant named Paul Corbin, whose connections with Ted Kennedy were thought to have been a motive to betray Carter. Corbin received a $1,500 payment from the Reagan campaign for "research" work three days before the debate. But there was no record of Corbin ever having been to the White House or the Carter campaign offices, so the mystery remained unsolved. Whatever their provenance, the Carter materials were a considerable embarrassment when they turned up in David Gergen's White House files in 1983. (Gergen had been on Reagan's debate preparation team.)

The "whodunit" aspect of this subplot to the campaign story overshadows a more basic question: Was there anything in the Carter debate papers that the political professionals in the Reagan camp could not already have anticipated? This late in a presidential contest, the strengths, weaknesses, and strategies of both sides are fairly transparent. Both sides knew what they needed to do in the debate, and how they would try to do it. Indeed, neither candidate said much in the debate that he had not said previously. This might be why Stockman so casually disclosed the story in his Optimist Club lunch. Stockman received the papers the day before his first mock debate with Reagan; it is hard to see how he could have discerned from seven hundred pages of material what Carter's specific debate strategy and tactics would be, and thereby provide Reagan a decisive, otherwise unattainable edge. Stockman later said, "The only person I can imagine this stuff was useful to was the guy who had to digest in one day the entire sorry history of the Carter administration."

It is also possible that the Carter administration broke the law; some of the material on Carter's briefing materials appeared to have come from analysts at the Office of Management and Budget, which would represent a political misuse of a federal government agency.

Another telling contrast between the two campaigns, reflecting the style of the candidates, emerges from this episode: While Carter's campaign produced nearly one thousand pages of debate preparation material, contained in four notebooks, Reagan had a single debate briefing book of only seventy-one pages. Carter's debate strategy was to convey his mastery of the job and the facts, and he crammed for the debate in the same dutiful, paperwork-heavy fashion in which he governed. He mentioned during his debate rehearsals that he was thinking about discussing the concern of his twelve-year-old daughter, Amy, about world peace. Carter's advisors thought it a bad idea and warned him against it.

One hundred million people—the largest political audience in American history, rivaled in size only by the Super Bowl—tuned in for the debate on October 28. Before the debate, Pat Caddell's tracking polls showed undecided voters breaking for Carter and had Carter ahead of Reagan by two points. Wirthlin's polls gave Reagan a small lead. Walter Cronkite introduced the debate by saying, "It's not inconceivable that the election could turn on what happens in the next ninety minutes." Carter won the coin toss, and opted to let Reagan answer the first question, which turned out to be about war and peace. Carter's strategists believed that Reagan might be nervous and stumble out of the starting gate. Reagan was a little halting and hesitant, but got out a pre-planned answer emphasizing that "our first priority must be world peace," and included his refrain about having seen four wars in his lifetime and not wishing to see another. Reagan settled into a relaxed rhythm for the rest of the debate and accomplished his most important objective, that of reassuring viewers that he was not a "mad bomber."

Carter, on the other hand, appeared stiff and uptight throughout the evening. *Washington Star* columnist Mary McGrory wrote, "Carter seemed stricken with nerves, so tense that he looked affronted when Reagan bounded over to shake hands before the hostilities began." Carter hit Reagan hard on the Republican's "out of the mainstream" views, and six times used the adjective "disturbing" to describe his policies. Conversely, Carter kept referring to the Oval Office, as though he thought viewers might have forgotten that he was the president. Reagan parried effectively, though a strict scoring of the debate would have awarded Carter points for consistently putting Reagan on the defensive.

The public, of course, does not judge presidential debates by careful scoring of points and counter-points. The demeanor and bearing of the candidates counts as much as, if not more than, the substance of the debate. The relaxed and confident Reagan showed some of his quickness and instinct for the cut and thrust of debate, especially during the argument over his economic plan. Carter repeated his charge that it would be inflationary. Reagan answered with a rhetorical question that focused viewers on his broader philosophical point about government: "I would like to ask the president why it is inflationary to let the people keep more of their money and spend it the way they like, and it isn't inflationary to let him take that money and spend it the way he wants?" Reagan also hoisted Carter on his own petard. In 1976, Carter had blasted Ford with the "misery index," the combination of inflation and unemployment, which was then 12.5. Carter had said, "[N]o man with that size misery index had a right to seek reelection to the presidency." Reagan observed that the misery index was now above 20.

Carter never did loosen up. One of Carter's own aides observed that in the TV cutaway shots showing Carter while Reagan was speaking, "Jimmy looked like he was about to slug him." Carter's one attempt at humanizing himself was a disaster. About two-thirds of the way through the debate, at the close of several questions about foreign policy and arms control, Carter said, "I had a discussion with my daughter, Amy, the other day, before I came here, to ask her what the most important issue was. She said she thought nuclear weaponry, and the control of nuclear arms." Reagan's line about having sons and a grandson had gone over fine, but Carter's line, delivered in a rapid-fire staccato burst, landed with a thud, and became a source of ridicule over the next week. Republican groups were quick with a bumper sticker: "Ask Amy, She Knows."

Carter then unwittingly set up one of the most famous lines of Reagan's career. "Governor Reagan," Carter charged, "began his political career campaigning around this nation against Medicare," and now Reagan was opposing any steps toward national health insurance. The camera swung to Reagan for his reply. Reagan nodded his head at Carter, and said, with a slight smile, "There you go again." The formal answer that followed didn't really matter. *There you go again* seemed to sum up both Reagan's easygoing character and the overreach of Carter's relentless attacks on his supposed extremism. It may well stand the test of time as the most memorable line of any presidential debate.

Carter's camp believed they had won hands-down. "We won, we won," Hamilton Jordan said immediately after the lights went down. So did much of the media, if only slightly. Hedrick Smith's lead in the *New York Times* news story the next day said, "The Presidential debate produced no knockout blow, no disastrous gaffe and no immediate, undisputed victor," though Smith gave the edge to Carter farther down in the story. "If anyone gains politically from the Tuesday night matchup," Morton Kondracke wrote in the *New Republic*, "it will be Carter.... [B]y every measure except aw-shucks niceness, Carter was the clearly superior performer."[18]

The viewing public didn't think so. Wirthlin conducted an overnight poll of five hundred voters that judged Reagan the winner by a two to one margin. Other polls by Lou Harris and the Associated Press found similar results. The most controversial spin on the debate came from ABC News, which promoted a call-in phone poll on *Nightline* after the debate. Bell Labs, which facilitated the phone poll, expressed "shock" when more than 600,000 people phoned in over the next hour, at a cost of 50 cents per call. The tabulation found Reagan the winner, again by a two to one margin. This self-selected phone-in "poll" was utterly unscientific and drew heavy criticism that it was no more accurate than the 1936 *Literary Digest* telephone poll that had predicted Alf Landon would defeat Franklin Roosevelt. Nevertheless, the poll took on a life of its own and received wide news coverage. "Whatever the poll's shortcomings," the *New York Times* suggested, "a margin that wide probably reflected something of substance about the debate's impact."[19]

The *Times* was right, though this didn't become clear until forty-eight hours before election day. Wirthlin's tracking polls, based on more than 10,500 phone calls in the week after the debate, detected Reagan's numbers moving up steadily, but public polls continued to find the race still within the margin of error—too close to call. Gallup reported the Sunday before the election: "Never in the forty-five year history of presidential election surveys has the Gallup poll found such volatility and uncertainty." On Sunday, the CBS/*New York Times* poll found Reagan and Carter dead even, as did Pat Caddell's daily tracking poll, which led Caddell to confess, "I just wish we hadn't debated."

Carter Goes Down

Carter, meanwhile, entered a fresh agony over the Iranian hostages. Late on Saturday, November 1, Iran announced four conditions for releasing the hostages, the most crucial of which was unfreezing billions of dollars of Iranian assets held in the United States. Carter canceled his campaign events on Sunday and flew back to the White House. The Reagan campaign feared that the "October surprise" was about to be sprung forty-eight hours before voters headed to the polls. Reagan held his tongue, telling reporters on a campaign stop in Ohio that "this is too delicate a situation." Henry Kissinger was less reticent, telling ABC News that the Ayatollah Khomeini was trying to manipulate the election, which was certainly plausible. One joke making the rounds went: "What's flat as a pancake and glows in the dark? Iran after Reagan becomes president."

Reagan's camp needn't have worried. Wirthlin had polled extensively for this contingency, and found that nearly half the voters would be skeptical of any last-minute hostage release deal, believing that Carter would manipulate the situation for political purposes. Carter came on television shortly after 6 p.m. EST Sunday (interrupting the NFL football games on the networks), with a carefully worded announcement reminiscent of his statement the morning of the Wisconsin primary. Iran hadn't formally transmitted its demands, but Carter said "they appear to offer a positive basis" for achieving a deal. "Let me assure you," Carter added, "that my decisions on this crucial matter will not be affected by the calendar." It was clear, though, that no deal was imminent. It was, coincidentally, the one-year anniversary of the beginning of the hostage crisis. On Monday night, Walter Cronkite signed off the CBS evening news, as he had for the past year, with the modification of his signature closing: "And that's the way it is, Monday, November third, 1980, the three hundred and sixty-sixth day of captivity for the American hostages in Iran."

The hostage crisis, which had revived Carter's political fortunes a year ago, had now become prominent among the factors that crushed him. In the last forty-eight hours, both Wirthlin and Caddell discerned a huge move toward Reagan in their tracking polls. Both arrived at the same conclusion—Reagan could win by ten points or more, and score an electoral landslide. The public polls—Gallup, CBS, and the others—were behind the curve, mostly because they had stopped surveying over the weekend, before the last-minute hostage drama. The media was still reporting that the election would be a squeaker. A week before the election, Morton Kondracke wrote, "It seems more likely by the day that Ronald Reagan is not going to execute a massive electoral sweep. In fact, the movement of the presidential campaign suggests a Carter victory."[20] Kondracke, a fine reporter, was nonetheless representative of media prognostications in 1980.

Washington was rainy and cool on election day. Caddell had seen "the bottom fall out" of Carter's poll numbers. He relayed the news to Jody Powell, who told Carter on board Air Force One en route from the West Coast. Carter later denied reports that he broke down in tears.

At 2 p.m. EST, the first exit poll results began coming in. Prior to 1980, no news organization had ever "called" a state solely on exit poll results alone, but NBC News decided it would be aggressive in "calling" states, scooping the other networks. Anchor John Chancellor opened the network's broadcast at 7 p.m. EST with the stunning news: "According to an NBC-AP poll, Ronald Reagan appears headed for a substantial victory." This, even though the polls were still open in forty-four states. Of the remaining six states, two (Florida and Alabama) had some polls still open, but NBC projected Reagan the winner in Indiana, Virginia, Mississippi, Florida, and Alabama, with

Carter carrying only his home state of Georgia. NBC was half an hour ahead of the other two networks in calling a state.

At 7:30 p.m., the polls closed in Ohio, a key Midwest state with twenty-five electoral votes. NBC called the state for Reagan forty seconds later. At 8 p.m., polls closed in thirteen more states. Within two minutes and forty seconds, NBC had called twelve of the thirteen—all went to Reagan. Included in this batch were such key states as Pennsylvania, New Jersey, Michigan, Illinois, and Missouri. Reagan's electoral vote total was already at 261, just nine short of assuring victory. At 8:15 p.m., two hours and forty-five minutes before the polls closed on the West Coast, NBC made it "official," flashing on the screen "REAGAN WINS." By this time NBC had projected the results in twenty states; ABC had called only ten; CBS had called only four. NBC projected that Reagan would be the fortieth president of the United States with less than 4 percent of the national vote total officially tabulated.

While NBC was calling the election for Reagan, Carter was on the phone to Reagan conceding. It was only a little after 5 p.m. in Los Angeles, where Reagan was, and Nancy Reagan had to get him out of the shower to take Carter's call. Carter knew all day that he was going to lose big, but what he did next was extraordinary. An hour and a half before the polls closed on the West Coast, Carter made his formal public concession. House Speaker Tip O'Neill was livid; he told Carter's congressional liaison, Frank Moore, "You guys came in like a bunch of pricks, and you're going out the same way."[21]

It was Carter's final insult to his Democratic colleagues in Congress, because there were still several close House and Senate contests on the West Coast, which the Democrats lost, including an incumbent senator (Warren Magnuson) in Washington and the powerful chairman of the House Ways and Means Committee, Al Ullman of Oregon. "One wonders if the President entertained the idea of conceding even before the polls opened," the *Nation* wrote; "it might have rescued a few of the more worthy Democrats who the President brought down with him."[22]

By the end of the night, Reagan had won forty-four states, for an electoral vote landslide of 489 to forty-nine for Carter. Reagan won 50.8 percent of the total popular vote to Carter's 41 percent, and rolled up huge majorities among the Protestant evangelicals who had enthusiastically backed Carter in 1976. Reagan also received 45 percent of the Catholic vote and an astounding 35 percent of the Jewish vote, which helped him carry New York.

Many liberals blamed Carter for their defeat as a way of deflecting searching questions about the decadence of liberalism. Carter Cabinet exile Joseph Califano told a gathering of Democratic leaders at a post-election meeting that "Jimmy Carter was the most incompetent Democratic president in history." Carter lost, Daniel Patrick Moynihan said, because the voters saw a Democratic Party that believed "government should be strong and America should be weak." Moynihan added, "Even Herbert Hoover got more electoral votes than President Carter."

In the last days of his presidency, Carter managed to extricate the hostages from Iran through a complicated deal that involved returning frozen Iranian assets. The deal represented, in essence, ransoming the hostages with Iran's money. The Iranians' fear of what incoming President Reagan might do undoubtedly contributed to the resolution of the crisis. During the transition, Reagan had repeatedly made comments along the lines of "I don't think you pay ransom for people that have been kidnapped by barbarians." The *Washington Post* speculated, "Who doubts that among Iran's reasons for coming to terms now was a desire to beat [Reagan] to town?"[23]

Immediately after Reagan was sworn in, the suddenly ex-president Carter flew to West Germany to greet the hostages. There were some tense moments, as some of the former hostages couldn't understand why Carter hadn't bombed Iran, even if it meant a risk to their lives. Others thought their honor was compromised by a deal that could be regarded as paying a ransom. Most of the hostages were in a generous mood, however, understanding that their plight figured prominently in the factors that cost Carter his reelection.

Rejected by the voters and his own party, Carter had delivered his apologia a week earlier in a televised farewell address. Having campaigned for office in 1976 as an optimist about America's third century and about his own ability to deliver "a government as good as the people," Carter gave a pessimistic speech, opening with excuses for why he could not succeed as president. The presidency, he said, "is at once the most powerful office in the world and among the most severely constrained by law and custom." He continued:

> Today we are asking our political system to do things of which the Founding Fathers never dreamed.... Today, as people have become ever more doubtful of the ability of the government to deal with our problems, we are increasingly drawn to single-issue groups and special interest organizations to ensure that whatever else happens, our own personal views and our own private interests are protected. This is a disturbing factor in American political life. It tends to distort our purposes, because the national interest is not always the sum of all our single or special interests....

To the bitter end, Carter refused to confront or acknowledge his own weaknesses as a leader. As Carter prepared to leave office, he was privately predicting that Reagan was certain to fail as president, and a number of liberal thinkers, led by Carter's White House counsel Lloyd Cutler, began advocating sweeping constitutional reforms to make the presidency more "effective." Liberals had complained about the "imperial presidency" when Nixon was in the White House; now, at the end of Carter's presidency, liberals thought the presidency wasn't nearly imperial enough.

All the talk of needing to amend the constitution vanished over the next few years as Reagan proved that effective presidential leadership is as possible today as it has ever been. The contrast between Carter's vacillating self-righteousness and Reagan's confident application of consistent principles is one of the greatest lessons leaders and citizens alike can learn at any time. Instead of reflecting on this experience as an elder statesman, Carter was determined to be useful—in effect, to carry on Carterism with the prestige of an ex-president. Carter's latent liberalism was about to become even more pronounced—and dangerous.

CHAPTER ELEVEN

Becoming the American Gandhi

"Terrible is the temptation to be good."

—BERTOLT BRECHT

N
ot since Theodore Roosevelt has an ex-president been as peripatetic or troublesome to his successors as Jimmy Carter. Teddy Roosevelt supremely annoyed William Howard Taft and Woodrow Wilson, costing the former a second term in office and hammering the latter for his irresoluteness about the Great War in Europe. But Roosevelt left office on a wave of popularity, and thus remained politically potent. Carter left office rejected by the voters; he was a pariah in his own party and was thus seemingly impotent. Arkansas's young governor, Bill Clinton, was among those Democrats who attributed his 1980 reelection defeat to Carter's unpopularity. Yet Carter became a shaping force of the future Clinton White House and established himself as a popularly revered ex-president.

This is all the more astounding because Carter never exhibited the restraint and decorum that is expected of former presidents. Even during the transition, Carter found it impossible to hide his contempt for Reagan. Some of his gripes were petty. A few days before leaving the White House in 1981, Carter looked out the window of the Oval Office and remarked to Brzezinski, "I planted four trees in the White House garden. I hope Reagan doesn't cut them down."[1] But others made it seem that the election campaign rhetoric would never end. During the transition period, Carter's treasury secretary William Miller and chief economic advisor Charles Schultze both blasted Reagan's economic plan, saying it would drive up interest rates and create an economic emergency. The *New York Times* reported, "Both men, it was understood, had Mr. Carter's approval"[2] to criticize the incoming administration's economic agenda.

Carter appeared obsessed by his defeat at the hands of the former actor. He told the historian Douglas Brinkley in 1995 that "allowing Ronald Reagan to become president was by far my biggest failure in office."[3] Brinkley noticed that "[e]verything Reagan did drove Jimmy Carter crazy." Carter's petulance about losing to Reagan came out early and often.

In the early spring of 1981, Carter threatened to embarrass the Reagan administration by complaining to the media that he was not receiving security briefings. It was true that the new administration had not yet organized regular briefings for former presidents, but neither Gerald Ford nor Richard Nixon had complained or threatened to embarrass the new administration; only Jimmy Carter did. National security advisor Richard Allen was sent to soothe Carter's bruised ego.

On his first return visit to Washington, D.C., in October 1981, Carter appeared outside the White House, and before going inside for a face-to-face meeting with Reagan tore into the new administration. "Carter Is Critical of Reagan Policies," read the *New York Times* headline.[4] "This Administration and what it stands for, in my judgment, is an aberration on the political scene," Carter said. A year later Carter made headlines again, attacking Reagan's competence. "Carter Says Reagan Has Failed to Accept His Responsibilities," read the *New York Times* story. Of the Iran-Contra scandal that erupted in 1986,

Carter told Douglas Brinkley that it showed "Reagan was capable of just about anything underhanded." Nor did Carter rally around the flag when American servicemen were sent in harm's way. He criticized Reagan's 1986 bombing raid on Libya, which was retaliation for a Libyan-sponsored terrorist bombing in Berlin that killed two American servicemen, as a "serious mistake." In 1987, Carter took the extraordinary and unprecedented step of writing the Senate Judiciary Committee to oppose Reagan's nomination of Robert Bork to the Supreme Court. No other former president has ever challenged a sitting president's nomination of a candidate to the Supreme Court.

Carter's Habitat

Carter's high-profile good works have eclipsed these and later transgressions of American political etiquette. Most famous has been Carter's assistance to Habitat for Humanity, transforming it from a small, fledgling nonprofit housing enterprise into a worldwide presence. Unlike most politicians, Carter didn't just show up, hammer in hand, for an hour of photo-ops at Habitat construction sites; he would spend the entire day sawing wood and driving nails. He would then come back the next day, along with a crew of volunteers, and the day after that, for a week or more. Carter made an annual event of assembling a team to work on a Habitat project, often in troubled neighborhoods like the south Bronx.

It is common to hear people, even in the media, refer to "Jimmy Carter's Habitat for Humanity," as though he founded the organization. Carter himself reports that Habitat is the most frequently mentioned aspect of his life when he meets people on planes and elsewhere. In fact, a fellow Georgian, Millard Fuller, founded Habitat for Humanity in 1976, while Carter was campaigning for the White House. Fuller, a successful businessman and later a Christian missionary, recruited Carter to take up Habitat's cause after he left the White House. At first Carter resisted, but ultimately agreed to serve on Habitat's board, with his role eventually expanding to fund-raising and hands-on work. It ranks among the most counterintuitive and remarkable steps ever taken by an ex-president. As Douglas Brinkley rightly notes, "The notion of a former president dressed in overalls and work boots, with a red bandanna tied around his neck, actually doing menial labor of the most unpleasant and backbreaking kind seized the public's imagination."[5]

Carter's other prominent humanitarian crusade was the elimination of the obscure guinea worm disease, a horrendous affliction that struck as many as five million people a year in Africa and Asia. Guinea worm disease is water-borne, and can be prevented with basic water purity techniques, making it easily eradicable. Starting in 1986, Carter raised large sums of money and traveled to guinea worm hot spots to promote a program of eradication. After ten years of effort, the number of new guinea worm cases has fallen by more than 90 percent.

Carter's Very Own UN

Habitat for Humanity and the elimination of guinea worm disease are laudable causes, and, as Douglas Brinkley has written, Carter was "obsessed with being useful." But Carter's main post-presidential occupation has been founding and promoting the Carter Center as part of his presidential library. Here he would have a forum to advocate the same kind of ideas that brought ruin to his presidency.

As with all of Carter's endeavors, his presidential library had to be "the best." Several presidential libraries, including Nixon's, Johnson's, and Reagan's, have adjunct centers for public affairs to promote scholarship and public discussion of issues. Carter wanted his center to have a real-world mission. Carter spoke oddly of applying "new theories of conflict resolution" to perennial conflicts around the world. The Carter Center, Peter Bourne explained, "was not to be a think tank in the traditional sense, turning out position papers or learned treatises. It was to be an action center, where its direct intervention would influence events."[6] Or, as former secretary of state Dean Rusk put it, "Carter wanted to create a mini-United Nations in downtown Atlanta."[7]

Carter had become enamored of "two-track diplomacy," according to which the knottiest conflicts in the world can sometimes be best addressed through low-key "back channel" contacts rather than through the formal structures of State Department and foreign ministry diplomacy. There is something to this idea, of course, but it is dependent on the president directing both tracks and on the back channel contact operating discreetly, even anonymously. But Carter had no intention of keeping a low profile or of putting himself under the direction of the president. Instead, he has carried on as a free agent, even at times apparently seeing himself as a citizen of the world more than as a citizen of the United States. As a humiliated president, Carter initially fared poorly trying to raise money for the Carter Center, so it was slow to take shape. His largest single contribution the first year was $50,000 from the Rockefeller Brothers Fund, a tiny grant for this charitable behemoth. Many of the major contributors to his presidential run declined to make commitments. Carter asked Tom Watson, the retired chairman of IBM and former ambassador to the Soviet Union, to serve on the Center's board of directors. Watson declined. Perhaps Carter would have done better had he not eschewed the route Gerald Ford took in joining numerous boards of Fortune 500 companies, where the old-boy network opens its wallet easily for fellow members of the club.

Eventually, a more determined fund-raising effort netted $10 million for the Center in 1983, and today the Carter Center boasts a major donor list of some of the leading left-liberal foundations and individuals, including the Charles Stewart Mott Foundation, the MacArthur Foundation, the Ford Foundation, the late Joan Kroc, Paul Newman, Norman Lear, and numerous other prominent Democratic Party donors. The Center also enjoys considerable support from major Georgia-based corporations, including Home Depot, United Parcel Service, Delta Air Lines, and Coca-Cola. The Carter Center's current annual budget is more than $35 million, and has accumulated an endowment of more than $200 million. Carter has ensured that his activist legacy will long survive him.

Much of the Carter Center's early major funding, however, came from foreign sources—some of them questionable at best. Tadao

Yoshida, owner of the Japanese manufacturing firm YKK, kicked in $2.5 million. Another major Japanese backer was Ryoichi Sasakawa, a shipping tycoon with a murky and controversial reputation, which included support for Japanese fascism before and during World War II. Later, he was a major donor to enterprises as various as the United Nations and the Reverend Sun Myung Moon's Unification Church. Sasakawa offered Carter $1.7 million in 1981, and accompanied him on several foreign trips, supplying his private jet for their transportation.

Carter also raised prodigious sums from Arabs and wealthy Palestinians. Saudi Arabia's King Fahd supplied $1 million, and the notorious Saudi arms dealer Adnan Khashoggi underwrote a fund-raising auction. Another major funder was Hasib Sabbagh, a prominent Palestinian businessman close to Yasir Arafat, who hoped Carter would help propel the "Middle East peace process" between Israel and the Palestinians. Sabbagh would also make his private aircraft available to Carter for his travels to the Middle East. The complete list of major foreign donors to the Carter Center includes the Sultan of Oman, the government of the United Arab Emirates, the Saudi bin Laden Group (yes, *that* bin Laden Group), the Saudi Fund for Development, the OPEC Fund for International Development, and Prince Abdallah of Morocco.[8]

But by far the donor who raised the most eyebrows was Aga Hassen Abedi, the head of the Bank of Commerce and Credit International (BCCI). Abedi initially donated $4 million to the Carter Center in 1985, and gave an additional $17 million in 1988. Once again, transportation was also donated; Carter traveled several times to the Middle East, Africa, and Asia aboard what Douglas Brinkley described as "BCCI's palatial airplane." Carter's prestige likely assisted BCCI's efforts to establish substantial banking centers in the same countries Carter and Abedi visited together. After BCCI collapsed in the early 1990s amidst one of the largest banking scandals in history, Carter said, "He [Abedi] may have snookered me."

Peter Bourne explained that "Carter's attitude was that as long as these people were giving their money for the center's humanitarian

"I'm basically a redneck," Carter once told reporters; cynically seeking the "redneck" vote was central to Carter's Georgia campaigns.

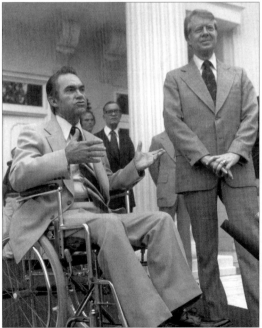

Carter always courted George Wallace and his supporters, even though he privately disdained Wallace.

The Carter brothers relax in Billy's service station in Plains.

Carter's peanut-farming past in 3-D.

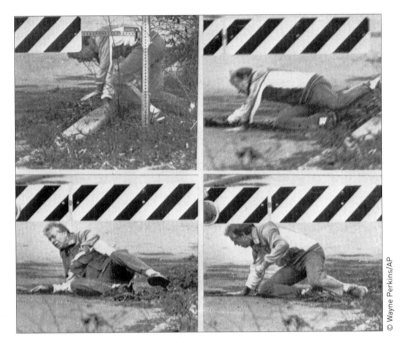

Carter stumbled not just in politics, but in several reported jogging mishaps, like this one in Plains in January 1981.

Jimmy lays the groundwork for the future Boy President.

Champions of Unintended Consequences: Jimmy Carter, the man who elected Ronald Reagan, and Ralph Nader, the man who elected George W. Bush.

© AP

The man he would betray: Carter toasts the shah of Iran, whose fall to the Ayatollah Khomeini on Carter's watch spawned the resurgence of fundamentalist Islamist terrorism that is now the War on Terror.

© Bettmann/CORBIS

Cuban dictator Fidel Castro gives Carter some baseball pointers.

Carter makes nice with Leonid Brezhnev.

Two "great" leaders: Kim Il Sung of North Korea and Jimmy Carter, the man who thought North Korea could be trusted not to develop nuclear weapons.

© Reuters

© Max Trujillo/Getty Images

Nicaraguan dictator Daniel Ortega considered Carter "a good friend."

From one "moderate" Southern Democrat to another: Clinton awards
Carter the Medal of Freedom.

Two of a kind: global ambassadors for bad-mouthing America—Jesse
Jackson and Jimmy Carter.

Carter listens to his favorite Middle Eastern tyrant, Yasir Arafat.

Former presidential candidate Howard Dean is all smiles for Carter, who helped advise Dean's failed campaign.

programs with no strings attached, he was happy to receive it."[9] But were these Arabic donors motivated purely by humanitarian purposes, or were they seeking to exploit Carter's increasingly anti-Israeli and pro-Palestinian attitudes? As we shall see, Carter's pro-Palestine, anti-Israel tilt has become more pronounced with the passage of time.

Hating Reagan

The primary target of the Carter Center's independent diplomacy in its first years, however, was President Reagan. Douglas Brinkley judged that Carter "thought [Reagan] immoral to the core," and seemed to relish opportunities to undermine Reagan's foreign policies. He even appeared at an anti-Reagan protest in New York in 1982. Speaking to the Council on Foreign Relations, Carter blasted Reagan for his "one-sided attitude of belligerence toward the Soviet Union," which begs the question of what an "even-handed" attitude of belligerence would be. In 1983, Carter criticized the Reagan administration policy of encouraging Japan to increase its defense spending—and did so on Japanese television, violating the unwritten rule that former presidents do not criticize the current administration on foreign soil. Reagan's policy, Carter said, was "not only ill-advised, but counterproductive."[10] In 1985, Carter told *60 Minutes* that he "could not think of a single international or diplomatic achievement that's been realized by Ronald Reagan." At times, Carter would nearly hyperventilate about Reagan, remarking once that "Under Reagan, military madness had taken hold," and, during the election campaign of 1984, he described Reagan as "extreme" and even "crazy."[11]

Carter's most egregious lapse in judgment might have been his visit in early 1984 with Soviet ambassador Anatoly Dobrynin. As Dobrynin recalls the scene:

> Jimmy Carter paid me an unexpected visit on January 30 to voice concern at the extent of Reagan's arms buildup. He described Reagan's peace rhetoric as a pure campaign maneuver. The former president was "utterly convinced" that there

would not be a single agreement on arms control, especially on nuclear arms, as long as Reagan remained in power.

Dobrynin was too discreet to let on whether Carter said or was hinting that the Soviets should do something to help out Walter Mondale's candidacy against Reagan that year. The Reagan policy that rankled Carter most was his missile defense plan, the Strategic Defense Initiative (SDI) more commonly known by the epithet Ted Kennedy successfully attached to it, "Star Wars." Carter called it "an absolute stupid waste of money" and "a scam." Even Carter's sympathetic biographer Douglas Brinkley acknowledged that "it never occurred to him to think that the Republicans were simply devising a bargaining-chip hoax to get a psychological upper hand on the bankrupt Soviet government."[12]

Starting in 1983, the Carter Center began holding high-profile "consultations" on arms control, to which Carter eventually succeeded in attracting senior Soviet officials to attend. And if senior Soviets were attending, senior American officials could hardly stay away without looking churlish. It helped that Carter managed to persuade Gerald Ford to co-host the Center's 1985 consultation, held a few months before Reagan's first summit at Geneva with Gorbachev.

The Soviet representatives made it clear that "Star Wars" was an implacable obstacle to any progress on arms control—and Carter agreed. The plain purpose of Carter's 1985 consultation was to bring pressure on Reagan's arms control policy and negotiation strategy—an astounding move by an ex-president.

Carter relished attacking Reagan's position that strategic arms reductions, not mere limitations, could be achieved by a policy of "peace through strength." "If the American people get the idea, which is mistaken, that a nuclear arms race on our side is going to cause the Soviets to quit building nuclear weapons on their side, they are silly," Carter said, in yet another miscalculation. In the real-world test of reducing arms, it was Reagan who succeeded where Carter had failed miserably.

Carter's independent foreign policy missions soon put him the company of some of the most loathsome dictators in the world, a practice he freely criticized in others. The late Michael Kelly memorably quipped that "Carter has put in more amiable sofa time with more despots than anyone except, perhaps, UN secretary-general Kofi Annan." Sometimes Carter behaved commendably, confronting dictators about some of their egregious human rights abuses and standing up for the honor of the United States. In Zimbabwe in 1986, for example, he walked out of an anti-American diatribe by the foreign minister. He no doubt gave Fidel Castro a case of heartburn during his 2002 visit to Cuba, as we shall see. Just as often, though, Carter would offer effusive and embarrassing praise for his abhorrent host, combined with gratuitous slaps at the United States. He said of Ethiopia's homicidal dictator Mengistu Haile Mariam, "I found him to be charming," and added that Mengistu's wife was "one of the most beautiful women I've ever seen in the world; she was like King Solomon's daughter, eloquent and personable." *Time* magazine's Lance Morrow observed, "Carter, citizen of the world, seems to have missed class the day we learned that even a character like Hitler can turn on the charm."

Presiding Over the Third World

Carter's foreign missions often proceed under the guise of fighting hunger or disease, in which case it is possible to shrug off his actions as the necessary price for achieving some good in the dismal third world. Carter has also become the world's premier poll watcher, and is invited to monitor elections in troubled or fledgling democracies, such as Haiti and the Philippines.

One of his most significant election monitoring efforts came in Panama in 1989, with the encouragement and full cooperation of the first Bush administration. Carter forcefully rebuffed Panamanian strongman Manuel Noriega's attempts to limit the number of poll watchers he wanted to bring to the country and to restrict his access to polling places. When Carter observed obvious vote-counting manipulations, he boldly and publicly declared the election to be a fraud. Noriega nullified the election, sent tanks into the streets, and declared martial law. Carter successfully lobbied the heads of other Latin American governments to denounce Noriega's actions. It was one of Carter's finest moments, partially vitiated, however, by his subsequent opposition to U.S. military intervention in Panama to remove Noriega. Carter even opposed pressuring Noriega with a *threat* of intervention. "Do not make any statement threatening armed intervention in the country," Carter urged in a memo to President Bush's national security advisor. Carter wanted further mediation and negotiations, preferably through the Organization of American States. Noriega actually strengthened his grip on power in the months after the nullified election, and the stubbornness with which he resisted the eventual U.S. military intervention suggests that Carter's preferred approach would have been fruitless. (A CBS poll after the invasion reported that a staggering 92 percent of Panamanians approved of the U.S. intervention.[13])

More problematic was Carter's election watching in Nicaragua in 1990. Nicaragua's unelected president, Daniel Ortega, bowing to international pressure, agreed to hold the nation's first free elections since the Sandinista revolution in 1979. With the growing crisis of Soviet communism in 1989 (culminating in the fall of the Berlin Wall in November), Nicaragua's Marxist-Leninist regime was in trouble, and needed relief from American economic sanctions (and pressure from the weakened but still fighting Contras) if it was to survive. Ortega thought he and his Sandinista Party would win the election, in part because it was better organized and funded than the scattered opposition parties (the Sandinistas even hired foreign campaign consultants), and in part because it had no hesitation to use the low arts of intimidation and propaganda typical of ideological leftist parties. Carter called complaints about Sandinista tactics "exaggerated," but did pressure Ortega to desist from a few measures. At one point, Ortega threatened to cancel the election unless the U.S. ended its humanitarian aid to the Contras, a blunder that backfired when liberal Democrats in Congress joined the Bush administration in renewing pressure for the election to go forward.

Early polls showed Ortega with a huge lead over the opposition candidate, Violeta Chamorro. Carter's blessing on the election, Ortega thought, would "certify the right wing's defeat." Ortega considered Carter "a good friend." The two men had held twelve hours of cordial talks in a 1986 visit Carter made to Nicaragua, and Carter hosted Ortega at one of his Habitat for Humanity projects in New York in 1987. Carter, expecting a Sandinista victory, dismissed charges of Sandinista malfeasance, and practically seemed to be taking the side of the Sandinistas. He *liked* the Sandinistas. After one of his earlier visits to Nicaragua, Carter declared that under the Marxist Sandinistas there was "as much free enterprise, private ownership, as exists in Great Britain." Now, as a poll watcher, he told reporters that the biggest problem he foresaw was demobilizing the Contras after the election. That the Sandinistas might need to be disbanded never crossed his lips. Costa Rican president Oscar Arias publicly broke with Carter and criticized Carter's election monitoring team for its lax attitude toward Sandinista election manipulations.

Even the Bush administration anticipated a Sandinista victory, so the shock was total when, early in the evening on election night, a "quick count" of the first 10 percent of the vote showed Chamorro winning a substantial victory throughout the nation. The Sandinista directorate called an emergency meeting and ordered a news blackout on election results. It appeared they might try to "fix" the election, Chicago-style. The presence of Carter and more than seven hundred UN election monitors made such chicanery problematic. Carter leaned on Ortega to relent, but also pressed Chamorro not to claim victory publicly until Ortega conceded, potentially disastrous advice if Ortega nullified the election. When the final votes were tallied, Chamorro beat Ortega 55 to 41 percent, gaining majorities among all age groups and in nearly every region of the country.

The result was shattering for liberals in the United States (including Carter), who saw the election as a referendum on Reagan-Bush policy toward Nicaragua and who thought a Sandinista victory would vindicate their criticisms of American support for the Contras. Instead, the election result revealed that the main premise of Reagan-Bush policy was correct: The Sandinistas were unpopular with most Nicaraguans (after the election there were numerous accounts of Nicaraguans who had lied to pollsters about their voting preferences out of fear of the Sandinista regime), and that without the persistent pressure from the Contras, it is doubtful a free election would have taken place. In the end, the Sandinistas agreed to surrender most of their power, given that even their supporters had to concede that their legitimacy was gone.

Arafat's Friend

In recent years Carter has—to use his own favorite phrasing—"injected himself" into several hot spots, including Bosnia and North Korea. But nowhere have his foreign interventions been more dubious than in the Middle East. He has made a mission of extending his one foreign policy success—the 1978 Camp David agreement between Israel and Egypt—to the entire region. But Carter has increasingly abandoned his status as an honest broker and revealed himself to be anti-Israel and pro-Arab. Both Brzezinski and Vance said in their memoirs that Carter's anti-Israeli sentiments began during his presidency, when he described Israeli prime minister Menachem Begin as a "psycho." Vance wrote that Carter intended to sell out Israel if he had been reelected.

Carter wants a Palestinian state on the West Bank. This requires, among other things, the rehabilitation of the Palestinian political leadership, especially Yasir Arafat, and other Arab leaders who have made war on Israel or supported terrorism, such as Syria's Hafez Assad. Carter proved himself more than willing to play the role of legitimizer. In 1983, when he made his first post-presidential visit to Israel, he wanted to meet Arafat. However, he reluctantly yielded to Reagan administration and Israeli government requests that he not do so. It was about the last time Carter deferred to American foreign policy.

Carter did meet with Syria's dictator Hafez Assad on his 1983 trip. The two held four hours of talks that Carter described as "constructive." *New York Times* columnist Abe Rosenthal noted Syria's "record of execution, torture, imprisonment of its own citizens, and in peacetime, could and does fill volumes," and added that Syria "year after year has been host, trainer and paymaster to one of the most murderous gangs of terrorists on earth."[14] Yet Carter has said virtually nothing about Syria's abysmal human rights record.

This was not Carter's first meeting with Assad; he had met him in Switzerland in 1977, early in his presidency, and his account of the meeting in his book on the Middle East, *The Blood of Abraham*, provides an excellent example of his penchant for swooning before strongmen and despots, and checking his human rights badge at the door. Finding Assad "gracious," Carter went on to describe the meeting as if he and Assad were part of a Rat Pack stand-up act in Las Vegas: "We began to enjoy the discussion, parrying back and forth and attempting to outdo each other in precipitating laughter in our audience of aides and advisers around the table."[15] A contemporary entry in Carter's diary read: "It was a very interesting and enjoyable experience. There was a lot of good humor between us."

Carter further observed of Assad: "Athough Assad depended heavily on Soviet aid and shared many goals with the Kremlin, he was not a subservient puppet." There were more than five thousand Soviet advisors in Syria during these years. A year after Carter's laugh-filled meeting with Assad, the Syrian dictator denounced Egypt's Anwar Sadat for making peace with Israel, and Damascus openly celebrated Sadat's assassination in 1981.

By the time Carter saw Assad again in 1983, Assad's army had occupied Lebanon and reduced it to a vassal state—a condition that continues to exist today. In 1984, after American peacekeeping troops had withdrawn from Lebanon, Assad declared, "Our principal enemy is the United States, and not Israel." Syria's close ties with Iran since the 1980s extends to cooperation in the spread of Iranian-sponsored terrorism. It is hard to escape the conclusion that the truck bombing of the Marine barracks in Beirut in October 1983 could not have occurred without Syrian complicity (if not direct sponsorship), and before long, the State Department officially designated Syria to be a "state sponsor" of terrorism. In December 1984, the Syrians were caught red-handed in an attempt to blow up an Israeli airliner. The Reagan administration recalled its ambassador and banned high-level contacts between American and Syrian officials.

Carter was not about to abide American foreign policy restrictions on Middle East contacts. "It just didn't apply to me," Carter told Douglas Brinkley. So when he went back to the Middle East in 1986, he sent the State Department a false itinerary that omitted mention of his planned trip to Damascus to see Assad. By now Syrians understood more clearly that Carter was on their side. Whereas during his 1983 visit, Carter had been blasted in the state-controlled Syrian press and protested in the streets as a lackey of the American State Department, in 1986 he received a warm hero's welcome. Carter met with Assad for nine hours, describing the talks as "very interesting, broad-ranging, and pleasant."

Carter's object in talking repeatedly to Assad was to bring Syria into the Camp David peace process with Israel. Carter discounted Assad's repeated public and private professions of "pan-Arabism," along with Assad's view that Middle Eastern borders were meaningless, which was a clever way of avoiding a commitment to respect any border adjustments Israel might agree to as a part of a peace agreement. Carter thought he was succeeding in bringing Assad along, but Syria never entered serious negotiations with Israel.

Meanwhile, the main object of Carter's affections remained Yasir Arafat. Indeed, Douglas Brinkley wrote, "there was no world leader Jimmy Carter was more eager to know than Yasir Arafat." Carter recruited Mary King, a former Peace Corps volunteer with extensive Middle East contacts, to serve as his "unofficial" liaison with Arafat, and said publicly that the U.S. should recognize the PLO and meet with Arafat. Carter told Douglas Brinkley that he thought "Arafat had been, to a substantial degree, unfairly maligned in the Western press."

Can there be a more squalid and duplicitous "head of state" in recent decades than Arafat? Former Romanian intelligence officer Ion Pacepa describes Arafat as "a career terrorist, trained, armed, and bankrolled by the Soviet Union and its satellites for decades."[16] Carter describes Arafat as "well-educated," but does he know that part of this education was at a Soviet special operations school? Among other terrorist outrages linked to Arafat, according to evidence pried loose from the State Department under a Freedom of Information Act request, is that he personally ordered the assassination of two American diplomats in 1973. A previously classified State Department cable from that year reads, "Fatah leader Yasir Arafat has now been described in recent intelligence as having given approval to the Khartoum operation [that killed the American diplomats] prior to its inception."[17] Arafat also sponsored the "Black September" militants who hijacked and blew up several passenger airliners in the desert that same year. Arafat bragged to Pacepa, "I invented the hijackings [of passenger airplanes]."

Arafat's strategy from the time of the Carter administration has been to assert that he is prepared to break with terrorism and recognize Israel in order to win concessions from Israel and the West. Israel saw through the strategy and so have many others. Douglas Brinkley criticizes Carter for not recognizing "the duplicitous side" of Arafat. Even President Bill Clinton's chief Middle East negotiator, Dennis Ross, has come to recognize the ugly truth about Arafat. "Is there any sign that Arafat has changed and is ready to make historic decisions for peace?" Ross asked in a recent article in *Foreign Policy*. "I see no indication of it." Ross adds, "I have never met an Arab leader who trusts Arafat or has anything good to say about him in private."[18]

Carter apparently trusts Arafat more than Arab leaders do, and has plenty good to say about him. He writes in *The Blood of Abraham*, "After he was chosen as chairman of the Central Committee of the PLO, Arafat was able to constrain some of the more radical terrorist groups among the Palestinians.... Yasir Arafat has generally taken a more moderate line, claiming: 'The PLO has never advocated the annihilation of Israel.'"[19] Carter accepts Arafat's English-language claim at face value, choosing to ignore Arafat's repeated statements in Arabic about the PLO's goal of eradicating Israel. Elsewhere in *The Blood of Abraham*, Carter writes as a value-free social scientist, describing the PLO as a Middle Eastern version of the United Way: "The PLO is a loosely associated umbrella organization bound together by common goals, but it comprises many groups eager to use diverse means to reach these goals."[20]

In the late 1980s, Carter kept in touch with the PLO through the Carter Center's Palestinian financial backers. According to Douglas Brinkley, Carter even helped a Palestinian activist named Mubarak Awad write pacifist pamphlets that were distributed on the West Bank and inside Israel. Brinkley adds, "Carter began the long process of trying to persuade Arafat to make statements that would be regarded as responsible in the United States," though it is unclear whether Carter and Arafat were in direct contact at this time.[21]

By 1990, President George H. W. Bush was himself engaged in formal diplomatic contacts with Arafat. Carter used this shift in American diplomatic policy as an excuse to meet Arafat in Paris, where he told the PLO leader, "I would like an easy relationship with you so that I might be able to help you because my heart is torn with anger and anguish and sorrow when I observe the suffering of the Palestinian people." Carter suggested that the phrases in the PLO Charter calling for the destruction of Israel be removed, but Arafat waved him off, saying that "fanatics" among the Palestinians wouldn't let him, an explanation Carter apparently accepted. Carter's sympathy extended so far that he and Arafat sobbed together about Israeli atrocities against the Palestinians. After the meeting, Carter told the press, "Chairman Arafat has done everything he can, I think, in recent months to promote the peace process."

Carter and Arafat were in constant contact in the weeks after their Paris meeting, culminating in the extraordinary step of Carter writing a long letter to Arafat outlining a speech Arafat should give for Western consumption. "The objective of the speech," Carter wrote, "should be to secure maximum sympathy and support of other world leaders, especially including Americans and Israelis. [Here Carter had in mind the "peace" party in Israel, led by Shimon Peres.] The Likud leaders are now on the defensive, and must not be given any excuse for continuing their present abusive policies."[22]

Carter's increasingly explicit anti-Israeli tilt was too much even for one of his top staffers at the Carter Center, Middle East expert Ken Stein. Stein wrote to Carter, "If you continue on the course of only criticizing or minimizing Israel in your public presentations, you will be doing yourself a potentially devastating disservice, particularly if you want to be reengaged in any capacity in future Middle East diplomacy."[23]

Four months after Carter's meeting with Arafat, Iraq invaded Kuwait, and Arafat blundered by publicly siding with Hussein, who was perhaps the only Arab leader less liked than himself by other Arab leaders. Carter responded by contacting foreign heads of state. He tried to dissuade them from supporting President Bush's military coalition to force Iraq out of Kuwait and tried to pry them away from supporting the UN resolution calling for Iraq's withdrawal. Carter thought sanctions against Iraq were the right answer to its aggression. And, incredibly, he thought the key to peaceful resolution of Iraq's invasion of Kuwait was for Israel to give up the West Bank. Along with Saddam Hussein, Arafat was the big loser of the first Gulf War. Arafat was excluded from the postwar Madrid conference, where the Bush administration attempted to revive the Israeli-Palestinian peace process. Arafat kept in close touch with Carter, though, and Carter was not about to abandon his friend. Douglas Brinkley wrote that "together they strategized on how to recover the PLO's standing in the United States."[24] Because he sided with Iraq, Arafat lost millions of dollars in support from Arab nations opposed to Saddam Hussein's invasion of Kuwait. Arafat appealed to Carter to help revive this funding. Carter flew to Saudi Arabia on what Douglas Brinkley described as "essentially a fund-raising mission for the PLO," imploring Saudi King Fahd to restore Saudi funds for the PLO.

Much of Carter's game plan was taken over by the Clinton administration, which brokered the Israeli-PLO peace accord in Oslo in 1993. When Arafat arrived in Washington to sign the Oslo agreement, Carter greeted him by saying, "You have been so patient and wise." Carter would later gush even more effusively, "I am so proud of you." At Oslo, Israel recognized the Palestinian Authority as a legitimate political entity, ended the PLO's exile in Tunisia, and allowed Arafat to return to the West Bank and set up a government. The PLO, for its part, was to recognize Israel and renounce terror and the incitement of terror.

Today, of course, the Oslo framework lies in tatters, with Israel having suffered another decade of terrorism and Arafat having rejected a Clinton-brokered follow-up offer at Camp David in 2000 that would have given Arafat a Palestinian state on 97 percent of the West Bank and a capital city of East Jerusalem. While Bill Clinton was bitter that Arafat rejected an unprecedented Israeli offer to accommodate an independent Palestinian state, Carter wasn't; he professed to understand Arafat's point of view. Carter said, "Arafat could not have survived politically if he had accepted." There is little doubt that Arafat is complicit in the wave of suicide bombings that have come in the wake of the collapse of the 2000 Camp David negotiations. One has to assume that Carter considers such terrorism understandable and acceptable.

Carter continues to soldier on in his quixotic quest to legitimize Arafat and isolate Israel, culminating in a December 2003 peace conference in Geneva (Hollywood actor and noted foreign policy expert Richard Dreyfus acted as master of ceremonies), where Carter and a host of out-of-office Israeli and Palestinian politicians came up with a new "peace plan" that essentially reiterates the Oslo Accords (which Israeli abided by and the PLO did not) but offers further concessions to the Palestinians, including granting the Palestinian Authority control of the entirety of Jerusalem, and puts in place no reliable safeguards to protect Israeli borders, which would return to where they were in 1967. "This is not a peace treaty," columnist Charles Krauthammer observed. "It is a suicide note."

If Carter's barely concealed anti-Israeli sentiments were not enough (he is virtually persona non grata in Israel nowadays), at the Geneva conference Carter embraced the popular leftist theme that America is responsible for creating the climate of terrorism that led to September 11. "There is no doubt that the lack of real effort to resolve the Palestinian issue is a primary source of anti-American sentiment throughout the Middle East and a major incentive for terrorist activity," Carter said. A "senior Israeli government official" commented to the *Jerusalem Post*, "Does anyone really care what Carter has to say?" At the end of the Geneva conference, Carter let slip a comment that ranks up close with his "ethnic purity" remark in the 1976 campaign: "Had I been elected to a second term, with the prestige and authority and influence and reputation I had in the region, we could have moved to a *final solution*." (Emphasis added.) Strange that such a politician of such prestige, authority, and influence would use that particular phrase.

Chapter Twelve

The Second Carter Administration

> "A great deal of intelligence can be invested in ignorance when the need for illusion is great."
>
> —SAUL BELLOW

While Jimmy Carter never got that second term in the White House, he did experience a virtual second term with the arrival of President Bill Clinton in 1993. Personally, Clinton never liked Carter, though no former president played a greater role in shaping Clinton's presidency. At the intersection of the administration and Congress, however, Clinton tended to tack right, in reaction to a Republican-controlled Congress and to maintain his political viability, while Carter tacked left. Clinton biographer Rich Lowry says that on foreign policy Carter "could out-appease even Bill Clinton."[1]

Carter endorsed Clinton in 1992, but very late in the primary process, long after Clinton's nomination was assured. The Clintons returned the favor by giving Carter the cold shoulder at the inauguration in January 1993. Nevertheless, Carter, or the spirit of Carterism, of feckless appeasement, could be said to have been at the heart of Clinton's foreign policy, such as it was. Clinton's front-line foreign policy players, starting with his first secretary of state, Warren Christopher, were retreads of the Carter administration. Indeed, Carter lobbied hard for Christopher to be selected as secretary of state right after the 1992 election. Other prominent Carter alumni who played key roles for Clinton included Clinton's first national security advisor, Anthony Lake, the author of Carter's infamous "inordinate fear of communism" speech in 1977; Richard Holbrooke, who served Clinton as UN ambassador; and Sandy Berger, Clinton's second national security advisor.

And then there was Carter himself. He grabbed a much more center-stage role with his foreign policy freelancing during the Clinton years. Indeed, for a period during Clinton's first term, it seemed as though Carter was Clinton's de facto secretary of state. Carter attempted to inject himself into the Somalia mess, hoping to be named the official U.S. negotiator. When the White House nixed this ambition, Carter simply invited a Somalian delegation representing the wanted warlord Mohammed Farah Aidid to visit him at the Carter Center in Atlanta. Aidid was the warlord U.S. Army Rangers were hunting in the summer of 1993 during the "Black Hawk Down" incident. Aidid's goons killed seventeen American soldiers. Carter criticized UN attempts to capture him as "regrettable."

Adventures in Haiti, Bosnia, and North Korea

In 1994, Carter thrust himself into the civil war in Haiti, the ferocious ethnic violence in Bosnia, and the appeasement of saber-rattling of North Korea—assignments he undertook with plenty of media hype. In Haiti, the Clinton administration had resolved to go beyond its initial trade embargo and use military force to oust General Raoul Cedras, the strongman who had seized power in a coup, and to restore the elected president, Jean-Bertrand Aristide, a leftist former priest.

Cedras tried to stave off American military action by playing the Carter card, telephoning Carter in Atlanta and asking him to intervene as a mediator. Cedras had met Carter when Carter monitored

Haitian elections in 1990, and had kept in frequent contact by phone during the current crisis. Carter eagerly jumped into the fray. He disagreed strongly with Clinton's policy toward Cedras and later told the *New York Times* that he was "ashamed" of it. But Carter did something that Cedras didn't anticipate; he invited Georgia senator Sam Nunn to join his negotiating effort. In turn, Nunn suggested adding Colin Powell, recently retired chairman of the Joint Chiefs of Staff.

Despite opposition in the State Department and National Security Council, Clinton gave Carter's mission his approval. "The only thing Carter was authorized to discuss on behalf of Clinton," a White House aide told reporters, "was the modalities of departure" for Cedras. Nonetheless, Carter immediately began negotiating his own policy once he arrived in Port-au-Prince. He drafted an agreement that set no firm deadline for Cedras to step down, promised the lifting of the U.S. trade embargo, and made no mention of restoring Aristide.

Cedras foolishly rejected Carter's appeasement, and Clinton, exasperated with Carter, ordered the planned military invasion of Haiti to begin. Carter then hurriedly got Haiti's provisional president Emile Jonassaint (whom the United States did not recognize as a legitimate political authority) to sign Carter's draft agreement, with Cedras's reluctant consent. Carter flew back to Washington and called CNN to arrange a live press conference to give details of the deal before he went to the White House to brief President Clinton. Carter told the press, "The problem last night and in a number of places around the world causes it to be necessary for the Carter Center to act." Despite the Carter Center's action—and its slap at the Clinton administration—it was American troops, not Carter's agreement, who restored Aristide to power.

In Bosnia, Carter brokered a cease-fire agreement that was announced with great to-do, but which was hardly groundbreaking. There had been thirty cease-fires since 1992, and there was little reason to suppose this deal would hold any longer than the others had. Indeed, stopping the violence in Bosnia ultimately required the intervention of U.S. troops in 1996—and U.S. troops are still there today. Carter displayed his usual affinity for anti-American thugs by sympathizing with the chief architect of "ethnic cleansing" in Bosnia, Radovan Karadzic, telling him, "I cannot dispute your statement that the American public has had primarily one side of the story." This was too much for the *New Republic*, which editorialized that "Carter is a menace," his agreement "an indecent farce," and suggested that "a statue of the vain, meddling, amoral American fool should stand in every ethnically cleansed square."[2]

But worse than his meddling in Haiti and Bosnia was Carter's third escapade in 1994: his peacemaking mission to North Korea. By 1994, it was evident that North Korea—still ruled by the last Stalinist, Kim Il Sung—was progressing with a nuclear weapons program. Clinton viewed the matter with sufficient alarm that he ordered the Pentagon to beef up American military forces in the region and to prepare a plan to bomb North Korea's nuclear facilities—a step that would likely have set off a general war on the Korean peninsula. The main strategy, however, was to seek UN sanctions. UN ambassador Madeleine Albright was making headway at the UN to impose severe economic sanctions on North Korea. The UN Security Council, always preferring sanctions over military force, was ready to go along.

Jimmy Carter stood squarely in the way.

Carter had a long history with both South and North Korea. He had come into office in 1977 pledging to withdraw American troops from South Korea. Unknown to the public is that Kim Il Sung had written to Carter right after the 1976 election proposing a rapprochement. Douglas Brinkley wrote that Kim was "eager to bond with Carter," and Carter was eager to reciprocate. Kim sent several letters to Carter via such worthy intermediaries as the communist dictators of Yugoslavia and Romania, Tito and Ceausescu. Kim's main purpose was to reinforce Carter's intention to withdraw American troops; he also held out the prospect of negotiations about the reunification of North and South Korea—provided that the South Korean government was excluded from the talks.

Kim referred to Carter as "a man of justice." Carter reciprocated these flatteries by lifting the U.S. ban on travel to North Korea. When

Carter floated the idea of a Camp David–style summit between himself, Kim, and South Korean president Park Chung Hee, the State Department blew a gasket and worked every channel to get Carter to drop the idea. Carter acquiesced, but he did make South Korea's Park a major target of his human rights policy. Carter did not like President Park, who had taken power in a coup in 1961; their only meeting was, Richard Holbrooke told Douglas Brinkley, "the worst imaginable exchange between two treaty allies." In Carter's mind, there was close to a moral equivalence between South and North Korea.

In the fall of 1979, the chief of South Korea's intelligence service murdered President Park. Carter's ambassador to South Korea, William Glaysteen, judges that "U.S. actions and words unwittingly contributed in a significant way to Park's downfall."[3] Army general Chun Doo Hwan deposed Park's successor, Choi Kyu Ha, in a military coup less than two months later, after which martial law was declared amidst violent student demonstrations. The already strained relations between the U.S. and South Korea took a turn for the worse. It was Carter's third human rights–related catastrophe in one year (along with Iran and Nicaragua.) Stiff U.S. protests and the intervention of President-elect Reagan were required to convince President Chun to commute a death sentence South Korea had imposed on human rights activist Kim Dae Jung.

Even after Carter left the White House, Kim Il Sung continued to court him, inviting him to visit North Korea on at least three occasions. Carter wanted to go, and in the last instance, in late 1993, only Secretary of State Warren Christopher was able to talk him out of going. When the North Korean crisis intensified in the spring of 1994—North Korea was extracting spent fuel rods from their reactors, a precursor to making weapons-grade material—Carter inserted himself in the middle of the Clinton administration's maneuvering. Clinton sent Assistant Secretary of State Robert Gallucci to Plains to brief Carter personally. Douglas Brinkley laconically records this remarkable summary of Carter's attitude: *"Carter informed Gallucci that his patience was wearing thin,"* almost as if he were co-president or secretary of state.[4] (Emphasis added.) Carter underscored his view of his own indispensability when he later told Brinkley, "Kim Il Sung's invitation to talk was something I couldn't turn down; it was perhaps the only hope left before war commenced."[5]

The next day Carter informed Vice President Al Gore that he was strongly inclined to accept North Korea's invitation to visit; in other words, Carter was going to go to Pyongyang with or without Clinton's approval. Gore lobbied Clinton to approve Carter's proposed mission, and Clinton ultimately yielded, against the wishes of much of the State Department. Clinton's condition was that Carter make clear that he would be traveling as a private citizen, and not as an official representative of the U.S. government.[6] As in Haiti, Carter was supposed to present the U.S. position; in this case, the U.S. was demanding that North Korea halt its nuclear program, surrender its spent fuel rods, and allow UN inspections to resume.

The fiction that Carter was going as a private citizen fooled no one, least of all Kim, who had previously rejected Clinton's proposal to send two senators to negotiate officially. Kim wanted Carter, and only Carter. The practical result of giving the green light to Carter's North Korea mission was that Clinton lost control of U.S. policy toward Korea, which is a measure of both the chutzpah of Carter and the endemic weakness of Clinton. Carter immediately abandoned the policy constraints with which Clinton had tried to bind him, and began negotiating from his own position.

Carter thought the threat of UN sanctions backed Kim into an unacceptable corner. Indeed, Carter believed North Korea's threat that it would attack the South if the UN imposed sanctions. Carter saw his intervention as having averted a war; so he took it upon himself to offer Kim an alternative agreement: that North Korea freeze its nuclear program in return for the U.S. agreeing to further talks. Carter dropped American demands that UN inspections resume and that North Korea surrender its spent fuel rods. Kim agreed to Carter's proposal.

Kim's one concession was enough for Carter to announce publicly on CNN—without first informing the White House, which knew neither of Carter's proposal nor that he had brought CNN camera crews with him—that the crisis was over. Carter even said that the U.S. was dropping its support for sanctions at the UN, which wasn't true. Clinton was furious, but if he repudiated Carter, he would look like a fool for having allowed Carter to go in the first place. Carter reacted angrily himself when the White House insisted on stronger terms, and Carter's terms were eventually adopted. The U.S. agreed to send fuel oil and light water nuclear technology in return for North Korea's "cooperation."

More disturbing than the diplomatic outcome was Carter's behavior toward Kim Il Sung. If Carter brought up North Korea's human rights record with Kim, there is no mention made of it in any of the accounts of his mission. By any scale, North Korea ranks as one of the worst human rights violators of the last century. In a nation of twenty-three million souls, an estimated 1.5 million people have been killed in North Korea's concentration camps, which are still operating today. More than 100,000 have been executed in party purges right out of the pages of a Stalinist nightmare. North Korea can't even make the Cuba-style boast that at least it provides its people with literacy and health care. Collectivized agriculture has created chronic famine. World Vision International estimates that as many as two million have died from starvation; the German Red Cross estimates that ten thousand children are dying of malnutrition every month.[7] Rumors of cannibalism are rife. But Carter, ever gullible with America's enemies, remarked that he saw supermarkets in North Korea that were just like Wal-Mart.

Carter's first session with Kim ended "with a warm embrace," according to Brinkley. It was his most sickening performance yet. "[W]hen the Great Leader and the Man from Plains first laid eyes on each other," Brinkley wrote, "it was all smiles, as if they had known each other for years. . . . From Carter's born-again perspective, Kim was not by nature evil."[8] Carter said that he was impressed by "the reverence with which [North Koreans] look upon their leader," and later told his Plains, Georgia, church congregation that North

Koreans regard Kim "as almost a deity, as a George Washington, as a Patrick Henry, as a worshipful leader all rolled into one."[9] Carter had apparently forgotten that he had said the same thing about the Iranian shah less than a year before he was toppled by his adoring people.

Carter joined Kim for an outing on the presidential yacht on the Taedong River, which Kim called a "peace celebration" for the benefit of the CNN cameras he allowed to tag along. Carter and Kim discussed their mutual interest in hunting and fishing, with Carter promising to send biologists and fly fishermen to North Korea to analyze North Korea's fishing potential. He talked to Kim about Christianity, and reported that Kim was "deeply interested in Christianity." On the diplomatic front, Carter got Kim to agree to a summit between North and South Korea, the first since the end of the war in 1953. This, too, was not a policy objective of the Clinton administration; Carter once again exceeded his instructions. It emerged later that North Korea demanded a payment of tens of millions of dollars from the South as a condition of attending the summit, which produced little progress.

Carter declared the purported success of his mission to be a "miracle." When Kim Il Sung died shortly after the Carter mission, a popular joke around the State Department and the White House was that Kim died of laughter from negotiating with Jimmy Carter. North Korea did not abide by Carter's agreement for a single minute, admitting in late 2002 that it had continued developing nuclear weapons under Kim's successor (his son, Kim Jung Il) and was now in possession of several warheads. North Korea blamed the U.S. for the breakdown of the deal, since the Clinton administration had not built the two promised replacement reactors. Writing in the *New York Times* in October 2002, Carter essentially agreed with the North Korean position; it was our fault.[10] He went further in a February 2003 column about North Korea in the *Washington Post*, writing that Bush administration belligerence "helped cause many in that country to assume that they were next on America's hit list after Iraq."[11] *National Review* wondered: "He is the former president of whose country?"

President Clinton refused even to meet with Carter upon his return from North Korea. In fact, the Clinton administration didn't want to see him at all, but Carter came to the White House anyway, where no senior member of the administration agreed to meet him. He had to settle for a tense and difficult meeting with his own former aide Anthony Lake. Finally, in 1995, after indulging further Carter escapades in Haiti and Bosnia, the Clinton administration refused to sanction or approve any other Carter foreign adventures.

Dismissing Dubya

There was never much chance that Carter would find favor with President George W. Bush. Only six months into Bush's presidency, Carter told the Columbus (Georgia) *Ledger-Enquirer*, "I've been disappointed in almost everything he [Bush] has done." He went on to complain that Bush is "strictly conforming" to the wishes of hardline right-wingers like Dick Cheney and Donald Rumsfeld. Carter reasserted his posture of near-sole ownership of human rights by dismissing the president, saying, "I don't think that George W. Bush has any particular commitment to preservation of the principles of human rights."

When Carter's comments about Bush made the international news wires (the comments made it as far as Agence France-Presse wire service) and caused a stir, Carter claimed the *Ledger-Enquirer* reporter had double-crossed him; his comments were supposed to be off the record. No one over the age of six bought this excuse; Carter is too intelligent and experienced a politician to have forgotten the basic Washington rule that nothing a president says can be considered off the record, no matter how high the stack of Bibles on which the journalist swears.

Uncharacteristically, Carter apologized to Bush at a White House event a few weeks later; Bush told him to forget about it. But when Bush identified Iraq, Iran, and North Korea as the "axis of evil," Jimmy Carter, the avatar of human rights, was not only quick to criticize Bush's formula as "overly simplistic," he added, "I think it will

take years before we can repair the damage done by that statement."
And as he did during the Reagan administration, Carter continues to
attack missile defense, calling Bush's plans "technologically ridicu-
lous" and saying that missile defense "will re-escalate the nuclear
arms race"—though of course the "arms race" ended under Ronald
Reagan's watch.

Carter and Castro

In the spring of 2002, Carter became the first American ex-president
to visit Cuba. (The Ford Foundation paid for this jaunt.) As with his
approaches to Arafat, Carter thought he could build bridges with the
pariah Fidel Castro. Carter had had his first telephone conversation
with Castro in 1995, a step that infuriated Clinton and drew an
enraged phone call from Vice President Al Gore. Contacting Castro
without the approval of the U.S. government was bad enough for
Clinton and Gore; in 1995, Clinton was sagging in the polls and
did not want Carter causing trouble for him with Florida's voters in
the 1996 election.

The 2002 trip had all the portents of another groan-inducing
embarrassment. Shortly before Carter's trip, Undersecretary of State
John Bolton told the media that Cuba was suspected of having a bio-
logical weapons research program. The Bush administration subsequently backed away from Bolton's charge, almost surely for larger
strategic reasons (wanting to maintain a stable relationship with
Cuba for the time being). Considerable evidence exists that Bolton's
assessment is correct.[12] Nonetheless, Carter went public with the
claim that his own intelligence information refuted the charge, and
that the Bush administration was purposely trying to undermine his
trip: a typical Carteresque compound of arrogance, presumption, and
disregard for a sitting administration.

A visit by an American ex-president was a major propaganda coup
for Castro, and the Cuban dictator undoubtedly assumed that Carter
would play the role of "useful idiot." Carter certainly issued the pre-
dictable pre-trip announcements about "establishing a dialogue with

Castro" and "reaching out" to the Cuban people, and repeated the familiar tropes about Cuba's "superb systems of health care and universal education." Carter had several long, cordial meetings with Castro, during which Carter seemed to have accepted Castro's "genuine belief in maintaining equity of treatment and an absence of class distinctions for Cubans and determination to retain the tightest possible control over all aspects of life in the nation."

Carter had asked for and received permission to make a prime-time televised address to the Cuban people. This time he embarrassed not the United States, but his dictator host. Giving his address in Spanish, Carter announced that the American embargo of Cuba was not the source of Cuba's economic problems. Noting that nearly every Latin American nation was now a legitimate democracy, Carter chided Cuba for being behind the times: "Cuba has adopted a socialist government where one political party dominates, and people are not permitted to organize any opposition movements. Your constitution recognizes freedom of speech and association, but other laws deny these freedoms to those who disagree with the government."

The day before, Carter had visited Oswaldo Paya, leader of the Varela Project, a Cuban human rights group. The Varela Project had managed to generate more than ten thousand signatures for a pro-democracy petition—no easy feat in a nation where paper is scarce and copy machines, when available, are state-regulated. Any news of the Varela Project had been suppressed in the Cuban media, but it could not be ignored if Carter shined a spotlight on it: "It is gratifying to note that Articles 63 and 88 of your constitution allow citizens to petition the National Assembly to permit a referendum to change laws if ten thousand or more citizens sign it. I am informed that such an effort, called the Varela Project, has gathered sufficient signatures and has presented such a petition to the National Assembly. When Cubans exercise this freedom to change laws peacefully by a direct vote, the world will see that Cubans, and not foreigners, will decide the future of the country." Carter's public praise of the Varela Project elevated Paya's status such that Castro could not include him among the hundreds of democracy activists he jailed when the Iraq war distracted public attention in the spring of 2003.

Castro is in firm control of the National Assembly, so no referendum has occurred, constitution or no. Yet, as Latin American scholar Mark Falcoff observed, "Castro could not have been pleased to listen to Carter publicize and praise the Varela Project." Falcoff adds, "Carter's visit to Cuba was arguably more important than the Pope's." Falcoff notes that Cuban journalists who had been keen to cozy up to American journalists at the beginning of Carter's visit were noticeably distant and wary of American reporters and Carter's entourage at the end of the trip.[13]

Carter, the Energizer Bunny of ex-presidents, who turns eighty in 2004, can still surprise, and, as in Cuba, not always entirely badly.

The Myth of St. Jimmy

> "Jimmy Carter's reputation for idealism has been one of the great swindles of American politics for two decades. In fact, he is the man in his time who will have done most to damage the prestige of idealism, and the prestige of peace. For peace is never lasting or true when it is based on the belief that there is nothing worse than war; but that is Carter's belief."[1]
>
> —The *NEW REPUBLIC*

Garrison Keillor once described an annoying *Prairie Home Companion* character as "a good person—in the worst sense of the word." It is a characterization well suited to Jimmy Carter. He trades on popular admiration for his good works with Habitat for Humanity and other charitable causes to widen his latitude for his usually embarrassing and often disastrous peace missions around the world. The only prominent Americans who can rival Carter for bad-mouthing sitting presidents, coddling murderous dictators, and criticizing American policy while on foreign soil are Jesse Jackson and Ramsey Clark. It is not an accident that Carter's popularity overseas is highest among the nations that hate the United States the most. Yet Carter's moral authority is such that he is consistently absolved of behavior that he would be the first to condemn in anyone else.

How to sum up this maddeningly contradictory man? He is a famously professed Christian, and yet a particularly unhumble and mean-spirited politician. He is a Baptist from the conservative South, yet his liberal theology and leftward politics put him on the fringes of his religious denomination and region. He is held up as a model ex-president, and yet by any objective assessment Carter must be regarded as America's *worst* ex-president: a man whose record of accomplishments is almost entirely negative, and yet who cannot leave foreign policy to the elected government of the Unites States and travels the world speaking ill of his successors in the White House. He is a very smart man, and yet seems incapable of learning anything. Even Neville Chamberlain came around on the Nazis—that they had to be defeated militarily—but Carter never did come around on the Soviet Union, and he remains hopelessly credulous about Yasir Arafat, North Korea, and a long list of other mendacious dictators and regimes.

Meeting with these dictators provides a stage for him. Through them he can attract the media, creating an audience for his proclamations of his own initiatives for peace. Carter clearly craves public attention; there is a portion of his soul that cannot be satisfied without being in the center of the limelight. The late liberal columnist Murray Kempton wrote in 1994 that Carter "has no clear idea of the shrine he seeks except that it is built for him."[2] His insatiability for attention can be seen beyond his political grandstanding. He has published a children's book, a book of poetry that even his admirers admit is not very good, a book about aging, and most recently a historical novel. He is prolific, but his works seem juvenile compared to Nixon's meditations on foreign policy, and will never challenge Theodore Roosevelt's for interest or scope. They seem to lack any ultimately greater purpose than that of promoting Jimmy Carter.

Carter bears a deep and abiding wound from the electorate's humiliating rejection in 1980. The combination of his restless energy, ambition, idealism, and overweening pride makes it impossible for him to settle into comfortable ex-presidential retirement. He seeks vindication for himself and his principles—indeed, his political agenda has become a religious mission for him. Douglas Brinkley wrote a chilling evaluation of Carter's theo-politics: "Because Carter saw himself doing God's will, he in effect made himself the final arbiter of God's will. His belief [was] that he was beyond reproach, as if he were the last Christian in the Colosseum of modernity...."[3]

In retrospect, it can be seen that although Carter acted aloof toward his party and antagonized many of its leading liberals, he represents a transition figure between the older, hard-headed anti-communist liberalism of the early Cold War era (the Truman-JFK-Scoop Jackson Democrats) and the post-McGovern liberalism that embraces principles of weakness in foreign affairs and thinly veiled socialism in domestic affairs. Clinton biographer Rich Lowry called Clinton's foreign policy "McGovernism without a conscience." Carter, perhaps, represents McGovernism redoubled by self-righteous arrogance, which is a pretty good description of modern liberalism as represented by the likes of the Clintons, Al Gore, John Kerry, and Howard Dean. During the 2004 Democratic primaries, Howard Dean actually took counsel from Carter, but John Kerry and John Edwards were in their various ways plowing Carter's fields: Kerry with his flip-flopping foreign policy of appeasement, his calls for "regime change in the United States," and his leftist agenda (at least partly obscured by his decorated Navy service); and Edwards as yet another liberal "moderate" Southern Democrat.

Although Carter's judgment and principles are doubtful, and his presidential record one of enormous failure, many people are inclined to give Carter the benefit of the doubt, saying, "at least his heart is in the right place." But is it? It is impossible to know how much Carter is driven purely by ego and how much by do-gooding. But even with the best of intentions, idealism has its limits. The idealist can point the way forward, but the realist has to get us there.

Carter's human rights policy produced some salutary results during his presidency; he helped secure the release of political prisoners from several African nations, for example. And as ex-president, Carter has helped secure the release of thousands of political prisoners through his moral suasion alone. Presidents Reagan and George W. Bush in their own way used the bully pulpit of the presidency to advance the idea of human rights, too, in some ways more expansively than Carter did. The Reagan administration echoed Carter in declaring explicitly that "human rights is at the core of our foreign policy." On the Ronald Reagan and George W. Bush side of the ledger, one records firstly the collapse of global communism and secondly the liberation of Afghanistan and Iraq as part of an ambitious effort to inject Western ideals of human rights into some of the most repressive regimes in the world.

On the other hand, according to the annual Freedom House survey of democracy and liberty around the globe, there was almost no increase in freedom during Carter's presidency.[4] Instead, both Iran and Nicaragua, principal targets of Carter's human rights policy, became human rights disasters; the Soviets cracked down on human rights activists Anatoly Scharansky and Aleksandr Ginzburg; and Carter's foreign policy weakness encouraged the Soviets to invade Afghanistan. The aftershocks of Carter's foreign policy failures reverberate most powerfully in the Islamic fundamentalist terrorism we have today. It was the Soviet invasion of Afghanistan that created the *mujahadeen*, who revived the idea of *jihad*. More important, the fall of the shah in Iran gave Islamic fundamentalist radicalism an enormous state sponsor and inspiration and made being an American ally in the Middle East seem more dangerous than being an American foe. Carter's idealism failed in confronting communism during his presidency and later in confronting communist North Korea. Carter idealism—if it can be called that—in the Middle East would have us side with the terrorist PLO rather than with democratic Israel, and would have us on a perpetual merry-go-round of talks aimed at appeasing Arab dictators rather than toppling them or challenging them to reform and cease sponsoring terrorism.

Ronald Reagan consigned communism to the dustbin of history. It would be nice to consign Carterism there as well; but, like the man himself, it keeps coming back in the Democratic Party, which has been transformed by him even as it has hated him. It is tragic but true that the foreign policy future of the Democratic Party is likely the foreign policy past of President Jimmy Carter. His record should be a warning to the electorate: Don't go down that road again.

Acknowledgments

P art of the purpose of this book is to bring to a new generation of readers many aspects of the Carter story that were well known to journalists and authors who pondered him when he was president, but whose works are now long out of print and forgotten, such as Betty Glad, James Wooten, and Gary Fink. All writers are indebted to Douglas Brinkley, who chose the counterintuitive approach of writing exclusively about Carter's post-presidential career. Although Brinkley is woefully uncritical of Carter, his book *The Unfinished Presidency* is the most comprehensive account of any president's post–White House days ever written, and as such is an essential resource for anyone pondering Carter's recent activities.

A number of my colleagues at the American Enterprise Institute deserve thanks for their insights and recollections, starting with AEI's president Christopher DeMuth, whose unflagging support of the resident scholars provides a model of what should be the standard for academic freedom. Mark Falcoff, Michael Novak, Jeane Kirkpatrick, and Ben Wattenberg all gave me useful advice on how to think about Carter. My research assistant, Ryan Stowers, and AEI librarian Gene Hosey helped track down endless requests for sources and documents. The Rev. Richard B. Yale was invaluable in sorting out the internecine theological disputes in the Southern Baptist Convention.

Regnery uber-editor Harry Crocker, an old friend I've said "no" to on numerous occasions, convinced me that I was the right person to undertake this project. I am glad I took his advice.

Notes

Chapter One: The Conscience of the World

1. Lance Morrow, "The Lives of the Saint," *Time*, May 11, 1998.
2. Jules Witcover, *Marathon: The Pursuit of the Presidency, 1972–1976* (New York: Viking, 1977), 211.
3. Howard Norton and Bob Strosser, *The Miracle of Jimmy Carter* (Plainfield, NJ: Logos Books, 1976), 93.
4. Douglas Brinkley, *The Unfinished Presidency: Jimmy Carter's Journey Beyond the White House* (New York: Viking, 1998), 7.
5. Cited in Betty Glad, *Jimmy Carter: In Search of the Great White House* (New York: Norton, 1980), 298.
6. Gary Fink, *Prelude to the Presidency: The Political Character and Legislative Leadership Style of Governor Jimmy Carter* (Westport, CT: Greenwood, 1980), 19.
7. Patrick Anderson, *Electing Jimmy Carter: The Campaign of 1976* (Baton Rouge: Louisiana State University Press, 1994), 164.
8. Margaret Thatcher, *Downing Street Years* (New York: Harper-Collins, 1993), 69. Carter's first encounter with Thatcher went so disastrously—Thatcher lectured Carter on foreign policy, according to Carter's aides—that Carter told his staff never again to schedule him to meet with a foreign opposition leader. For her part, Thatcher found Carter "personally ill-suited for the presidency, agonizing over big decisions and too concerned with detail.... [I]n leading a great nation decency and assiduousness are not enough."

9. Kenneth E. Morris, *Jimmy Carter: American Moralist* (Athens, GA: University of Georgia Press, 1996), 169.

10. Glad, 199.

11. Morris, 155.

12. Glad, 476.

13. Reg Murphy, "The New Jimmy Carter," *The New Republic*, January 14, 1976. According to one account, Carter tried to blackmail Murphy during the 1970 campaign for governor by threatening to release documents showing Murphy had allowed Carter's rival, Carl Sanders, to pay some of Murphy's travel expenses. It was not true: Murphy had paid cash to Sanders for his expenses; Sanders bundled the expenses of several other cash-paying reporters and charged them to his credit card.

14. Jeff Chu, "The Peace Process: Inside the Committee That Gave Jimmy Carter a Nobel," *Time* (international edition), October 21, 2002. Republican senator William Roth sponsored a resolution in the Senate in 1978 recommending Carter for the Nobel Prize.

15. That the Nobel Peace Prize has been politicized is not breaking news. Among other dubious awards in recent years include Rigoberta Menchu, a Guatemalan human rights activist whose autobiography was subsequently revealed to be a fabrication, and Yasir Arafat, whose "commitment to peace" scarcely requires comment.

16. "The Ignoble Peace Prize," *New York Daily News*, October 12, 2002, 24.

17. Brinkley, 339.

18. Jimmy Carter, "Just War—Or a Just War?" *New York Times*, March 9, 2003.

19. Monica Crowley, *Nixon Off the Record: His Candid Commentary on People and Politics* (New York: Random House, 1996), 21.

20. Cited in Brinkley, 217.

Chapter Two: The Plain Man from Plains

1. William Alexander Percy, *Lanterns on the Levee* (New York: Alfred A. Knopf, 1941), 313.
2. Peter Bourne, *Jimmy Carter* (New York: Scribner, 1997), 9.
3. *I'll Take My Stand: The South and the Agrarian Tradition* (Baton Rouge: Louisiana State University Press, 1978), 176.
4. Bourne, 23.
5. Jimmy Carter, *Why Not the Best?* (New York: Bantam, 1976), 36–37.
6. Ibid., 24.
7. Jimmy Carter, *Always a Reckoning, and Other Poems* (New York: Times Books, 1995), 44.
8. Betty Glad, *Jimmy Carter: In Search of the Great White House* (New York: Norton, 1980), 48.
9. Ibid., 53.
10. Bourne, 64.
11. Glad, 62.
12. Bourne, 70.
13. Carter, *Why Not the Best?*, 59.
14. Glad, 64.

Chapter Three: Rising Politician

1. Peter Bourne, *Jimmy Carter* (New York: Scribner, 1997), 80–81.
2. James Wooten, *Dasher: The Roots and the Rising of Jimmy Carter* (New York: Summit Books, 1978), 320.
3. Jimmy Carter, *Why Not the Best?* (New York: Bantam, 1976), 66.
4. Betty Glad, *Jimmy Carter: In Search of the Great White House* (New York: Norton, 1980), 78.
5. Ibid., 84.
6. Ibid., 85.
7. Bourne, 119.
8. Joe Hurst was later convicted and sent to prison for federal voter fraud violations in another election.
9. Glad, 92.

10. Ibid., 94.

11. Bourne, 134.

12. Glad, 107.

13. Bourne, 165.

Chapter Four: The Born-Again Governor

1. John 3:3–7 (King James version) makes clear that the second birth is of the spirit: " 'Verily, verily, I say unto thee, Except a man be born again, he cannot see the kingdom of God.' Nicodemus saith unto him, 'How can a man be born when he is old? Can he enter the second time into his mother's womb, and be born?' Jesus answered, 'Verily, verily, I say unto thee, unless a man be born of water [baptized] and of the Spirit, he cannot enter into the kingdom of God. That which is born of flesh is flesh, and that which is born of the spirit is spirit. Marvel not that I said unto thee, Ye must be born again.' "

2. Betty Glad, *Jimmy Carter: In Search of the Great White House* (New York: Norton, 1980), 108.

3. James Wooten, *Dasher: The Roots and the Rising of Jimmy Carter* (New York: Summit Books, 1978), 276.

4. Ibid., 278.

5. Kenneth E. Morris, *Jimmy Carter: American Moralist* (Athens, GA: University of Georgia Press, 1996), 151.

6. One of the best short accounts of Niebuhr's thought came from the pen of Whittaker Chambers in a cover story in *Time* magazine ("Faith for Lenten Age," March 8, 1948), and is reprinted in Terry Teachout, ed., *Ghosts on the Roof: Selected Journalism of Whittaker Chambers, 1931–1959* (Washington, D.C.: Regnery Gateway, 1989), 184–193.

7. Arthur Schlesinger, Jr., "God and the 1976 Election," *Wall Street Journal*, April 28, 1976.

8. Garry Wills, *Lead Time: A Journalist's Education* (New York: Doubleday, 1983), 255–256.

9. Morris, 155.

10. Cited in Gary Fink, *Prelude to the Presidency: The Political Character and Legislative Leadership Style of Governor Jimmy Carter* (Westport, CT: Greenwood, 1980), 9.

11. Glad, 333.

12. Ibid., 223

13. Peter Bourne, *Jimmy Carter* (New York: Scribner, 1997), 210.

14. Wooten, 282.

15. Steven Brill, "Jimmy Carter's Pathetic Lies," *Harper's*, March 1976.

16. Glad, 127.

17. Ibid., 129.

18. Bourne, 191.

19. Glad, 131.

20. Bourne, 192.

21. Glad, 310.

22. Jimmy Carter, *Why Not the Best?* (New York: Bantam, 1976), 103.

23. Bourne, 193.

24. Glad, 193.

25. Morris, 180.

26. Jimmy Carter, *Turning Point: A Candidate, A State, and a Nation Come of Age* (New York: Times Books, 1992), 192.

27. Carter writes of "frequent references from the White House to 'welfare queens'" during the Reagan administration. There is not a single mention of "welfare queens" by Reagan during his entire presidency, according to a word search of the electronic files of the Public Papers of the President, 1981–1989.

28. Reinhold Niebuhr, *Moral Man and Immoral Society* (New York: Scribner, 1932), 244.

29. Cited in Morris, 189.

30. Glad, 199.

31. Jules Witcover, *Marathon: The Pursuit of the Presidency, 1972–1976* (New York: Viking, 1977), 113.

32. Fink, 108, 175.

33. Ibid., 38–39.

34. Ibid., 145.

35. Ibid., 116.

36. Glad, 180.

37. Ibid., 198.

38. Ibid., 206.

39. Bourne, 225.

40. Another member of the Trilateral Commission in the late 1970s was former CIA director George H. W. Bush.

41. Nor was this speech atypical of Carter. In a 1976 memorial service for Congressman Jerry Litton, who died in a place crash, Carter used the person pronoun forty-four times in his eulogy. By contrast, when Ronald Reagan boasted of the achievements of his governorship in California, he almost invariably used the pronoun "we" instead of "I." Reagan explained in a letter, "I use the plural 'we' because as governor I had the help of some very fine people."

42. Glad, 220.

43. Howard Norton and Bob Strosser, *The Miracle of Jimmy Carter* (Plainfield, NJ: Logos Books, 1976), 58–59.

44. Glad, 202.

Chapter Five: Jimmy Who?

1. Nathan Miller, *Star-Spangled Men: America's Ten Worst Presidents* (New York: Touchstone, 1998), 25.

2. Christopher Matthews, *Hardball: How Politics Is Played by One Who Knows the Game* (New York: Summit Books, 1988), 60.

3. Kenneth E. Morris, *Jimmy Carter: American Moralist* (Athens, GA: University of Georgia Press, 1996), 191.

4. Peter Bourne, *Jimmy Carter* (New York: Scribner, 1997), 250.

5. Jules Witcover, *Marathon: The Pursuit of the Presidency, 1972–1976* (New York: Viking, 1977), 195.

6. Betty Glad, *Jimmy Carter: In Search of the Great White House* (New York: Norton, 1980), 368.

7. Witcover, 118, 13.

8. Bourne, 251.

9. Howard Norton and Bob Strosser, *The Miracle of Jimmy Carter* (Plainfield, NJ: Logos Books, 1976), 9.

10. *Newsweek*, October 25, 1976.

11. Bourne, 305.

12. Norton and Strosser, 57.

13. Patrick Anderson, *Electing Jimmy Carter: The Campaign of 1976* (Baton Rouge: Louisiana State University Press, 1994), 93.

14. Cited in Richard Harwood, ed., *The Pursuit of the Presidency 1980* (New York: Putnam, 1980), 202.

15. Glad, 314.

16. Anderson, 14.

17. Glad, 311.

18. Ibid., 294.

19. Anderson, 162.

20. Witcover, 225.

21. Glad, 306.

22. Witcover, 336.

23. Bourne, 279.

24. Witcover, 207.

25. Norton and Strosser, 106.

26. *National Review*, April 16, 1976.

27. *New Republic*, March 6, 1976.

28. *Newsweek*, August 30, 1976.

29. Witcover, 306.

30. Matthews, 60.

31. Brill, 79.

32. *National Review*, October 15, 1976.

33. Bourne, 299.

34. Morris, 245.

35. *National Review*, October 1, 1976.

36. Morris, 247.

37. John Coyne, "Niceguyin' His Way to the White House," *National Review*, May 14, 1976.

38. Burnham, "Jimmy Carter and the Democratic Crisis," *New Republic*, July 3, 1976.

39. Anderson, 65.

40. *National Review*, October 1, 1976.

41. *New Republic*, July 24, 1976.

42. *National Review*, October 29, 1976.

43. *Atlantic Monthly*, July 1976.

44. *New Republic*, October 23, 1976.

45. *New Republic*, July 31, 1976.

46. Witcover, 524.

47. John Robert Greene, *The Presidency of Gerald Ford* (Lawrence, KS: University Press of Kansas, 1995), 183.

48. *National Review*, November 26, 1976.

Chapter Six: President Carter at Home

1. Tip O'Neill, *Man of the House* (New York: Random House, 1987), 310–311.

2. Charles O. Jones, *The Trusteeship Presidency: Jimmy Carter and the United States Congress* (Baton Rouge: Louisiana State University Press, 1988), 1.

3. Robert G. Kaufman, *Henry M. Jackson: A Life in Politics* (Seattle: University of Washington Press, 2000), 342.

4. Jones, 149.

5. *National Review*, November 26, 1976.

6. Robert Shogan, *Promises to Keep* (New York: Thomas Y. Crowell, 1977), 282–283.

7. Peter Bourne, *Jimmy Carter* (New York: Scribner, 1997), 416–417.

8. Burton I. Kaufman, *The Presidency of James Earl Carter, Jr.* (Lawrence, KS: University Press of Kansas, 1993), 53–54.

9. *New Republic*, December 23 & 30, 1978.

10. *National Review*, May 27, 1977.

11. Jones, 154.

12. Kenneth E. Morris, *Jimmy Carter: American Moralist* (Athens, GA: University of Georgia Press, 1996), 245.

13. Bourne, 421.

14. James Fallows, "The Passionless Presidency," *Atlantic Monthly*, July 1979.

15. Gary Fink, *Prelude to the Presidency: The Political Character and Legislative Leadership Style of Governor Jimmy Carter* (Westport, CT: Greenwood, 1980), 163.

16. Warren T. Brookes, *The Economy in Mind* (New York: Universe Books, 1982), 85.

17. *National Review*, October 24, 1975.

18. *National Review*, April 28, 1978.

19. *National Review*, May 26, 1978.

20. "Carter Shaped Energy Plan with Disregard for Politics," *New York Times*, April 24, 1977.

Chapter Seven: President Carter Abroad

1. Cited in Nathan Miller, *Star-Spangled Men: America's Ten Worst Presidents* (New York: Touchstone, 1998), 23.

2. Jeane Kirkpatrick, *Dictatorships and Double Standards* (Washington DC: American Enterprise Institute, 1982), 92, 91.

3. Michael Ledeen and Bernard Lewis, *Debacle: The American Failure in Iran* (New York: Alfred A. Knopf, 1981), 71.

4. James Fallows, "The Passionless Presidency," *Atlantic Monthly*, June 1979.

5. *Harper's*, October 1977.

6. Kirkpartrick, 45, 37.

7. Ledeen and Lewis, 67.

8. Robert G. Kaufman, *Henry M. Jackson: A Life in Politics* (Seattle: University of Washington Press, 2000), 365.

9. Robert Shogan, *Promises to Keep* (New York: Thomas Y. Crowell, 1977), 217.

10. Kaufman, 370–371.

11. Godfrey Hodgson, *The Gentleman from New York: Daniel Patrick Moynihan* (Boston: Houghton Mifflin, 2000), 295.

12. Norton and Slosser, 77.

13. *New Republic*, June 4, 1977.

14. *New Republic*, February 9, 1980.

15. Peter Bourne, *Jimmy Carter* (New York: Scribner, 1997), 366.

16. *Time*, April 4, 1978.

17. "The Junior Varsity," *New Republic*, February 19, 1977.

18. Jay Winik, *On the Brink* (New York: Simon and Schuster, 1996), 84.

19. *National Review*, February 18, 1977.

20. Daniel Patrick Moynihan, "Further Thoughts on Words and Foreign Policy," *Policy Review*, Spring 1979.

21. Carl Gershman, "The World According to Andrew Young," *Commentary*, August 1978.

22. Ibid., 28–29.

23. Bourne, 382.

24. Michael Barone, *Our Country: The Shaping of America from Roosevelt to Reagan* (New York: The Free Press, 1990), 569.

25. Ledeen and Lewis, 36.

26. Walter Laqueur, "Why the Shah Fell," *Commentary*, March 1979.

27. Tom Bethell, *The Noblest Triumph: Property and Prosperity Through the Ages* (New York: St. Martin's Press, 1998), 218.

28. Ledeen and Lewis, 124.

29. Gary Sick, *All Fall Down: America's Tragic Encounter with Iran* (New York: Penguin Books, 1986), 193.

30. Ledeen and Lewis, 126; Sick, 43.

31. Sick, 36.

32. Ledeen and Lewis, 158.

33. Ibid., 144–145.

34. Sick, 195.

35. Ibid., 142.

36. Ledeen and Lewis, 233.

37. Ibid., 149.

38. Sick, 219.

39. Robert Moss, "Who's Meddling in Iran?" *New Republic*, December 2, 1978.

40. Ledeen and Lewis, 163.
41. Sick, 183.
42. Laqueur, "Why the Shah Fell."
43. Robert Kagan, *A Twilight Struggle: American Power and Nicaragua, 1977–1990* (New York: The Free Press, 1996), 31.
44. Robert Gates, *From the Shadows: The Ultimate Insider's Story of Five Presidents and How They Won the Cold War* (New York: Simon & Schuster, 1996), 126.
45. Kagan, 52.
46. Ibid., 736.
47. *Washington Post*, August 3, 1978.
48. Kirkpatrick, 74.
49. Gates, 128.
50. Robert W. Tucker, *Foreign Affairs*, Winter 1979/1980.
51. *Commentary*, November 1979.

Chapter Eight: President Malaise

1. *New Republic*, August 4, 1979.
2. *Newsweek*, July 16, 1979.
3. *National Review*, August 3, 1979.
4. *New Republic*, August 4, 1979.
5. *New Republic*, May 21, 1977.
6. *Time*, July 30, 1979.
7. New York: W. W. Norton, 1978.
8. *New Yorker*, August 27, 1979.
9. Peter Bourne, *Jimmy Carter* (New York: Scribner, 1997), 442; Steven M. Gillon, *The Democrats' Dilemma: Walter Mondale and the Liberal Legacy* (New York: Columbia University Press, 1992), 262.
10. Gillon, 262.
11. *Time*, July 30, 1979.
12. *New Republic*, August 4, 1979.
13. Anatoly Dobrynin, *In Confidence* (New York: Times Books, 1995), 422.

Chapter Nine: Carter Held Hostage

1. Kenneth E. Morris, *Jimmy Carter: American Moralist* (Athens, GA: University of Georgia Press, 1996), 276.
2. Peter Bourne, *Jimmy Carter* (New York: Scribner, 1997), 389.
3. Strobe Talbott, *Endgame: The Inside Story of SALT II* (New York: Harper & Row, 1979), 75.
4. Robert Gates, *From the Shadows: The Ultimate Insider's Story of Five Presidents and How They Won the Cold War* (New York: Simon & Schuster, 1996), 178–179.
5. Edward Luttwak, "Ten Questions About SALT II," *Commentary*, August 1979, 28.
6. Morris, 276.
7. Bourne, 455.
8. Gates, 130.
9. Ibid., 148.
10. Gary Sick, *All Fall Down: America's Tragic Encounter with Iran* (New York: Penguin Books, 1986), 343.
11. *National Review*, March 21, 1980.
12. Robert W. Tucker, "America in Decline: The Foreign Policy of 'Maturity,'" *Foreign Affairs*, Winter 1980.
13. *Washington Post*, December 30, 1979.
14. Robert G. Kaufman, *Henry M. Jackson: A Life in Politics* (Seattle: University of Washington Press, 2000), 397.
15. *New Republic*, February 9, 1980.
16. Jay Winik, *On the Brink* (New York: Simon and Schuster, 1996), 100; Author interview with Ben Wattenberg, September 29, 2000.
17. *New Republic*, August 2 & 9, 1980.
18. Godfrey Hodgson, *The Gentleman from New York: Daniel Patrick Moynihan* (Boston: Houghton Mifflin, 2000), 291.
19. Nelson Polsby, "The Democratic Nomination," in Austin Ranney, ed., *The American Elections of 1980* (Washington, D.C.: American Enterprise Institute, 1981), 45.
20. Ranney, 147.

Chapter Ten: Reelect President Vicious

1. Peter Bourne, *Jimmy Carter* (New York: Scribner, 1997), 459.
2. Ibid., 460.
3. Daniel Wattenberg, "Clinton's Hard-Line Appeaser,"*American Spectator*, February 1993.
4. Richard A. Gabriel, *Military Incompetence: Why the American Military Doesn't Win* (New York: Hill and Wang, 1985), 86.
5. Elizabeth Drew, *Portrait of an Election: The 1980 Presidential Campaign* (New York: Simon & Schuster, 1981), 313.
6. *National Journal*, October 11, 1980.
7. *National Review*, August 22, 1980.
8. *National Review*, September 5, 1980.
9. *New Republic*, September 27, 1980.
10. *Washington Post*, September 18, 1980.
11. Anatoly Dobrynin, *In Confidence: Moscow's Ambassador to America's Six Cold War Presidents* (New York: Times Books, 1995), 460.
12. Ibid., 462.
13. Kornienko's account appeared in an untranslated 1995 Russian book, *Khocodnaia Voina: Svidetel'stvo ee Unchastnika*, and is recounted in Peter Schweizer, *Reagan's War* (New York: Doubleday, 2002), 94.
14. Dobrynin, 457.
15. Austin Ranney, ed., *The American Elections of 1980* (Washington, D.C.: American Enterprise Institute, 1981), 165.
16. Richard Harwood, ed., *The Pursuit of the Presidency 1980* (New York: Putnam, 1980), 300.
17. Drew, 410–411.
18. *New Republic*, November 8, 1980.
19. *New York Times*, October 30, 1980.
20. *New Republic*, October 25, 1980.
21. John A. Farrell, *Tip O'Neill and the Democratic Century* (Boston: Little, Brown, 2001), 536.

22. *Nation*, November 15, 1980.

23. "President Reagan's America," *Washington Post*, January 21, 1981.

Chapter Eleven: Becoming the American Gandhi

1. Zbigniew Brzezinski, *Power and Principle* (New York: Farrar, Straus & Giroux, 1983), 513.

2. Ed Cowan, "Miller Asserts Talk of Economic Crisis Could Create One," *New York Times*, December 20, 1980.

3. Douglas Brinkley, *The Unfinished Presidency: Jimmy Carter's Journey Beyond the White House* (New York: Viking, 1998), 3.

4. *New York Times*, October 14, 1981.

5. Brinkley, 154.

6. Peter Bourne, *Jimmy Carter* (New York: Scribner, 1997), 489.

7. Brinkley, 91.

8. The complete list of Carter Center donors is available in the Center's annual reports, available online at www.cartercenter.org. In addition to Middle Eastern funders, other foreign sources of support include the governments of Nigeria, the United Kingdom, Denmark, Japan, Portugal, the Netherlands, Norway, and Finland. Adding to the Center's feel as a quasi-United Nations are grants from the World Bank, Inter-American Development Bank, various United Nations agencies, the National Endowment for Democracy, and the U.S. Institute for Peace.

9. Bourne, 481.

10. "Carter Assails Demands on Tokyo," *New York Times*, July 21, 1983.

11. Brinkley, 122, 127, 136.

12. Ibid., 127–128.

13. Ibid., 293.

14. A. M. Rosenthal, "Silence Is a Lie," *New York Times*, March 22, 1990.

15. Jimmy Carter, *The Blood of Abraham: Insights into the Middle East* (Boston: Houghton Mifflin, 1985), 65–66.

16. Ion Pacepa, "The KGB's Man," *Wall Street Journal*, September 22, 2003.

17. See Scott W. Johnson, "Who Murdered Cleo Noel?" www.front-pagemagazine.com/Articles/ReadArticle.asp?ID=10855 (accessed December 9, 2003).

18. Dennis Ross, "Think Again: Yasir Arafat," *Foreign Policy*, September/October 2003.

19. Carter, 105, 118.

20. Ibid., 119.

21. Brinkley, 241.

22. Cited in Brinkley, 331.

23. Ibid., 322.

24. Brinkley, 344.

Chapter Twelve: The Second Carter Administration

1. Cited in Rich Lowry, *Legacy: Paying the Price for the Clinton Years*, (Washington, D.C.: Regnery, 2003), 239.

2. "Merry Christmas, Mr. Karadzic," *New Republic*, January 5, 1995.

3. William H. Glaysteen, Jr., *Massive Entanglement, Marginal Influence: Carter and Crisis in Korea* (Washington, D.C.: Brookings Institution, 1999), 61.

4. Douglas Brinkley, *The Unfinished Presidency: Jimmy Carter's Journey Beyond the White House* (New York: Viking, 1998), 398.

5. Ibid., 400.

6. As with several previous trips, the Rockefeller Foundation, not the U.S. taxpayer, covered Carter's travel expenses to Korea.

7. See Stephane Courtois, et al., *The Black Book of Communism* (Cambridge, MA: Harvard University Press, 1999), 562–564.

8. Brinkley, 401.

9. Ibid., 409.

10. *New York Times*, October 27, 2002 (available through the Carter Center website, www.cartercenter.org/viewdoc.asp?docID#1099&submenu=news).

11. *Washington Post*, January 14, 2003 (available through the Carter Center website, www.cartercenter.org/viewdoc.asp?docID#=1137 &submenu=news).

12. See Mark Falcoff, *Cuba: The Morning After* (Washington, D.C.: American Enterprise Institute, 2003), 111–116.

13. Author interview, December 11, 2003.

Conclusion: The Myth of St. Jimmy

1. *New Republic*, January 9, 1995.

2. Murray Kempton, "St. Jimmy's Halo Askew," *Newsday*, September 22, 1994.

3. Douglas Brinkley, *The Unfinished Presidency: Jimmy Carter's Journey Beyond the White House* (New York: Viking, 1998), 456.

4. The exceptions to this statement are Spain and India, which both restored democratic rule during Carter's presidency. However, neither country was a target of Carter's human rights policy, and the U.S. had little to do with the restoration of democracy in those nations.

Index